EDUCATION
WITH AN
ATTITUDE

TEACHER EDUCATION WITH AN ATTITUDE

Preparing Teachers
to Educate Working-Class
Students in Their
Collective Self-Interest

EDITED BY

Patrick J. Finn
and
Mary E. Finn

State University of New York Press

Cover Image: Brandon Laufenberg, iStockphoto

Published by
STATE UNIVERSITY OF NEW YORK PRESS
ALBANY

For information, address
State University of New York Press
194 Washington Avenue, Suite 305, Albany, NY 12210-2384

Production by Judith Block
Marketing by Fran Keneston

Library of Congress Cataloging-in-Publication Data

Teacher education with an attitude : preparing teachers to educate working-class students in their
    collective self-interest / edited by Patrick J. Finn, Mary E. Finn.
        p. cm.
    Includes bibliographical references and index.
    ISBN-13: 978-0-7914-7035-0 (alk. paper)
    ISBN-13: 978-0-7914-7036-7 (pbk. : alk. paper)
        1. Teachers—Training of—Curricula—United States.   2. Multiculturalism-—Study and
teaching (Higher)—United States.   I. Finn, Patrick J.   II. Finn, Mary E.

LB1715.F455 2007
370.71'173—dc22   2006013429

10 9 8 7 6 5 4 3 2 1

For our grandsons
Harry, Lewis, Moe, and PJ

Contents

III. Social Justice Teacher Education in Graduate School

IV. Social Justice Teacher Education through Professional Development

Acknowledgments

Chapter 2, "Labor Deserves Credit: The Popular Education Foundations of the National Labor College" by Susan J. Schurman is a revised version of Chapter 8, Article 4, "Labor Deserves Credit: The Popular Education Roots of the National Labor College," in *Teaching for Change: Popular Education and the Labor Movement*, L. Delp, M. Outman-Kramer, S. J. Schurman, and K. Wong (eds.), Los Angeles, CA: UCLA Center for Labor Research and Education (2002), pp. 204–218.

Chapter 13, "Popular Education in Los Angeles Classrooms: Collective Bargaining Education Project," by Linda Tubach is a revised version of Chapter 8, Article 3, "Labor in the Schools: Collective Bargaining Education Project," in *Teaching for Change: Popular Education and the Labor Movement*, L. Delp, M. Outman-Kramer, S. J. Schurman, and K. Wong (eds.), Los Angeles, CA: UCLA Center for Labor Research and Education (2002), pp. 198–202.

We are very grateful to UCLA Center for Labor Research and Education for permission to reprint revised versions of these chapters.

Introduction

Patrick J. Finn and Mary E. Finn

TEACHER EDUCATORS USUALLY ESCAPE THE intense public scrutiny and criticism to which classroom teachers, principals, school board members, parents, and students are subjected when high-stakes test results are announced. Free-market ideologues, however, continue their maneuvers to reduce the power and influence of traditional routes to teacher certification through teacher education programs in colleges and universities. Conservatives call for more liberal arts and science involvement in teacher education programs, which in itself is not a bad idea. But the old saw that all one needs to be a good teacher is a good grounding in one of the arts or sciences continues to be floated, even though traditionally certified teachers who have graduated from higher education-based programs consistently outperform those who are on emergency certificates, or who have gone through alternative programs (Darling-Hammond 2000; Wayne & Young, 2003).

Teacher education critics on the left complain about the emphasis many teacher education programs place on subject area methods courses; however, they would replace them with cultural studies, social theory, and courses on multiculturalism, antiracism, and social class (Giroux, 1997). These subjects have much to recommend them, but they are not always well received by school practitioners who are looking for more immediate ways to cope with extraordinary challenges, and whose efforts are being graded F and labeled underperforming, or worse, on the front pages of local newspapers and in state and national reports.

Some urban districts with many underperforming schools, desperate for better test scores and the funding tied to them, are developing their own teacher preparation programs. Others, frustrated with the inability of graduates of teacher education programs to provide the desired results, are looking outside traditional university-based programs altogether for the help their teachers need. Textbook companies are only too happy to supply professional development for teachers in districts that buy their books. Their practical how-to workshops make it relatively easy for teachers to use the teacher-proof materials that program developers and publishers promise will improve students' test results. Charter and voucher-supported schools often hire people to teach who have had none of the above training, frequently with discouraging results.

Teacher educators, however, can't be held accountable for the products of their programs without some sense of the standards by which parents, students, school districts, and taxpayers can evaluate their efforts. For the authors of articles in this volume, whether they prepare teachers in undergraduate or graduate programs or through professional development activities, that standard is how well teacher educators prepare teachers to educate working-class students in their collective self-interest. The students to whom we refer are usually found in urban, rural, and first-ring working-class suburban schools. Their parents, guardians, and families may be the working poor; they may be consistently under- or unemployed, or they may have moved up economically as a result of labor union benefits, but they still identify culturally as working class. They may be native, white, black, Hispanic, or from a multitude of immigrant groups.

Preparing social justice teachers for these classrooms is a challenging job, given the difficult time economically under-resourced families have in supporting their children's education, as well as the social class, ethnic, racial, linguistic, geographical, and cultural differences between many urban teachers and their students. The racial and social class achievement gap is often attributed to these differences, and many education reforms, such as standards and high-stakes testing, claim to address them. These reforms have only illuminated the problems, however; they have not solved them.

DEMOCRACY AND EDUCATION: DEWEY AND FREIRE

We believe that not enough attention has been paid to the advice John Dewey (1933) gave educators seventy years ago, when he argued that the educator's relation to the social problems of the day, the "crisis in education" produced by the Great Depression, was not that of an outsider. He warned teachers they needed to remove "the illusion many of them have entertained—that their vocation and vocational interests are so distinctive, so separated from that of other wage earners and salaried persons as to justify them in an attitude of aloofness" (Dewey, 1933, p. 386). Solving the crisis in education, he said, requires seeing an identity of interest between educators, farmers, and factory workers. Teachers are workers who must recognize their part in the community of interest they share with other workers, all of whom are "genuine producers of social necessities." Once this community of interest is recognized, he urged educators to form "an alliance in sympathy and action" to break down the "moral barriers which now divide teachers from members of other groups and make the latter more or less suspicious of them" (Dewey, 1933, p. 388).

Finding solutions to the problems of economic imbalance must be done by people "who understand one another and sympathize with one another," according to Dewey (1933, p. 389). Educators will not have a share in solving social problems unless they break down "personal remoteness and indifference as to the things they have in common [with other workers] . . . and have ceased to think of their interest being separate or exclusively linked with those of purely professional groups" (p. 390). To closely connect "with actual social responsibility" in solving social problems, educators must start with their work in their schools:

> Teachers [need] to assert themselves more directly about educational affairs . . . in both the internal conduct of the schools by introducing a greater amount of teacher responsibility in administration, and outside in relation to the public and the community. The present dictation of policies for schools by bankers and other outside pecuniary groups is more than harmful to the cause of education. It is also a pathetic and tragic commentary on the lack of social power by the teaching force. (Dewey, 1933, p. 390)

Social justice teacher educators, whose ideas and experiences are included in this volume, strive in various ways to prepare teachers with social power and social responsibility. They are aware that their views and their acts will cause some to accuse them of politicizing education. But in rebuttal, they argue that education is inherently political; it either reinforces the status quo by reproducing the existing hierarchy of social and economic relationships, or it offers a new vision of society, a revitalized democratic vision (Singer & Pezone, 2003, p. 1). They know education either domesticates students or liberates them.

Social justice teacher educators prepare teachers to strengthen democracy through education by helping them develop "critical consciousness," Freire's (1973) term for the will to address society's injustices and inequities. Freire, like Dewey, wants "students to become 'agents of curiosity' in a 'quest for . . . the why of things,' " but Freire is more direct than Dewey in stating that this educational goal "can only be achieved when students are engaged in explicitly critiquing social injustice and actively organizing to challenge oppression . . ." (Singer & Pezone, 2003, pp. 2–3). This translates into education for understanding and challenging the government's social, political, and economic policy decisions that have such a negative impact on working families. At least one urban district superintendent believes that achievement scores would go up if the minimum wage were raised, a major goal of organized labor today.

The potential role in teacher preparation of organized labor, historically the most potent force in challenging the hierarchical social structure and championing the cause of working families, however, has largely been ignored, even by those who acknowledge that American schools continue to reproduce society's social and economic status quo. One basis for collaboration between progressive teacher educators and progressive labor is the fact that many in both camps consider themselves either to be disciples of Paulo Freire or at least are interested in incorporating aspects of his ideas, such as the role of critical consciousness, into their educational work.

The road to critical consciousness follows various paths, and each author in this volume has taken his or her own route based on a variety of experiences and inspirations. Not all use the language of Freire and Dewey. Some are more comfortable with Vygotsky (1978), Dorothy Day (1952), or Saul Alinsky (1946, 1971), but these different roads lead to the same end task: preparing critical teachers; that is, teachers who understand, and help their students understand, the inequities and injustices of the social and economic power structure, and who actively collaborate with their students and others to change the economic and educational polices that keep the hierarchical structure in place.

Social justice teacher educators know this understanding cannot be derived from lectures or readings alone. They also provide experiences that help teachers acquire new information and test old theories, and they offer opportunities to reflect on the experiences, individually and in groups, that build a sense of community and allow for dialogue among equals. Providing teachers with opportunities to experience inquiry, reflection, community, and dialogue around issues of social justice makes explicit the powerful analytic/critical thinking and literacy skills their students need "to read the word and to read the world" (Freire, 1970). These experiences also help teachers recognize they have a social responsibility to act on their new knowledge and understanding—to connect their practice to their theory. Social justice teachers prepared in the undergraduate and graduate teacher education and professional development programs, described in this volume, develop their own educational and political power and agency alongside their students. They see schools as sites of struggle for democracy and urge their students to direct their attitude toward outcomes that are in their collective self-interest.

SOCIAL CLASS IN AMERICA: IS OUR DEMOCRACY IN DANGER?

Forty-five percent of Americans identify as working class, a larger percentage than might be expected in a society that has historically downplayed social class distinctions (Linkon, 1999, 2003; Russo & Linkon, 2005). This self-identified social group no doubt includes a fairly wide range of incomes and net worth, and probably an even wider range of definitions of working class. Michael Zweig (2004), an economist at SUNY Stony Brook, defines class as based on power, the power to make decisions on the job, and not on income alone. So "a truck driver is working class but a truck driver who owns his own rig is an independent contractor and is therefore middle class. By this measure . . . 62 percent of the country's workforce is actually working class" (Cunningham, 2004, p. 3).

Janet Zandy (2001), a cultural studies professor at the University of Rochester, defines class more collectively, as "seeing individual identities in relation to others. . . . Class defined in collective terms as shared economic circumstances and shared social and cultural practices in relation to positions of power means more than the absence or presence of things." She urges educators to "decloak" class and make it visible in "Disney-saturated America." As a working-class professor in an institution of higher education, Zandy claims that even if "we've climbed a bit, we may still inherit certain values, attitudes, shared histories, uses of language and even bodily postures" that separate working-class professors from the middle-class sensibilities that pervade institutions of higher education. As a result, working-class faculty seldom call attention to or celebrate their working-class backgrounds (Zandy, 2001, pp. 247–279).

This tendency to ignore class affects the education received by the students in these institutions, including those preparing to become teachers. Ignoring class means that what is valued as academic knowledge is determined "by the interests of the ruling white elite"—corporate leaders who define what students "need to learn to get jobs in the new technological world order so they can become part of the global 'knowledge elite.' " Business interests are represented "as an all pervasive reality"; labor stories don't count. Zandy urges progressives and working-class educators to fight for the power to "construct, reconstruct, remember, reinvent, rediscover, reconnect, and struggle for the knowledge that belongs to the majority of people, the working class" (Zandy, 2001, p. 249).

Bill Fletcher, a labor activist in Chicago, says class is ignored in K–12 schools as well as in institutions of higher education. "Class is generally not discussed in schools. If it comes up, it is brief, and usually in the context of comments such as, 'Oh yea, by the way, there's a labor movement.' But there is rarely any discussion of the psychological impact of class" (Peterson, 1999a, p. 119). For Fletcher, a good way to get the subject of social class on the table in schools is for teachers unions "to demand regular training programs or institutes" in these issues:

> Teachers help to shape the minds of the future generation. One important role is [to] help build awareness about unions and the labor movement. Some teachers don't want to talk to their students about unions; they see it as somehow unethical and misusing their position. That's ridiculous. Teachers need to help sow the seeds of the future of unionism. (Peterson, 1999a, p. 119)

Social class historian Howard Zinn agrees: "The history of labor struggles in this country is one of the most dramatic of any country in the world . . . [but] the history of working people and the labor movement is not taught in this country. It's not in the school books and it's not in the mass media. So workers are unaware of past labor struggles, and this can have a debilitating effect" (Peterson, 1999b, p. 73). "If teacher unions want to be strong and well-supported it's essential that they not only be *teacher unionists* but *teachers of unionism*" (p. 76) (emphasis mine).

To those who ask if all this talk of class will lead to class war, Bill Moyers answers: "Class war was declared a generation ago . . . [when] William Simon, who was soon to be Secretary of the Treasury . . . called on the financial and business class, in effect, to take back the power and privilege they had lost in the depression and the New Deal." This class answered Simon's call "to trash the social contract" and to "starve the beast," that is, the government and what remains of the New Deal programs such as Social Security. According to Warren Buffet: "My class won" the class war, with the result that the gap in wealth between the top 20 percent and the bottom 20 percent, which in 1960 was 30-fold, by 2000 was 75-fold (Moyers, 2004).

Jean Anyon (2002, 2005) argues that educators may have more success in the classroom if they focus on developing a "new civil rights movement," one that demands changes in the federal government's economic policy that, over the past thirty years, has created the enormous number of urban families in poverty, while at the same time, drastically increased the wealth of the ruling elites. One of her examples is the minimum wage, which was "higher between 1940 and 1970 than it was in 2000 (all in 2000 dollars)" (Anyon, 2005, p. 30).

Other recent economic statistics reinforce Anyon's point. To put the Bush tax breaks into perspective, the average worker takes home $517 a week and gets about $400 a year in tax breaks. The average CEO takes home $155,769 a week (United for a Fair Economy, 2004) and in 2003 alone received well over $50,000 in new tax breaks (Citizens for Tax Justice, 2003). In 1980, the ratio of CEO pay to average worker compensation was 41:1; in 2002 it was 531:1, a situation New York's Attorney General Eliot Spitzer calls "insane" (Buffalo News, 5/27/04).

The decades-long connection between economic status and education has been well documented (Bowles and Gintis, 1976). What demands attention today, and what verifies Moyer's account of the current class warfare, is indicated in these 1999 statistics:

> If you are in the top economic quarter of the population, your children have a 76 percent chance of getting through college and graduating by age 24. . . . If you're in the bottom quarter, however, the figure is 4 percent. . . . In 1979, it was 27 percent. . . . (Howey and Post, 2002, p. 267)

In addition, in 2003, 35 percent of students from families with less than $25,000 annual income attended college, while 80 percent of those from families with more than $75,000 annual income did. Even among top achievers, "only 78 percent from low-income families [with high test scores] . . . attend college—about the same as the 77 percent of rich kids who rank at the bottom academically" (Symonds, 2003, p. 68). This means that if you have high test scores and are poor you have about the same chance of attending college as if you have low test scores but are wealthy.

We conclude that teachers being prepared to educate children in urban public schools should receive instruction in topics such as tax and wage policy, its impact on their students' families, and on their ability to increase their students' academic achievement. Not much has changed in teacher preparation on this topic, however, since 1941 when Counts and Brameld said:

> The evidence is conclusive that most teachers are not themselves informed, consistent, or clear-minded about the crucial issues of social, economic, and political life. Their views, too largely, are the reflection of [individualist] folkways and mores which are wholly incompatible with the realities of the present [interdependent] world. (Counts and Brameld, 1941, p. 257)

While this discussion focuses on the impact of class on education, it is also important to acknowledge the way class intersects with race and ethnicity in educational outcomes. Howey and Post (2002) note: "Contemporary American schools remain sharply segregated not only by race but also by social class. Unfortunately, these factors are too often highly correlated." They cite Orfield's (1997) study, which shows that 5 percent of segregated white schools "face conditions of concentrated poverty contrasted with an astounding 80 percent of segregated black and Latino schools" (Howey and Post, 2002, p. 256). While African-American and Hispanic minorities represent 28 percent of all 18-year-olds, only "12 percent of freshmen classes at the nation's top 146 colleges" are from this group (Symonds, 2003, p. 68). If the other top colleges are like Harvard, a large proportion of the African-American minorities will be blacks from Africa or the Caribbean, not products of the U.S. schools with concentrated poverty that Orfield studied (New York Times, 2004, p. 1).

However, class trumps race in nearly every statistic that Rothstein (2004) cites to describe the racial achievement gap; that is, poverty explains almost all of the difference in test scores between majority and minority students. It does not mean that the prejudice and discrimination of racism experienced by African-Americans and other minorities is any less devastating. There are numerous advantages to being white in this society, no matter what one's social class. But when it comes to statistically teasing out the factors that contribute to school success in terms of scores on standardized tests, social class accounts for most of the differences between white and black students; that is, poor students are at the bottom of this heap no matter what their race (Rothstein, 2004, pp. 51–56).

Social class and race clearly matter to educators, but there has been a profound disconnect between the desire to remedy the negative social and educational consequences of these differences and the development of practices that might really address the problem. Teacher educators must accept responsibility for their role in this continuing failure by putting social, political, and especially economic policy topics high on their teacher preparation agenda. Without direct intervention at this higher education level, schools will continue to reproduce the social and economic status quo. If we are to honor our democratic heritage, then the remedy is preparing social justice teachers whose attitude is that the social and economic power structure is unjust and needs to be changed.

While each chapter in this volume is based in theory, at our request, each author has limited the amount of space devoted to theory in order to make their findings, their experiences, and what they have learned, as accessible to the reader as possible. The papers are organized into four parts: (1) Addressing Issues of Class, Race, and Culture; (2) Social Justice Teacher Education in Undergraduate Courses; (3) Social Justice Teacher Education in Graduate School; and (4) Social Justice Teacher Education through Professional Development. The title of the concluding chapter is For Further Thought.

PART I. ADDRESSING ISSUES OF CLASS, RACE, AND CULTURE

To prepare teachers who understand that their personal and professional self-interest is intimately tied to the well-being of the families whose children they teach, teacher education programs need to acknowledge that in today's highly interrelated society, everyone's self-interest is best served when the well-being of the whole society is considered. "An owie to one is an owie to all."[1] For teachers who are being prepared to teach in urban schools, this translates into understanding the way the government's social, political, and economic policies impact children of working families, and why Freirean pedagogy is a good cure for what ails urban schools and society.

Teachers can acquire the social power to make government policies more democratic through closer connections with the families of their students and with the communities in which they teach. Preparing teachers with social responsibility and the skills to form powerful connections and alliances in the interest of their students, requires a type of teacher preparation that is different from what is most typical today. The following discussions of social class, culture, race, and labor and community organizing offer several possibilities for such preparation. They also provide background for the chapters in the rest of this volume.

Patrick Finn provides an overview of his earlier book, *Literacy with an Attitude: Educating Working-Class Children in Their Own Self-Interest* (1999) and describes the sort of teacher education program he believes can prepare teachers with the attitude that all children can acquire powerful literacy in their collective self-interest. Many of the papers in this volume refer to Finn's (1999) book, and all of them contain ideas and suggestions consistent with the need to consider the role of social class and culture in teachers' education. Susan Schurman explains the Frierean, popular education foundations of the National Labor College that strives to develop critical consciousness in labor educators and organizers and suggests a model for preparing social justice teachers. Alex Caputo-Pearl, Kahllid Al-Alim, and Frances Martin describe how to translate social justice theory into practice through the Coalition for Educational Justice, where students, parents, and teachers organize social change campaigns to address the inequities they face.

PART II. SOCIAL JUSTICE TEACHER EDUCATION
IN UNDERGRADUATE COURSES

With few exceptions, we can say confidently that teachers do not want to domesticate their students. The problem is that far too many prospective teachers don't know what that means, or that it's possible to teach differently from what they personally experienced. So social justice teacher educators emphasize the social, political, and cultural contexts of teaching and learning, topics that are too often slighted in the rush to prepare new teachers with methods of covering content. And they provide hands-on experiences to contextualize the new learning. Combined with reflection through journals and dialogue in groups, these experiences help prospective teachers learn how to bring down the barriers between them and their students, and to recognize and value their differences of class, culture, and race. They can then act to counter the inequities built into the social and economic power structure by replacing domesticating education with powerful education.

Gillian Richardson and Rosemary Murray lead their undergraduate students from middle-class suburbs through a "research theory, experience, dialogue, action cycle" in order to help them develop critical reflection about themselves and their role as urban educators. Dennis Shirley describes the difficulties and rewards of organizing diverse communities to demand school reform. The teacher education programs that participate in the Massachusetts Coalition for Teacher Quality and Student Achievement, which he directs, prepare teachers to engage in their students' communities in an effort to promote such organizing. Rosalie Romano's undergraduate students, typically underinformed about the political, economic, and social class nature of educational reality, learn to see their students and their role as teachers differently through their experiences in a service learning course that includes Freirean theater exercises.

PART III. SOCIAL JUSTICE TEACHER EDUCATION
IN GRADUATE SCHOOL

Social justice teacher education prepares teachers who challenge the domesticating education found in most U.S. schools through new views of what constitutes literacy and social justice curricula, as well as powerful teaching methods such as inquiry, critical literacy, and intercultural dialogue. To become critical teachers who provide students with powerful education, teachers need experiences that help them connect what they learn about social justice in university classes to their own lives and their classrooms.

Reading the world as well as the word means having the power of structural analysis, that is, the skill to analyze, synthesize, theorize, think critically, and inquire into the structure of society and the nature of social, political, and economic relationships. Social justice teacher educators devise methods of teaching these skills so their students can adapt and translate them into their own classrooms and explore their political implications with their students. Inevitably these skills are developed through experiences—often of research or inquiry, and inevitably in conjunction or community with others—with the end goal of developing praxis, that is, combining theory with action consciously aimed at social justice or democratic outcomes.

Suzanne Miller and Suzanne Borowicz broaden teachers' views of what constitutes literacy through experiences with digital video production in studio-like classes where students actively direct their learning through engagement with others. Diane Zigo realizes her desire to prepare social justice teachers by structuring her classes around the framework of inquiry that gives students the experience of powerful literacy that is necessary to differentiate it from less powerful forms of literacy. Peter Hoffman-Kipp and Brad Olsen work with new teachers who struggle to translate the social justice theory of their graduate university preparation into social justice practices in their classrooms. Vladimir Ageyev cites the need to prepare teachers to conduct intercultural dialogues in their classrooms to bridge the cultural gap between American teachers and newly arrived students from Russia and Eastern Europe. His analysis of the culture gap applies equally well to minority and working-class U.S. students.

PART IV. SOCIAL JUSTICE TEACHER EDUCATION THROUGH PROFESSIONAL DEVELOPMENT

Social justice teacher educators recognize and take steps to reduce the isolation social justice teachers often face. Professional development opportunities for critical dialogue and reflection help teachers change the world by bringing social justice into the classroom and into the school and wider educational system through collaboration with peers, parents, and students. Such thoughtful, purposeful actions, by social justice teachers who combine dialogue and reflection on theory with practice, produce the praxis that can replace the dominate banking model of education with culturally relevant content and pedagogy.

Jeff Duncan-Andrade conducts inquiry groups with teachers striving to replace domesticating practices with methods that reflect more closely their desire to contribute to their students' educational, economic, and social well-being. John Otterness challenges teachers and administrators to see beyond a narrow conception of education based in transmitting subject matter, and through readings, observations, reflection, and dialogue, to broaden their views of what constitutes effective educational practice. Linda Tubach conducts roleplays that simulate trade union negotiations to engage students in learning that brings issues of equity and justice into the curriculum and models popular education methods for classroom teachers. Lauri Johnson provides a history of a social justice teachers union in New York City between the two world wars that actively promoted social justice professional development. She suggests teacher education programs include preparation for teachers' nearly inevitable participation in teachers unions.

In the concluding chapter, "For Further Thought," Mary Finn offers a rationale for Freirean teacher educators to collaborate with Freirean popular-worker educators.

NOTE

1. Slogan on children's tee-shirts for sale at the National Labor College in Silver Springs, MD.

REFERENCES

Alinsky, S. (1946). *Reveille for radicals*. Chicago: University of Chicago Press.

Alinsky, S. (1971). *Rules for radicals: A practical primer for realistic radicals*. New York: Random House.

Anyon, J. (2002, October 17). Social policy, urban education, and a new civil rights movement. Charlotte Acer Lecture, University at Buffalo.

Anyon, J. (2005). Radical possibilities: Public policy, urban education, and a new social movement. New York: Routledge.

Bowles, S., & Gintis, H. (1976). *Schooling in capitalist America: Education reform and contradictions of economic life*. New York: Basic Books.

Buffalo News. (2004, May 27).

Citizens for Tax Justice. (2003, September 23). We're paying dearly for Bush's tax cuts.

Counts, G., & Brameld, T. (1941). Relations with public education: Some specific issues and proposals. In T. Brameld (Ed.), *Worker education in the United States* (pp. 249–277). New York: Harper & Brothers.

Cunningham, B. (2004). "Across the Great Divide," *Columbia Journalism Review*, 3, May/June 2004 [online at www.cjr.org/issues/2004/3/cunningham-class.asp].

Darling-Hammond, L. (2000). How teacher education matters. *Journal of Teacher Education*, 51 (3), 166-173.

Day, D. (1952). The long loneliness: The autobiography of Dorothy Day. New York: Harper & Row.

Dewey, J. (1933). Education and our present social problems. *Educational Method*, XII (7), 385-390.

Finn, P. (1999). *Literacy with an attitude: Educating working-class children in their own self-interest*. Albany: State University of New York Press.

Freire, P. (1970). *Pedagogy of the oppressed*. New York: Seabury.

Freire, P. (1973). *Education for critical consciousness*. New York: Seabury.

Giroux H. A. (1997). Is there a place for cultural studies in colleges of education? In H. A. Giroux & P. Shannon, (Eds.), *Education and cultural studies: Toward a performative practice* (pp. 231–248). New York: Routledge.

Howey, K., & Post, L. (2002). A strategy for the reform of teacher preparation in urban centers in the United States. *Asia Pacific Journal of Teacher Education*, 5(2), 256–272.

Linkon, S. (Ed.) (1999). Teaching working class. Amherst: University of Massachusetts Press.

Linkon, S. (2003, December 9). National Public Radio interview.

Moyers, B. (2004, June 3). This is the fight of our lives. Keynote Address, Inequality Matters Forum, New York University. [online at www.commondreams.org.]

New York Times (2004, June 24), 1.

Peterson, R. (1999a). Defending the public sector: An interview with Bill Fletcher. In R. Peterson & M. Charney (Eds.), *Transforming teachers unions: Fighting for better schools and social justice* (pp. 117–119). Milwaukee, WI: Rethinking Schools.

Peterson, R. (1999b). Why teachers should know history: An interview with Howard Zinn. In R. Peterson & M. Charney (Eds.), *Transforming teachers unions: Fighting for better schools and social justice* (pp. 73–76). Milwaukee, WI: Rethinking Schools.

Rothstein, R. (2004). *Class and schools: Using social, economic and education reform to close the black-white achievement gap*. New York: Teachers College, Columbia.

Russo, J., & Linkon, S. (Eds.) (2005). New working-class studies. Ithaca: Cornell University Press.

Singer, A., & Pezone, M. (2003). Education for social change: From theory to practice. In E. Wayne Ross (Ed.), *Workplace: A Journal for Academic Labor*. [online at www.cust.educ.ubc.ca/workplace.]

Symonds, W. (2003, April 14). College admissions: The real barrier is class. *Business Week*, pp. 68–69.

United for a Fair Economy. (2004, April 14). CEO pay/worker pay ratio reaches 301-1. Common Dreams Progressive Newservice. [online at www.commondreams. org.]

Vygotsky, L. (1978). *Mind in society*. Cambridge, MA: Harvard University Press.

Wayne, A. J., & Young, P. (2003). Teacher characteristics and student achievement gains: A review. *Review of Educational Research*, 73, pp. 89–122.

Zandy, J. (2001). Traveling working class. In J. Zandy (Ed.), *What we hold in common: An introduction to working class studies* (pp. 241–252). New York: Feminist Press at the City University of New York.

Zweig, M. (Ed.). 2004. *What's class got to do with it? American society in the 21st century*. Ithaca, NY: Cornell University Press.

Part I

Addressing Issues of Class, Race, and Culture

1 Teacher Education With an Attitude: Completing the Revolution

Patrick J. Finn

PATRICK J. FINN, ASSOCIATE PROFESSOR EMERITUS, University at Buffalo, State University of New York, presents T. H. Marshall's proposition that in the unfolding of democracy, citizens have been granted civil rights by the courts, political rights by the legislature, and social rights by public schools. Finn argues the process is not complete because of the inferior education offered in the schools to poor and working-class students, and that process will not be complete without political struggle for more equal education. He addresses the role of teachers and university teacher education departments in this continuing struggle.

In a famous essay written in 1950, the British sociologist T. H. Marshall proposed that the modern idea of citizenship was born with the industrial revolution and the migration of the population from the countryside into towns. *Citizenship* captures the idea that although there can be enormous differences between people in a society, there is an underlying equality we can all claim—that is, we all have inalienable rights. Marshall conceived of citizenship as three kinds of rights—civil, political, and social—that were won first by the upper classes beginning about 1700 and passed down to the less fortunate. Civil rights are necessary for individual freedom of movement, speech, thought, and religion; the right to own property and conclude contracts; and the right to justice. Political rights enable one to participate fully in the political process: to vote, hold office, assemble, demonstrate, form political parties, and petition.

The concept of social rights would have sounded very strange to America's founders, but they were on the agenda on both sides of the Atlantic by the middle of the twentieth century. Marshall defined social rights as the right to economic security and to live the life of a cultivated human being according to the prevailing standards of the society. More specifically, social rights are the right to a decent standard of food, housing, clothing, health care, childcare, education, and access to the common culture of the nation—books, theater, and concerts, for example.

15

Marshall asserted that in the past, citizens went to the courts to secure civil rights and to the legislatures to win political rights. Citizens now looked to the schools to secure social rights. This is an astonishing concept. It is social rights that need winning, and it is the schools that guarantee citizens social rights, just as the courts and legislatures granted civil and political rights in previous centuries. The schools are, therefore, the final frontier in the 300-year march toward full citizenship and full democracy.

Here's how Marshall thought it worked. First, schools provide children with knowledge and skills that give them access to the economy. This is the job training function of the schools. Schools prepare you to make a decent living. A decent living provides you with a decent standard of housing, clothing, food, and health care. Second, schools provide children with the knowledge and skills that give them access to the culture of the nation through the study of the liberal arts and sciences—history, art, music, literature, mathematics, and science.

Since civil and political rights had already been won in the courts and in the legislatures, all that remained to extend full citizenship to everyone was to give every child a standard of education that would provide them with social rights, first through job training, and second through transmission of the common national culture. But Marshall recognized that children appear to have unequal capacities for this kind of learning and that they are not equally willing to put in the effort this kind of learning requires, and so this scheme would not provide equal income and equal access to the national culture for every citizen.

His plan was to enable all students to compete for high-status educational programs and to select students for those programs on the basis of examinations. Theoretically, if you are smart and work hard, you get a place in a high-status program. If you are not very smart or you don't work hard, you don't get a place in a high status program—regardless of the socioeconomic status or background of your family. Of course, high-status school programs lead to high-status, highly paid occupations, which in turn lead to more economic security and the ability to participate more fully in the national culture. The setup Marshall described came to be called "meritocracy." It is reminiscent of Thomas Jefferson's 200-year-old concept of a "natural aristocracy."

The history of citizenship in the U.S. is somewhat different from that of Great Britain, but we are at a similar place as far as Marshall's analysis is concerned. Theoretically, all American adults have civil and political rights. We depend on our schools to provide job training and access to the national culture. We recognize social inequalities, but we believe in equal opportunity. We sort children based on standardized tests, the grand-daddy of them all being the Scholastic Aptitude Test (SAT), and we believe the unequal distribution of income and status that results is fair because it is done on the basis of aptitude and willingness to work—not on social class.

I believe this model of the citizenship has entered the American psyche and is accepted, perhaps unconsciously, by most American teachers. It is a myth, however, because it is based on the falsehood that when children enter school at around age six, they are all more or less on the same footing, and that aptitude and willingness to work are randomly distributed. But we all know this is not true, and we know that achievement and willingness to work, as reflected in standardized test scores, are highly correlated with the socioeconomic status of children's families. Conservatives feel comfortable with this fact. Their explanation is: Poor people are not as smart, and they are certainly not as willing to work hard. That's why they are poor people. Conversely, rich people are smarter and they work harder. That's why they are rich.

In answer to that, I give you our forty-third President, who is alleged to have a very modest SAT score but was admitted to his father's alma mater, Yale, where he brags about being a "C" student, who winks about raising hell till he was forty, and who was admitted to Harvard's MBA program. On merit? But one privileged child's story doesn't prove the point. There are empirical studies that show that social rights are not distributed evenly or fairly in our schools.

SCHOOLING FOR POOR AND WORKING-CLASS STUDENTS

Jean Anyon (1980) observed fifth-grade classrooms where students' families were in different socioeconomic brackets.[1] These are some of the facts she reported: In "working-class" schools, knowledge was presented as isolated facts and skills. Work was easy; it consisted of copying the teacher's notes from the board and writing answers to test questions. A student's capacity for creativity and planning was denied or ignored. The students' movement and access to materials were tightly controlled. When asked, "Can you create knowledge?" nearly all students answered, "No." The dominant theme was Resistance. Students vandalized school property, interrupted the teacher, refused to answer questions, and expressed boredom. Work called for nothing beyond functional literacy—the ability to read easy texts, write words or phrases in answer to questions, and write short, personal narratives.

In "affluent professional" schools, Anyon (1980) found student work was challenging. In science, students experimented in their own way to discover principles and facts. They discussed methods and ideas with other students. When asked, "How should I do this?" the teacher answered "You decide. What makes sense to you?" Control involved constant negotiation. Students asked for reasons for teachers' decisions and challenged the validity of the reasons. When asked, "Can you create knowledge?" most students answered, "Yes." The dominant theme was Individualism. Emphasis was on thinking for oneself, creativity, and discovery. Work regularly called for informational literacy—the ability to read typical school texts and write reports. Work frequently called for powerful literacy—the ability to read, evaluate, analyze, synthesize, and criticize textbook writing and to use oral and written language to reason, solve problems, and create new knowledge. Powerful literacy is the language of negotiation. It is based on a consciousness of one's power, the ability to recognize one's interests, identify issues, marshal facts, and formulate arguments and plans.

Anyon (1980) argues that working-class students were prepared for wage labor, labor that is mechanical and routine, and where workers have little autonomy, while affluent, professional students were prepared for work as artists, intellectuals, lawyers, scientists, and professionals, work that is inherently interesting and where workers have a great deal of autonomy. Her study supported the findings of earlier observers of American schools that confirmed the theory of economic reproduction (Bowles & Gintis, 1976). Working-class children are taught to do mechanical low-paying work, and they learn to resist authority in ways sanctioned by their community. Affluent professional children are taught to create products and art—symbolic capital—and to negotiate with Anyon's (1980) "executive elites" who make the final decision in our society on how real capital is allocated.

Paul Willis (1977) observed a group of English working-class boys who were referred to by their teachers as "the lads." The most basic characteristic of the lads was opposition to authority. They cut classes, violated the dress code, indulged in sex, drinking, and smoking, and they flaunted it. They valued violence, sexism, and racism as manly traits. They valorized physical strength and practical know-how and had only disdain for useless abstract theoretical knowledge. They viewed middle-class culture with disdain. The lads had developed "oppositional identity" (Ogbu, 1991). With oppositional identity, I define *me* as *not you* (the dominant class culture, the culture represented by teachers). I refuse to accept the values, attitudes, beliefs, and behaviors associated with your culture, and I insist on expressing values, attitudes, beliefs, and behaviors associated with my culture. If that is offensive to you, so much the better.

Willis (1977) proposed that in real schools, that is, schools attended by middle-class and wealthier students, the teacher has the high-status knowledge students want. It will buy them good grades, high test scores, diplomas, and entrance into high-status colleges. In order to obtain it, students cooperate—more or less. But what if the students are "the lads"? What if they see no advantage in gaining high-status knowledge or are, in fact, repelled by it? You can try regimes of massive force and ever more strict control and punishment, but it does not work. In order to gain even a modicum of cooperation, teachers make the school work easier and easier, and when school work is easy enough, students cooperate enough to make it look as if school is in progress. What you get are "make-believe" schools. Unfortunately, that's what we have in most of our schools that are attended by poor and working-class students.

So now you have some of the reasons why Marshall's vision of equality through the concept of citizenship is a myth. It relies on the belief that civil and political rights were "passed down" and that social rights (the final ingredient in equality through universal citizenship) are distributed fairly, if not equally, in our schools. The facts are: (a) Every advance in civil and political rights was preceded by agitation perpetrated by parties who were denied their rights; and (b) Social rights are not distributed equally or fairly in our schools. Schools are failing in their function of securing social rights for working-class students, and it will take agitation to change this. But in this case, it is children who are short changed. Who is to agitate on their behalf? I believe it is the teachers and parents of working-class students (and perhaps older students themselves) who must act.

SOCIAL CLASS DISCOURSE AND SCHOOL DISCOURSE

The causes of class-related differences in schooling are a lot more complicated than teachers, students, or parents behaving badly. There are constellations of forces at work that produce what Anyon (1980) observed in her working-class and affluent professional classrooms. For example, Bernstein (1971) put forward the argument that working-class communication tends to be implicit and middle-class communication tends to be explicit because of differing values, attitudes, beliefs, and behaviors of the two classes. Working-class parents also tend to be more authoritarian. Picture a father and a ten-year-old:

Go to bed.

Why?

Because I said so.

Middle-class parents tend to be less authoritarian, more inclined to negotiate. Picture a father and a ten-year-old:

Go to bed.

Why?

Because you have to go to school tomorrow.

I was up later last night.

[And on, and on, and on. Junior finally goes to bed having won an extra ten minutes and just a little more experience in negotiating.]

Working-class society tends to demand more conformity.

You know what we think about those war protesters around here.

Yeah.

Middle-class society tends to demand less conformity.

I think war protesters ought to support our troops.

I think war protesters do support our troops.

I agree with them, but I think they energize pro-war voters.

[And on, and on, and on. No one changes their opinion much, but there's a lot of talk and everyone has a little more practice at what they are already very good at—argument and persuasion.]

Bernstein (1971) further argues that working-class people tend to live in a more intimate society where contacts are family, neighbors, people at work and at church, and lifelong friends—people with similar backgrounds, education, and beliefs. They are often not accustomed to talking to people who are very different from themselves, and therefore, they habitually imply meanings or leave them unspoken. Middle-class people, on the other hand, tend to be in frequent communication with absolute strangers in business, professional, and social situations; therefore, they habitually state things explicitly because they don't know what the person they are addressing knows or believes.

Middle-class people are conscious of their social and political power. They form associations, often with strangers, to address social, civic, and political grievances. This often calls for fact finding, arguing, persuading, debating, and negotiating—all of which require explicit language. Working-class adults feel relatively powerless, and so they seldom form such associations. Once more, they refrain from occasions calling for explicit language.

Shirley Brice Heath's (1983) study of professional people in a small city and textile mill workers in a nearby town describes social class contrasts similar to Bernstein's. Heath refers to the textile mill workers as Roadvillers. They live in an intimate society, value conformity, and believe in strict discipline for children. They prefer to rely on the spoken word rather than print. Rather than read the rules for a new game, for example, they learn to play it from someone who knew how. In assembling purchases, they use common sense rather than read the directions.

There was little writing done in the home except for letters and notes occasionally written by the mother. People did not engage in literacy beyond the functional level. At about age one, children were introduced to alphabet books and books with pictures of familiar objects such as trucks. When storybooks were introduced, at about age three, parents focused on teaching the child to sit still and listen. After a story was read, children were asked factual questions—not *how* and *why* questions—and they were discouraged from considering *what-if* questions.

I'll refer to the professional city dwellers in Heath's (1983) study as Maintowners. Maintown homes and communities tended to be less authoritarian. A parent's friends and associates tended to include professional and business contacts—people with dissimilar or unknown backgrounds, education, and beliefs. Maintowners tended to feel powerful, and they relied on print for information and advice. They chose movies on the basis of reviews and made purchases on the recommendations of consumers' guides. Both parents did work-related writing at home and wrote friendly letters as well as letters to politicians and newspapers. They regularly engaged in powerful literacy.

Parents began to read to children as young as six months. With the onset of speech, book reading sessions tended to be interactive with the parent following the child's lead and talking about what the child seemed to be interested in. Around age three, children learned to listen and to hold their questions until the story was over. Then parents asked factual questions followed by *why* and *how* questions, and finally critical questions—Did you believe it? Did you like it? How did it make you feel? Of course, this is the way of taking meaning from print that is used in the language of power, and Maintown youngsters are exposed to it before they enter kindergarten.

Whereas Bernstein (1971) and Heath (1983) talk about the ways culture and communication style interact, Gee (1994) proposes that both culture and communication are parts of a more complex system known as "discourse." He refers to groups of people who accept and conform to common values, attitudes, behaviors, beliefs, experiences, ways of learning, and ways of expressing what they know as "discourse communities." We acquire discourses we are immersed in without necessarily being consciously aware of the values, attitudes, ways of learning, and so on that make up the discourse. It appears to occur naturally, just as acquiring your native language in infancy seems to occur naturally.

We all acquire what Gee (1994) refers to as our "primary discourse" at our mother's knee, so to speak—the discourse of face-to-face oral communication with those close to us in the community where we start life. As we sally forth, we acquire "secondary discourses," those of the playground and Sunday school, for example. When we are exposed to a discourse community whose values, attitudes, and style of communication are in serious conflict with our own, we notice. If we are not ready to abandon ours and accept conflicting ones, we simply cannot acquire the new discourse or join that discourse community. This is another way of describing the source of the oppositional identity of such students as the lads. Their discourse conflicted with the discourse of school and they simply refused to accept it.

And so Marshall's idea that schools distribute social rights, not equally, but fairly, is a myth. Beginning long before they enter school, working-class children are not as well-prepared for the standardized tests, that will determine their share of social rights, as are children who are economically better off. The tests themselves are based on middle-class and affluent discourses.

MAKING MARSHALL'S VISION A REALITY

Gee (1994) makes an important distinction between acquiring a discourse and learning one. We can learn new discourses as Anyon (1980), Bernstein (1971), and Heath (1983) learned the discourses of the communities they studied. In order to learn a discourse, you must be consciously aware of the values, attitudes, ways of learning, that it comprises. Once we learn a discourse, we can critique it. We can think about what would have to change in order to accomplish specific goals—such as a teacher's attempts to impart powerful literacy to students whose discourse is in fact interfering with that goal. Having learned a discourse, we can suspend judgment and operate within it for our own ends, even if we do not accept its values—such as a male chauvinist selling computer software to the National Organization of Women. Working-class students can operate within the discourse of an affluent professional classroom in the same way. The challenge to educators is to find out how to motivate them to want to.

When I was a teacher education student in the 1950s, I was taught that there are two kinds of motivation. If you want to learn something because you are interested in it, the way some people are interested in science, history, or literature, that's called intrinsic motivation, and it is what we should strive for with our students (or so I was taught). If you want to learn something to get a good grade, or go to a good college, but otherwise you're not much interested in it, that is called extrinsic motivation; supposedly, it is not as good as intrinsic motivation.

After the social upheavals of the 1960s and 1970s, a third kind of motivation was suggested (Oller & Perkins, 1978). For example, if you go to an overcrowded high school where fewer than half the teachers are fully certified and more than half the students drop out, and you live in a part of town where unemployment is double the national average, and housing is substandard, and nearly everyone is without health insurance, and your little sister goes to a school where they just paved the playground for a teachers' parking lot, and you want to learn the discourse of power and become a teacher, organizer, or lawyer so you can fight to get families like those in your community a better deal, that is called Freirean motivation.

Motivation plays an interesting role in poor and working-class schools. Most teachers in these schools do not think much about intrinsic motivation, but they think about extrinsic motivation a lot. There are repeated references to learning things because they will be on the test. When teachers of poor and working-class students find outstanding students they usually encourage them with the promise of going to college and joining the middle class. Some refer to such students as border crossers—those who accept middle-class (real school) discourse and cross over. This is far different from Freirean motivation. The student with Freirean motivation learns middle-class (real-school) discourse not to cross over but to address the inequities and injustices suffered by his or her community.

I do not encourage teachers to stop looking for border crossers and helping them to cross. This has been going on for generations. I've had my share of success in this area myself, both as a student and as a teacher. It is what enables us to continue to think there are no real class barriers in America. But this process does not address the problems of educating the vast majority of poor and working-class students. Freirean motivation does address these problems and has the potential to transform poor and working-class classrooms into real classrooms, but with rather different objectives than traditional educators usually think about.

PAULO FREIRE AND SAUL ALINSKY

Freire (1970) was the widely known Brazilian educator who motivated the poor of Brazil to learn to read and write by leading them to reflect on their position in the world and the injustices they suffered, and to see that their plight was not God's will or the result of immutable fate, but instead, was the result of a social and political system of human invention. What humans have invented, humans can change. And so Freire started his literacy classes—not with reading and writing—but with literacy circles. He gathered his students together and showed them drawings representing familiar objects and scenes, and he encouraged discussion and dialogue.

For example, he would display a drawing showing a cow, a pig, some birds, and a man and a woman. The woman is holding a book and the man is holding a clay water jar. There are a rake and hoe on the ground and a well near by. Freire would ask how people were different from animals. In this discussion he would try to elicit the following ideas: People can make culture (the rake, the hoe, the jar, the book, and the well); animals cannot. People can communicate both with speech and graphic symbols; animals cannot. Such discussions led to generalizations such as the following: *The proper role of people is to be active and to communicate with others—not to be passive or to be used by others. Proper communication between people is dialogue between equals* (Brown, 1975).

Of course, Freire was asking his students to talk about something they already knew, but had perhaps never put into words—that people are entitled to liberty, equality, and fraternity; to life, liberty, and the pursuit of happiness; to dignity and justice; to democracy. This came into conflict with the reality of the lives of the poor people of Brazil. It comes into conflict with the reality of the lives of Anyon's working-class school children and of Willis' lads.

Freire believed that you didn't do people any favors by simply making them more conscious of their misery. Conscientization must motivate people to act to counter injustice because it is the victims of injustice who must act. Others may help, but they cannot do it for them. Nonviolent campaigns (the only kind that work, in the end) require powerful literacy. And so Freire's idea was to help the poor of Brazil see that learning to read and write was part of their struggle for justice for themselves and their children. He was successful enough to get himself arrested and then deported by the military junta that overthrew Brazil's first elected government in 1964.

Saul Alinsky, a graduate of the Department of Sociology at the University of Chicago, organized poor and working-class neighborhoods in Chicago around issues such as inferior municipal services. He organized citizens the way union organizers organized workers—and with a similar aim—to advance their collective self-interest. Through organizing and action, poor and working-class citizens learned to form associations with people beyond their usual circle, and they learned the language of negotiation and the attitudes and values it is based on (Alinsky, 1946, 1971). They were Roadvillers who learned the discourse of Maintown without becoming Maintowners. In fact, they were negotiating with Maintowners and their motivation was Freirean.

Many American teachers of poor and working-class students are disciples of Freire and Alinsky. These educators believe that if they are going to succeed, they must turn working-class schools into real schools, and therefore, they must make their students want the high-status knowledge they have to offer. They do this by making their students aware, on a conscious, political level, of what's at stake. Discussing social and political issues and how they affect students and their families is as much a part of their literacy curriculum as spelling. Then working-class students have a reason to cooperate and work hard, like rich students and for the same reasons. It is in their self-interest. This is what I call *literacy with an attitude—educating working-class children in their individual and collective self-interest*. The Institute for Democracy in Education at Ohio University, and the Institute for Democracy, Education, and Access (IDEA) at the University of California at Los Angeles, are among the centers of activity for such educators. The National Coalition of Education Activists in Philadelphia and the Coalition for Educational Justice in Los Angeles are among the centers of activity for such educators and their parent and student allies.

WHAT I'VE LEARNED WHILE LIVING OUT OF A SUITCASE

As I write this, *Literacy with an Attitude* (1999) has been out for over seven years, and during that time I have addressed groups and held workshops for principals, curriculum coordinators, teachers, parents, graduate and undergraduate teacher education students, and high school students in several states. These occasions have given me the opportunity to talk to many people in large and small group settings and in individual conversations.

Most of the teachers, parents, and students I've talked to found that Anyon (1980) confirmed what they already knew about schools attended by low-to-middle income versus high-income children, but they said they had never understood the connection between schooling and their students' future social and economic status so clearly. Most found the idea of economic reproduction new, but consistent with what they knew about American schools and society.

Occasionally, a teacher or principal would say that Anyon (1980) is probably correct for the most part, but *this* working-class school, or *my* working-class classroom really resembles the affluent professional school of Anyon's (1980) study. Almost always, another person in the same session would point out that, although there were bright spots in a few schools and classrooms, when you compare low-income schools with high-income schools district-wide, Anyon's (1980) description and analysis is quite accurate. This is, of course, consistent with the generally accepted belief that although teachers and principals can make a difference, they have little effect on the entire system, and the differences they do make are so difficult to maintain they often result in burnout and regression.

I have found there are three categories of readers when it comes to Freirean motivation. First, there are those who get it and love it. They are the choir, as in "preaching to the choir." Second, there are those who get it, but they don't love it. They say it's radical, politicizing education—depriving children of their childhoods—and class warfare. To them I say unequal educational outcomes related to class are unjust. It is equally political to pretend they don't exist, or to rationalize them as just the way it is.

Third, there are those who think they get it, but they don't. These are often good teachers who see themselves as progressive, but they see every new idea—Freire, whole language, outcomes-based education, for example—as "exciting." They do not see these ideas are inconsistent because they reinterpret every new idea to fit their assumptions—frequently unconscious, unexamined assumptions. They speak of Freire in the same breath as Marie Clay (1972) and Nancie Atwell (1987), people who were influential in promoting higher levels of literacy among students through progressive and humane methods, but people who would not give George W. Bush's Department of Education a moment's pause. It is my belief that if words and phrases like *call to action*, *speaking truth to power*, and *attitude* don't come to mind when you think of Freire, you don't get Freire.

There is also the question of why my book, which is based on studies ten- to twenty-years old, would be of use to anyone trying to promote a Freirean approach to the education of working-class students today. I believe the answer is that the vast majority of elementary and high school teachers I have met didn't know any of this and they find it astonishing. I've gotten comments like: "This explains what I've been observing in my classroom for ten years, but never understood." And, "This describes my educational history and the schools I went to. I suddenly understood what happened to me." A friend of mine, who taught history for thirty-five years in Buffalo high schools, called me after reading the chapter on the make-believe classroom and said, "I understand it all now. I wasn't a teacher; they weren't students; and it wasn't a school!"

TEACHER EDUCATION WITH AN ATTITUDE

What does it mean that classroom teachers did not know about these studies done ten and twenty years ago—studies they find fascinating and of vital relevance to their classroom practice? What's wrong with our preservice teacher education in colleges and universities and with our in-service professional development programs?

In departments of education at colleges and universities, subject matter is divided into departments and courses within departments in various ways, but there is one nearly universal divide. History, sociology, and philosophy of education are taught in one department, frequently called Social Foundations of Education, and curriculum and instruction are taught in another. When the prevailing philosophy of learning in Curriculum and Instruction departments leans toward empiricism and behaviorism, authors such as Anyon (1980), Willis (1977), Bernstein (1971), Heath (1983), and Gee (1994) are viewed as interesting but nonessential—to be read if students are interested and if there is room in their program. Even when the prevailing philosophy of learning in Curriculum and Instruction departments is constructivist, knowledge of these authors may be seen as important, but their students' other needs may seem more pressing. Knowledge of these authors is viewed as foundational; that's why they call departments where their students are supposed to learn it Foundations departments.

I believe it is the relationship between these two sides of teacher education that explains why these authors are unknown to students in many teacher education departments and to teachers in the field. There has been a firewall between Foundations departments and departments of Curriculum and Instruction. When I started teaching at the University at Buffalo in 1973, master's students were required to take six hours in Foundations. I didn't really know what they learned over there, because I had practically no contact with that department. Although I did read Bernstein in the late 1960s because of my interest in linguistics, and I read Freire in the early 1970s, I didn't read Anyon (1980) or Willis (1977) when they were published; I read them in the 1990s. By that time my interests had developed from linguistics, to psycholinguistics, to sociolinguistics, to the social context of schooling and learning, and finally to the politics of schooling, learning, and equity.

In the 1970s, when my students talked about the courses they took in Foundations, their comments were not usually positive. "They're all theory over there. Not real world stuff." In fact, I know just what they mean. I once had a student who was doing a master's thesis who asked me for a definition of working-class. I naively called a sociologist over there to see if he could help, and I got ten minutes of angry rhetoric that I am sure only a Marxist scholar would have understood. I am not a Marxist scholar. I thanked him kindly and looked elsewhere for an answer.

There was a certain dismissiveness on the part of faculty and students in each department towards each other. Foundations people saw us as people who were interested in rather pedestrian things such as how to teach spelling in fifth grade, and we saw them as people who were interested in somewhat irrelevant things which they presented in a really impenetrable discourse. By 1980, my department had dropped its requirement that masters degree students take two courses in Foundations without a word of protest from that department. Shame on both of us.

Of course, understanding social class, economic reproduction, oppositional identity, student resistance, conscientization, and liberating education is important to fifth-grade language arts teachers. The very process of raising our students' consciousness of injustice, of the failure of American schools to live up to American ideals, of helping our students and their students see their role in the problem, and in the solution, depends on the kind of insights that Foundations department faculty have. It is such work and inquiry that permitted Anyon (1980), Willis (1977), and others to look at the same things we were looking at and understand what was really happening. The rest of us, without this training, didn't get it. I had the same reaction when I read these studies that many readers of the book have reported to me—"My god, this explains what I've been looking at for years!" So why aren't my students over there beating down Foundation's doors to get these insights?

I think Foundations faculty should remember some very old-fashioned educational ideas. Instead of using the discourse that was used when I asked for a definition of working-class, they should gear their instruction to student's previous knowledge and their needs. They should ask: "Why should these students be interested in this? What's in it for them?" On the other hand, those of us in Curriculum and Instruction need to help our students understand why they need what folks in Foundations have to offer.

Of course, we mustn't forget that knowledge and skill in curriculum and instruction are equally important for teachers engaged in this struggle. I taught in urban schools all through the 1960s, mostly on the south side of Chicago, and saw many a flower child who had the struggle for justice part down pretty well, but apparently no knowledge of how to teach, and not much interest in the hard work teaching requires. It was not a pretty picture.

In my experience, the firewall has come down somewhat since I first joined a teacher education faculty in the 1970s. I think each generation of Curriculum and Instruction faculty after my own (and that's probably two or three generations) has been progressively more concerned about the social context of teaching and learning than my generation was. But we still have a long way to go. After talking to many younger faculty, my impression is that the ideas I discuss in *Literacy with an Attitude* (1999) are pretty new to many of them, or they are ideas they know about, but to which they haven't given much serious attention.

A COLLEGE FOR TEACHERS OF WORKING-CLASS STUDENTS

Students from poor and working-class backgrounds, who are preparing to become teachers and who will almost certainly teach poor and working-class children, are not educated as working-class people. I attended Chicago Teachers College forty years ago, where my classmates were overwhelmingly from poor and working-class homes, but our origins were totally ignored. In English courses we read such novels as *Studs Lonigan* as examples of American realism, without a mention of the fact that *Studs Lonigan* was about us, about our families, our neighborhoods, our place in American society in the middle of the twentieth century. In fact, the setting for *Studs Lonigan* was a twenty-minute streetcar ride from our campus.

We were not given any special preparation for teaching poor and working-class children, although we would almost certainly teach such students. We were treated as if we were middle-class college students who would teach middle-class K–12 students. If there was any reference to the fact that we would be teaching poor and working-class students it was in the context of how to make them middle-class adults, that is, to find border-crossers (which most of us were ourselves) and give them a hand. The idea of empowering working-class students as working-class students was simply not on anyone's mind. I don't think this situation has changed.

I've done considerable thinking about what the ideal teacher preparation program would look like if it were designed to prepare students to educate working-class children in their own self-interest. I believe such a program would attract mostly students who come from working-class families, but students from more affluent families would, of course, be welcome. (Some of my staunchest allies—Mary Finn, for example—come from middle-class or affluent professional families.) The first strand of the three-strand curriculum I have in mind would be a specialized curriculum for undergraduates. Each liberal arts department would develop one or two courses that examine their discipline through the lens of social class, such as:

- working-class literature, drama, film, art, and music

- the history of social change: such as the labor, civil rights, and womens movements

- the economics of poverty and globalization

- the sociology of class.

I've found that such courses are already offered at many institutions. There is no reason these courses could not be organized into a coherent course of study around the concepts presented in this paper, such as:

- identity formation (oppositional identity)

- the function of education in working-class lives

- the role of economic reproduction

- working-class discourse, including attitudes toward authority, conformity, isolation, power, and relationship to the printed word

- beliefs about learning

- the role of extrinsic and Freirean motivation in their lives.

Students could satisfy their core requirements with these courses and organize them into a program leading to a specialization in working-class studies.

The second strand would be a professional education component that would address curriculum and instruction as well as history, philosophy, psychology, and sociology of education. Assuming that we want to educate progressive teachers for all classes of American children, we've got our work cut out for us. Most students presenting themselves to be educated as teachers tend to be unconscious behaviorists because they have attended twelve years of American schools dominated by behaviorist assumptions. This is especially true if they attended working-class schools. If we do not address this problem explicitly and teach curriculum and instruction from a constructivist point of view, we will continue to find our recent graduates in schools teaching with a behaviorist point of view within a short time.

Economic reproduction, oppositional identity, student resistance, make-believe schooling, the kind of schooling found in affluent professional class-rooms, the concepts of discourse, Freirean motivation, and powerful literacy need to be presented as arguments favoring curriculum and methods of teaching from a holistic, constructivist, and sociological point of view. The notion of discourse and levels of literacy would be central throughout the curriculum, but particularly in language arts.

The objective of the third strand of the program would be to produce teachers who not only conscientize students, but their parents as well, and become both students' and parents' allies in taking action to end the injustices they face (Finn, Johnson, & Finn, 2005). Therefore, the third strand of the program would consist of courses in problem solving, organizing, and negotiation. It is, of course, important that we not simply make poor and working-class students aware of how bad off they are; we must also to give them the tools they need to combat the injustices they face. These topics would be taught in one-hour courses spread over three or four semesters. Students would also be able to earn credit for internships at union locals or community organizations such as those affiliated with the Industrial Areas Foundation that are active today in various parts of the United States (Shirley, this volume).

Progressive labor organizers who see education as their best hope in rebuilding membership and reclaiming the influence industrial unions once had in representing the political and economic interests of working families could be an important ally in developing and promoting this third strand. They have developed a whole new field of labor education called popular education, where they use Freirean techniques to teach democratic principles, workers' rights, economic survival, organizing, collective bargaining, and the history and structure of social relations. What they do in popular education has a lot in common with all three strands of my proposal (Schurman, this volume).

The objective of the Teacher Education with an Attitude program is to provide working-class students with teachers who motivate them to learn in their individual and collective self-interest, and who teach them powerful literacy to negotiate a better deal for the working class. Through collaboration, Freirean faculty in schools and colleges of teacher education and labor education could build a program to prepare teachers of working-class students that would achieve both groups' democratic and social justice objectives.

NOTE

1. Anyon actually observed four categories of schools: working-class, middle-class, affluent professional, and executive elite. I have confined this discussion to two categories.

REFERENCES

Alinsky, S. (1946). *Reveille for radicals.* Chicago: University of Chicago Press.

Alinsky, S. (1971). *Rules for radicals: A practical primer for realistic radicals.* New York: Random House.

Anyon, J. (1980). Social class and the hidden curriculum of work. *Journal of Education, 162*(1), 7–92.

Atwell, N. (1987). *In the middle: Reading, writing, and learning with adolescents.* Portsmouth, NH: Heinemann.

Bernstein, B. (1971). *Theoretical studies towards a sociology of education.* London: Routledge and Kegan Paul.

Bowles, S., & Gintis, H. (1976). *Schooling in capitalist America: Educational reform and the contradiction of economic life.* New York: Basic Books.

Brown, C. (1975). *Literacy in 30 hours: Paulo Freire's process in north east Brazil.* London: Centre for Open Learning and Teaching, Writers and Readers Publishing Cooperative.

Clay, M. (1972). *Reading: The patterning of complex behavior.* London: Heinemann.

Finn, P. (1999). *Literacy with an attitude: Educating working class children in their own self-interest.* Albany: State University of New York Press.

Finn, P., Johnson, L., & Finn, M. (2005). Workshops with an attitude. In L. Johnson, M. Finn, & R. Lewis (Eds.), *Urban education with an attitude* (pp. 193–217). Albany: State University of New York Press.

Freire, P. (1970). *Pedagogy of the oppressed.* New York: Seabury Press.

Gee, J. (1994). What is literacy? In C. Mitchell & K. Weiler (Eds.), *Rewriting literacy: Culture and the discourse of the other* (pp. 3–11). New York: Bergin & Garvey.

Heath, S. B. (1983). *Ways with words.* Cambridge, UK: Cambridge University Press.

Marshall, T. H. (1950). *Citizenship and social class and other essays*. Cambridge, UK: Cambridge University Press.

Ogbu, J. E. (1991). Cultural diversity and school experience. In C. Walsh (Ed.), *Literacy as praxis: Culture, language, and pedagogy*. Norwood, NJ: Ablex Publishing.

Oller, J., & Perkins, K. (1978). Intelligence and language proficiency as sources of variance in self-reported affective variables. *Language Learning, 28*, 85–97.

Willis, P. (1977). *Learning to labour: How working-class kids get working-class jobs*. Westmead, England: Saxon House.

2 Labor Deserves Credit: The Popular Education Foundations of the National Labor College

Susan J. Schurman

SUSAN J. SCHURMAN, PRESIDENT, National Labor College, argues that popular education, based in Freirean pedagogy, offers workers an opportunity to acquire the type of analytic skills necessary to act in their own interest that members of elite groups obtain through formal education. This version of worker education is surprisingly close to Finn's (chapter 1) call for social justice teacher education for working-class children. It emphasizes full citizenship for all as essential to democracy, values experience that learners bring to the classroom, focuses on solving problems through action, and understands the need to establish teaching-learning communities. Her description of how popular education is incorporated into the education of working-class adults contains potent suggestions for preparing teachers to educate their working-class children.

This chapter describes the Freirean, popular education roots of the National Labor College, a degree-granting institution of higher education that prepares labor leaders and organizers, and suggests how infusing popular education into teacher preparation can produce social justice teachers who educate working-class children in their collective self-interest. Because popular education has been associated almost exclusively with nonformal education, education that takes place outside and even in opposition to school-based education, there are some who insist that degree-based education cannot, by definition, be popular education (i.e., cannot educate for critical consciousness and social change).

Historically, it is hard to argue with this view. Popular education, developed by Paulo Freire (1973, 1982) in his adult literacy campaign in Brazil, was clearly an alternative to the state sanctioned formal education systems that controlled pathways to power and privilege by limiting access to educational credentials. In the United States, ideologies for restricting access to formal postsecondary education, based on such modern constructs as intelligence quotient (IQ) or test scores, have been the principal means of concealing the facts of educational and social inequality (Bowles & Gintis, 1976).

As John Hurst (2002) has made clear, popular education in the United States emerged specifically to help workers, minorities, and other oppressed groups acquire the kind of analytic skills to act in their own interest that members of elite groups obtain through formal education. Indeed virtually all forms of nonformal education have their roots in opposition to, or in compensation for, exclusion from the formal education system. Given this history, it should come as no surprise that an ideology has evolved asserting that the nonformal status of popular education is critical to its emancipatory role.

In this chapter I want to take issue with this claim. I want to argue that there is no inherent reason—apart from political power—that popular education methodology cannot serve as the foundation for formal workers' education, as well as for the preparation of teachers of working-class children. Indeed, if one reads Freire's (1973, 1982) work carefully, it is clear that his method was specifically designed to introduce illiterate people to the analytic processes associated with social research from both the Marxist and Western liberal traditions.

As Elaine Bernard (2002) and others rightly point out, neither popular education nor labor education is ideologically neutral. But neither is business education, economics, or even medicine, and some have argued effectively that teachers have historically been prepared to maintain the social and economic status quo, hardly a neutral stance (Bowles & Gintis, 1976). The difference is that the power of business and the medical profession to insert their point of view into the academic curriculum has grown in recent years while the power of labor education's traditional constituencies has weakened (Krause, 1999). As a consequence, after gaining a toehold in the academy during the second half of the twentieth century, academic labor education programs faced continuing pressure to adopt a more neutral or objective stance—which basically means to "stop teaching that class warfare stuff."

Business schools, however, can openly teach union avoidance in their classrooms as a matter of sound business policy, despite the fact that employees have the right to form or join unions—which is still the law of the land. Meanwhile, beneath the smokescreen generated by conservative academics such as Alan Bloom (1987) and E. D. Hirsch Jr. (1987)—who have been loudly screeching about the takeover of the academy by the "leftist professoriate"[1]— the disappearance over the past two decades of social class as a legitimate and important subject of study in the academy has been nothing short of spectacular (Rorty, 1998).

Arguing for popular education as the basis of formal degree-based instruction for workers, as well as the basis of teacher preparation, however, requires a focus on its content as well as its form (Bernard, 2002). I would rephrase Bernard's (2002) definition of popular education slightly for purposes of analysis: popular education (1) begins with recognizing and respecting people's own practical knowledge, gained through experience; (2) adds the core skills of theo-retical analysis and expression or literacy to validly understand and describe their own social, economic, and cultural condition in relation to other social actors; and (3) aims to empower them with the personal and collective efficacy to design actions that will enable them to advance their interests in a pluralistic society. Teachers who want to "educate working-class children in their own self-interest" (Finn, 1999) will need a sound preparation in this content.

While the second and third elements of this definition fall squarely within the historic mission of formal higher education—albeit mostly for the upper classes, the first element, the role of experience, is a point of intense political conflict. To bring popular education into the formal educational process for workers and for teachers requires the incorporation of experiential learning, a goal of progressive educators dating back a century and more. The National Labor College is intentionally constructed to incorporate all three of these essential elements of popular education into its curriculum and pedagogy. In the sections that follow I will try to describe how this has been accomplished so that teacher educators can determine what of our experiences might apply to their programs.

THE POLITICS OF EXPERIENCE: WHOSE GETS VALUED?

The question of whose experience gets valued in the formal educational curriculum lies at the heart of political contesting in all societies. Pipan (1989) defines curriculum as that aspect of "the cultural environment that has been selected as a set of possibilities for learning transactions." This definition calls attention to the fact that the cultural environment always contains multiple options for knowledge construction and transmission through the education process. The ways in which political interests are embedded in the curriculum can be examined through four basic questions:

1. Which aspects of cultural practice have been selected?

2. Who has the power to decide what is learned and by whom?

3. What is the specific character of the teaching-learning (pedagogic) practices?

4. What opportunities or prohibitions for action are implied in the learn-ing process?

John Dewey (1910), arguably one of the greatest U.S. philosophers, sum-marized the matter by pointing out that a system of education is the practical application of political philosophy. In the United States, the contest over cur-riculum does not follow simple partisan lines. In general, liberals and progressives advocate the incorporation of personal experience in the learning process while conservatives insist that the curriculum rest on selected experience from the past culled into a canon. Indeed, the insistence on the relevance of contemporary individual experience—in addition to or in place of the canon—is the hallmark of educational progressivism. However, many populists of all stripes want to throw out the entire formal education system, and attempts to do so (such as the home schooling movement) cut across the political spectrum.

It all boils down to a power struggle over who gets to decide the content of the curriculum. Even many progressives who otherwise advocate the inclusion of experiential learning in the formal education process, nevertheless want to confine to professionals the selection of which types of experience get counted, rather than allowing learners to participate. This poses serious problems within the context of adult worker and trade union leadership education for two primary reasons. First, adult learners possess rich experiential learning histories that contain what educational psychologists call the "basic empirical referents" to which all abstract concepts and theories refer. Indeed much of the formal learning process is really about discovering the power of theoretical knowledge to connect these basic referents in new ways to reveal new understandings (Novak, 1977; Novak & Gowin, 1985). Second, excluding the learners' experience deprives the teacher of a rich source of learning transactions on which to construct both the content as well as the instructional approach to the course.

Philosopher Gilbert Rile (1984) distinguished between practical knowledge (know how) and theoretical knowledge (know why). The former has always been the province of working people—the laboring classes; the latter owned by elites. The historical task of workers' education has been twofold: first to obtain recognition for the value of workers' practical knowledge; then to supply the theoretical tools that will enable workers to act more effectively in their own interests. In *Education for Critical Consciousness*, Paulo Freire (1973) clearly states the need to connect theory to practical knowledge in order to develop critical consciousness, the goal of popular education:

> Our traditional curriculum, disconnected from life, centered on words emptied of the reality they are meant to represent, lacking in concrete activity, could never develop a critical consciousness. Indeed, its own naïve dependence on high-sounding phrases, reliance on rote, and tendency toward abstractedness actually intensifies our naïveté.

Freire (1973) uses the term "praxis" to connote the explicit link between theoretical and practical knowledge in the development of effective action-change plans. Praxis is a Greek word that refers to action that is consciously aimed. It has come to represent an approach to social change in which interventions (actions) are grounded in the best available theories, and theories are amended based on the careful evaluation of the results of interventions. As

Freire's (1973) work demonstrated, it is entirely possible to develop a system of nonformal education to develop critical consciousness. But I doubt very much that he would have turned down the opportunity to embed his educational praxis inside the Brazilian formal education system, or in the preparation of teachers, if it were offered.

In the United States, the next important democratic project of labor education is to advance formal higher education opportunities for workers and trade union leaders, and to see that their children's teachers receive an education that prepares them to encourage and support these opportunities through their design of critical classroom experiences. But this cannot mean simply using organized labor's leverage to create better access to colleges and universities for working men and women. This was accomplished long ago with the advent of the community college. However, as the Brint and Krabel (1995) study of the community college system makes clear, access to institutions of higher learning does not mean access to the kind of instruction that leads to critical consciousness.[2]

Critical education—education that questions why things are the way they are—will not be accomplished without incorporation of the philosophy and pedagogy of critical consciousness into the formal educational system, and especially into the preparation of teachers of working-class children. The U.S. trade union movement must solidly anchor this philosophy and pedagogy within their own formal education, as well as press for its incorporation into the preparation of the teachers of their children. Such a project cannot be imposed from outside but must be generated within U.S. trade union institutions, which means overcoming the fact that very few unions encourage or promote the exercise of critical consciousness by their members (Bernard, 2002).

Union culture in the United States is based on strict notions of internal solidarity as the basis of collective power. Dissent is viewed as a threat to solidarity and therefore a threat to collective power. Such a culture makes it very difficult for unions to develop processes of critical reflection on their own practice. However, such processes are vitally important during periods of dramatic economic upheaval as unions seek to make the kind of changes required if they are to succeed in attracting more workers to the labor movement. Progressive teachers and teacher educators may find these thoughts about union culture similar to the culture of many schools, where dissent and asking "why?" is only minimally tolerated.

To succeed, such a process of collective reflection and learning must be firmly controlled by workers and their unions, or in the case of public education, by parents of working-class children. Outside experts and institutions can and must play an important role, but workers themselves and their representatives must initiate the process and shape the curriculum. Therein lies the central premise of the dialogic method in Freire's (1973) work. Dialogue is the method through which the concept of praxis is enacted:

Only dialogue, which requires critical thinking, is also capable of generating critical thinking. Without dialogue there is no communication, and without communication there can be no true education. . . . Thus, the dialogical character of education as the practice of freedom does not begin when the teacher-student meets with the student-teacher[3] in a pedagogical situation, but rather when the former first asks himself [sic] what he will dialogue with the latter about.

. . . For the dialogical, problem-posing teacher-student, the program content of education is neither a gift nor an imposition—bits of information to be deposited in the students—but rather the organized, systematized, and developed "re-presentation" to individuals of the things about which *they want to know more* [emphasis added].

The dialogic method, as Freire (1973) describes it, is anathema to the traditional higher education institution where most teachers receive their notions of what counts as knowledge and their beliefs about how it is to be delivered. What the typical teacher education student experiences throughout his or her education is what Freire termed the banking method of instruction: expert teachers depositing bits of information into the empty heads of students. Ironically, the techniques of learner-centeredness associated with popular education are being adopted by business schools rather than by liberal arts colleges (though business schools would describe their practice as customer-focused) (Boyatzis, Kolb & Cowen, 1995).

The National Labor College is explicitly structured to create a synthesis between the principles and practice of popular education and the best liberal arts traditions of the academy. This has required developing a system for converting nonformal work and union hall based education and training (which is often occupation or industry specific) into recognized credentials that are both portable and transferable. Without these characteristics, when a worker's employment relationship is severed, both the worker and the union lose their investment in education. The worker frequently cannot even obtain recognition for training from a different employer in the same industry.

A national skills standard has been proposed to address this problem, but the best system by far is the standard college credit system because it is a system that is based on the concept of generalizability; that is, knowledge that can be transferred to settings other than the one where it was acquired. Indeed, the essence of college level learning is not the subject matter taught but the ability to define and solve novel problems in novel settings. Importantly, over the past half century, a systematic methodology has been developed for assessing the college credit equivalence of work based and life based learning. It is this system that forms the foundation of the National Labor College.

THE ARCHITECTURE OF THE NATIONAL LABOR COLLEGE

Designing labor's college presented an extraordinary opportunity to rethink some basic assumptions about how higher education might be structured for adult trade union activists and members—and, by extension, for working people in general. I will briefly summarize a number of basic principles on which the college is constructed. Much of what I say about educating adult members of the working class also pertains to the education of their children. I leave it to teacher educators to determine how these principles might enrich their program.

RECOGNITION OF FULL AND EQUITABLE CITIZENSHIP

The frustration, resentment and, too often, self-doubt that many workers feel because the value of their experience seldom receives formal recognition is far deeper than is often appreciated—even by progressive educators. Freire repeatedly emphasizes this point. In *Pedagogy of the Oppressed* (1982) he powerfully describes the struggle of the oppressed for recognition as full human beings. As my friend and colleague Mike Merrill argues, the struggle by working men and women for recognition as adult human beings, with the same rights of citizenship as those possessed by elites, is a leitmotif in the development of democratic philosophy from Plato to Augustine, through Locke, Hegel, and Simmel, down to the present.[4] (It is also the topic addressed by T. H. Marshall's (1950) essay that Finn discusses in Chapter 1).

Workers form unions and demand recognition from their employers not just in the formal legal and pragmatic sense to improve their economic lot— though this is certainly a priority. They also seek recognition in the deeper psychological and social sense captured by Freire's emphasis on being acknowledged as fully human and entitled to political equality. Part of this psychological and social recognition involves valuing the contribution workers make to society through their work.

The strong desire for full recognition of the value of workers' practical knowledge and skill—in both economic and social terms—has been central to the labor movement in the United States for two centuries. As Jane Addams wrote a century ago in the *First Report of the Labor Museum at Hull House*, "to build on worker experience is vital for more than that the best 'education' cannot do for any of us."[5] More recently, Luis Moll (1998) described working families' "funds of knowledge" as valuable resources that teachers can draw on to make their curriculum and pedagogy more authentic.

In the United States, formal educational credentials are a powerful form of recognition for experience. In the history of postsecondary education, one of the great progressive victories of the last several decades was to "get beyond seat-time," that is, to establish a method of assessing the equivalence of learning in formal and certain nonformal or informal settings. Many colleges and universities now accept a certain number of credits earned through nonformal or informal learning experiences that are properly documented in an educational portfolio. However, very few accept the full value of the portfolio assessment and most charge full tuition for each portfolio credit, with the result that very few working people can afford to obtain fair recognition for their accumulated experience. In addition, the failure to acknowledge prior life and work experience as a valid part of the educational process means that these experiences cannot serve as the critical starting place for further reflection and problematizing.

The foundation of the National Labor College is based on the recognition, to the extent allowable within the limits of higher education statutes and accreditation standards, of both the individual's and the union's extraordinary investment in securing education, training, and development opportunities. Most of our students, whose average age is 42, enter the College with the maximum allowable credits—a total of ninety—through a combination of transfer credits from other institutions and portfolio. Our students' rich experience then serves as the basis of a curriculum built on the concepts of problem-posing (as opposed to problem-solving) and critical thinking, which provide learners with maximum flexibility to choose their own learning program.

VALUING EXPERIENCE

Experience is one of those fuzzy concepts that requires, as the great psychologist William James (1890) warned, that we "attach a definite meaning to that word." Experience per se does not automatically equate to formal learning, either in the best liberal arts tradition or in popular education practice. Experiences must be reflected upon to discover their meaning, assess their value, and locate them in one's existing store of knowledge. In John Dewey's (1910) famous description, the movement between reflection and action is the mechanism through which the human capacity for deductive and inductive thinking produces personal and social development.

Labor's college cannot be only an institution that trains activists in the skills required for action. It also needs to be an institution that promotes the skills of reflection, inquiry, and exploration of the consequences of alternative courses of action. Further, it needs to be a center of scholarship on the labor movement, accumulating and disseminating the knowledge acquired from individual and collective experience.

To meet these goals, the curriculum of the National Labor College places heavy emphasis on the skills of problem-posing, critical reading, writing, discussion, and debate. This begins in the first course students take, educational planning, where they learn to reflect on and document what they have learned from their experiences and to extract the generalizable knowledge they have acquired. However, many (but by no means all) of our students have developed what Finn (1999) terms an "oppositional identity" toward formal schooling. To defend their dignity in the face of negative schooling experiences, many adopt a stance that Kohl and Greer (1995) call, "I won't learn from you." Academically, our curriculum is very demanding and, in order to succeed, students must develop a new orientation to learning, one that moves past the resistance to education that many workers developed in their own school years.

The educational planning course begins by asking students to prepare essays describing their past relationship to education. These essays provide powerful support for Finn's (1999) and Kohl and Greer's (1995) theses. They are filled with stories of humiliation, poor teaching, lack of books and materials, economic deprivation, and low expectations—on the part of both parents and schools—that is prevalent in working-class education. They are also filled with stories about how the union became their school by providing opportunities for learning, occupational skill development, and leadership, in which they were able to experience success and to "realize that maybe I was smarter than I thought."

The course then shows students how to formally document the learning they acquired in their "union school." Their portfolio characterizes and classifies prior learning experiences gained through traditional education (transfer credit), preassessed training (apprenticeships, nursing programs, and so on), and knowledge acquired through work, the union, and community service. Although no two students share the same experience, the typical student transcript from our present student body—made up of elected union leaders, staff, and activists—reflects approximately 30 to 40 transfer credits, an additional 40 to 50 credits through third-party assessed training, and 15 to 20 credits through experience.

It is hard to overstate the impact on students when they discover that they are in fact college seniors instead of freshmen or sophomores and must only complete the thirty-credit major in labor studies in order to graduate. As one student put it, "this is the most incredibly motivating thing that's ever happened to me. I have dreamed about finishing my degree for 20 years—mostly because I want to set a good example for my kids—and now I realize I can actually do it."

Through the process of first recognizing the value of their experience themselves, and then having it formally recognized in the form of a college transcript, our students discover that they are fully ready for advanced college level study. This, combined with the problem-posing, critical reading, and writing emphasis in their first courses, and the respect afforded them by their teachers, shows them that a different approach to formal education is possible.

EMPHASIZING PROBLEM-POSING AND ACTION-TAKING

The hallmark of popular education is constructing educational environments in which working people can ask and answer questions about why the society they live in is structured the way it is and how it can be changed for the better.

The ability to ask these questions is also one of the hallmarks of a liberal arts education. This is precisely why conservatives want to limit access to it. In the lexicon of higher education, these are the skills of analysis, synthesis, theorizing, critical thinking, and research. In designing the National Labor College we decided to make these skills the fulcrum of the curriculum.

All students are required to take a research methods course and complete a senior seminar. Together, these two courses prepare them to design and complete an original research paper on a topic of their own choosing. They must first learn to pose researchable problems and then to design a method for studying the problem. Their conclusions should point to concrete actions that can be taken to change the situation.

The senior research papers cover a broad range of labor and industrial relations topics, from research into safety issues, such as the lack of two-way radio communications in California mass transit vehicles, to the relationship between engineer fatigue and locomotive accidents. In the former, the research became the basis for a successful legislative campaign to mandate such communication devices on all buses. The latter research is now the basis for union legislative and collective bargaining initiatives to reduce mandatory overtime and certain types of shift work in order to reduce the risk of fatigue related accidents. These are just two of the hundreds of original research papers that have been completed over the past four years by National Labor College students working under the guidance of a skilled thesis advisor. Collectively they make a significant addition to the corpus of trade union knowledge and experience.

CREATING A TEACHING-LEARNING COMMUNITY

National Labor College faculty and staff recognize that our students are our peers. We realize daily that we have as much to learn from them—perhaps more—as they from us. We have been able to attract a group of outstanding faculty members and that has helped attract a rapidly growing and diverse student body made up of dynamic trade union leaders from all over the country, and increasingly all over the world. In addition we have developed a unique set of articulation agreements with unions and academic institutions that allow them to partner with us in delivering the National Labor College curriculum. The result is an emerging community of colearners in which activism and scholarship are integrated.

FUTURE PROSPECTS

All of us connected with the National Labor College realize the fragility of our experiment. Resources are a constant problem. Learning to collaborate with other institutions—both union and academic—is difficult. And we are still learning how to better integrate the courses in the curriculum to make a coherent whole. We have, of course, faced intense criticism from those who question whether we are just a diploma mill, but our students are our best advocates. They are excited about their studies and highly motivated to complete their research. They, in turn, keep us motivated.

It is important to remember that what we are doing is not really new, except for the fact that it is formal instead of informal. As Hurst (2002) makes clear, we are following in the footsteps of the incredible network of hundreds of labor colleges that flourished in the early decades of the twentieth century. These colleges, of which Brookwood is the best known, represented an attempt by working people to create their own informal system of education outside the state sanctioned formal system to which they were denied access. None of these labor colleges survived.

The principal reason for the demise of labor colleges was not that they attracted the ire of the official educational establishment, but that they angered the official labor movement of the time, hence Bernard's (2002) caution about the risk contained in popular education's emphasis on critical consciousness. It can be turned on the union establishment itself with very negative consequences for the educational institution and/or the union teacher. Here it is vital to remember Freire's central point, that education should not be used for negative and destructive purposes. Rather, through the dialogic method, workers and union members must take responsibility for reshaping their institutions in constructive and politically accountable ways. This is the philosophy of the National Labor College.

In the early years of the last century, organized labor sanctioned corporate demands for the creation of a two-track system in United States public education: formal college for the few and nonformal vocational training for the many. At the time, it was in fact a step forward that eventually paved the way for the universal public high school. But it is time to take the next step toward democratizing education. In his 2001 State of the State address, Maryland Governor Parris Glendening proposed that it is now time to start preparing for universal access to publicly funded higher education, just as we did with high school in the twentieth century. Both the labor movement and workers' and labor education institutions should endorse this idea. But we must use our collective power to insist that the content and methods of popular education find a home in formal working-class education, and in the preparation of teachers of working-class students in schools and institutions of higher education.[6]

NOTES

1. For an excellent discussion of the impact of Bloom, Hirsch, and others in their genre on formal education see Aronowitz & Giroux (1991).

2. This study is just the latest in a long line of research that demonstrates the role of the community college in cooling out and redirecting the aspirations of working-class students away from baccalaureate instruction and toward vocational/technical instruction. See, for example, Bowles & Gintis (1976).

3. Freire's use of the terms "teacher-student" (referring to teachers) and "student-teacher" (referring to students) is his way of emphasizing that each person has something to learn and something to teach.

4. Michael Merrill, conversation with author, June 2001.

5. R. D. Reynolds, "Labour at leisure—not time to be wasted: Global professional sports, artistic endeavors and higher education" (paper presented at the International Labour Movement on the Threshold of Two Centuries conference, Stockholm, October 2002).

6. This chapter is adapted from an article in L. Delp, M. Outman-Kramer, S. J. Schurman, & K. Wong (Eds.), *Teaching for change: Popular education and the labor movement*. Los Angeles: UCLA Center for Labor Research and Education, 2002.

REFERENCES

Aronowitz, S., & Giroux, H. (1991). *Postmodern education: Politics, culture and social criticism*. Minneapolis: University of Minnesota Press.

Bernard, E. (2002). Popular education: Training rebels with a cause. In L. Delp, M. Outman-Kramer, S. J. Schurman, & K. Wong (Eds.), *Teaching for change: Popular education and the labor movement* (pp. 6–8). Los Angeles: UCLA Center for Labor Research and Education.

Bloom, A. (1987). *The closing of the American mind*. New York: Simon & Schuster.

Bowles, S., & Gintis, H. (1976). *Schooling in capitalist America*. New York: Basic Books.

Boyatzis, R., Kolb, D., & Cowen, S. (1995). *Innovation in professional education: Steps on a journey from teaching to learning*. San Francisco: Jossey-Bass.

Brint, S., & Karabel, J. (1995). *The diverted dream: Community colleges and the promise of educational opportunity in America 1900–1985*. Oxford, England: Oxford University Press.

Delp, L., Outman-Kramer, M., Schurman, S. J., & Wong, K. (Eds.) (2002). *Teaching for change: Popular education and the labor movement*. Los Angeles: UCLA Center for Labor Research and Education.

Dewey, J. (1910). *How we think*. Washington, DC: Heath.

Finn, P. (1999). *Literacy with an attitude: Educating working-class children in their own self-interest*. Albany: State University of New York Press.

Freire, P. (1973). *Education for critical consciousness*. New York: Seabury.

Freire, P. (1982). *Pedagogy of the oppressed*. New York: Continuum.

Hirsch, Jr. E. D. (1987). *Cultural literacy: What every American needs to know*. Boston: Houghton Mifflin.

Hurst, J. (2002). Popular education, labor, and social change. In L. Delp, M. Outman-Kramer, S. J. Schurman, & K. Wong (Eds.), *Teaching for change: Popular education and the labor movement* (pp. 9–18). Los Angeles: UCLA Center for Labor Research and Education.

James, W. (1890). *The principles of psychology*. New York: Holt.

Kohl, H., & Greer, C. (1995). *'I won't learn from you': And other thoughts on creative maladjustment*. New York: New Press.

Krause, E. (1999). *Death of the guilds: Professions, states and the advance of capitalism, 1930 to the present*. New Haven, CT: Yale University Press.

Marshall, T. H. (1950). *Citizenship and social class and other essays*. Cambridge, UK: Cambridge University Press.

Moll, L. (1998, February 5). Funds of knowledge for teaching: A new approach in education. Keynote address, presented to the Illinois State Board of Education.

Novak, J. D. (1977). *A theory of education*. Ithaca, NY: Cornell University Press.

Novak, J. D., & Gowin, D. B. (1985). *Learning how to learn*. New York: Cambridge University Press.

Pipan, R. (1989). Towards a curricular perspective of workplaces. In H. Leyman & H. Kornbluh (Eds.), *Socialization and learning at work: A new approach to the learning process in the workplace and society*. Aldershopt: Gowar.

Reynolds, R. D. (2002). "Labor at leisure—not time to be wasted: Global professional sports, artistic endeavors and higher education" (paper presented at the International Labour Movement on the Threshold of Two Centuries Conference, Stockholm).

Rile, G. (1984). *The concept of mind*. Chicago: University of Chicago Press.

Rorty, R. (1998). *Achieving our country: Leftist thought in twentieth-century America*. Cambridge, MA: Harvard University Press.

3 Coalition for Educational Justice: Antiracist Organizing and Teacher Education

Alex Caputo-Pearl, Kahllid A. Al-Alim, and Frances A. Martin

ALEX CAPUTO-PEARL, TEACHER, Kahllid A. Al-Alim, Parent, and Frances A. Martin, Student, in the Los Angeles Unified School District, argue for a pedagogy rooted in school- and community-based antiracist organizing and campaign development as the most effective transformative pedagogy for teachers, parents, and students. It is a pedagogy where teachers are organically connected to working-class communities and labor unions, where classrooms become spaces for critical pedagogy, where issues of racism and class bias abound, and where students and parents gather regularly in large multi-racial groups with opportunities for political engagement and for building and exerting power.

In a noisy high school classroom in South Los Angeles, groups of students draw maps of their communities on chart paper. They include positive and problematic elements in their communities—from the camaraderie and warmth of churches to homeless people and heavy police presence on the streets. Based on a lesson developed by Oakland's School of Unity and Liberation (SOUL),[1] the teacher asks the groups to identify the causes of the community problems. The majority of students blame individuals within their own communities: the homeless person was too lazy to find a job; the presence of gangbangers and criminals necessitate heavy police presence.

The teacher then leads a quick discussion on large alcohol and liquor companies and their targeted advertising in working-class communities and communities of color. He asks whether large institutions, like these companies, cause some of the community problems, such as high rates of alcoholism and crime. Soon, the students are focused on institutions and systems, pointing out the lack of living wage jobs and the high cost of housing as causal factors in homelessness, relating their comments to their own experiences. They give personal accounts of the media and police officers' profiling of young people of color, which creates fear among white and middle-class populations. These, the students say, along with the petty crime that comes with poverty, are among the causes for intense police presence and brutality in their communities. The teacher helps the

47

students understand the job market, high housing costs, media practices, the police department's behavior, and the fears of whites as different pieces of institutionalized or systematic oppression of working-class people and communities of color.

The teacher then reads through the Black Panther Party's 10-Point Program (the latest version of which was written in 1972) with the students.[2] Among other things, the Program includes a call for every person to have a job or a guaranteed income, for every person to have shelter, for true histories of oppressed peoples to be taught in schools, for an end to police brutality and military recruitment of oppressed peoples, and for Blacks to receive the reparations they were guaranteed after the Civil War. The students engage the questions of whether it is still important today to advocate for the policies included in the Black Panther Program, whether the Panthers were asking for too much, and whether an implementation of their program today would effectively combat institutionalized and systematic oppression.

The students' responses to these questions are passionate and reflective of deep experiences. Louis writes:

> Our communities would be a lot different if the Black Panther Program was a reality. Blacks wouldn't need to be on every corner selling coke, dimes, and nicks. Poor people wouldn't be at home living with they mammas. Blacks wouldn't be homeless. And, there would probably be less crime because people of color wouldn't be on the way to death. The young bloods like me, or any student here, wouldn't worry about death from the pressure to join the military, dropping out of school, and all the other bizarre things that we face.

Tyrone writes:

> We do need to control our destiny as Blacks. The government is controlling us by not putting books and real teaching in our schools—so students will have a reason to not want to go to school. The BP Program isn't asking for too much. If they had given us our 40 acres and a mule, then maybe we wouldn't have as much to ask for.

Angel makes it simple: "If the Black Panther Program existed today, I would feel safe."

Inspired by a lesson like this at a different high school in the mid-town area of Los Angeles, a student comes to a youth-led meeting of the Coalition for Educational Justice (CEJ) on her campus. After a few months, she is helping to lead break-out discussions at CEJ's mass student meetings. The small groups focus on demands students might make on the Los Angeles Unified School District (LAUSD) Board of Education to improve schools and challenge institutionalized oppression, including demands to limit military recruitment and school overcrowding. After another month, this student helps lead a meeting between twelve CEJ members and an LAUSD School Board member. She emerges from the meeting suggesting to her CEJ comrades that the organization needs to develop more alliances with other groups and needs to focus more on base-

building among parents. She also excitedly expresses a desire to learn how to write a School Board motion to propose to Board Members.

A third-year teacher who attended the same CEJ meeting with the Board Member had been, two years before, struggling to find ways to express opposition to the impending U.S. war on Iraq on her high school campus. She began working with her school's teacher union chapter, in which progressives had built influence in recent years, and an informal collective of antiwar teachers. They organized a lunch time march around the school's quad to oppose the war. Over thirty teachers and one hundred students participated. In the months following, the young teacher worked with the antiwar teacher collective to form a group called Progressive Teachers at her school. Now, Progressive Teachers is discussing their strategic direction. She believes that the group must continue to be explicitly antiwar and antiracist, but, at the same time, more embedded in determining the direction of local school policy.

Progressive Teachers, working with some teacher members of CEJ on campus and other education organizations, begins to explore how to effectively participate in the school's move towards breaking up into Small Learning Communities. Members of Progressive Teachers become deeply involved in the Small Learning Communities Steering Committee at the school. They focus on introducing grassroots democracy into the school transition process, bringing authentic and ongoing student, parent, and teacher leadership into the process, and putting forward proposals for a Youth, Social Justice, and Civil Rights Small Learning Community at the school that would be based on refining progressive pedagogical approaches and institutionalizing spaces at the school that encourage critical views on war, U.S. imperialism, racism, and oppression of gays and lesbians.

One Saturday, this young teacher attends a CEJ event: two hours of general membership meeting, followed by two hours as part of a global march against the U.S. occupation of Iraq. At the membership meeting, a discussion emerges on LAUSD's bureaucratic bloat and the priority that seems to be placed on maintaining that bureaucracy over providing the necessary resources to schools. A monolingual Spanish-speaking CEJ parent leader acknowledges the problem of bureaucratic excess, but says that she, as a parent activist, has found particular levels of the local bureaucracy helpful in empowering parents. She adds that parents and teachers at her school—partially with support from the local school bureaucracy—have successfully campaigned for the initiation of a fair, antiracist, justice oriented discipline plan for their middle school—one based on positive modeling, student self-knowledge, and student self-love rather than on-campus police, backpack searches, racial profiling, and high expulsion rates. A CEJ student leader at the general meeting responds, commending the discipline plan, and suggesting that engagement with the Black Panther Party's 10-Point Program could help students raise their self-knowledge and self-esteem.

The above are true accounts of the antiracist organizing experiences of various teacher, student, and parent leaders within the Coalition for Educational Justice (CEJ) in Los Angeles. They reveal important insights into educating working-class children in their collective self-interest (Finn, 1999), and preparing teachers to do so.

ANTIRACIST ORGANIZING AND TEACHER EDUCATION

CEJ is an antiracist, politically independent, grassroots organization composed of hundreds of teachers, parents, and students. CEJ centers its work on building its base and developing pressure campaigns, organized efforts to recruit regular people into a coherent political formation that demands antiracist policy changes from politicians and brings democratic, electoral, and public pressure on those officials to make these changes. Linked to these pressure campaigns, CEJ develops political education pedagogy and curriculum for classrooms, and caucus-building efforts within the Los Angeles Unified School District (LAUSD) teachers union, the United Teachers of Los Angeles (UTLA).

CEJ originated in 1999 in response to the rise of high-stakes tests. It was initially a group composed mainly of teachers, many of whom had cut their teeth organizing against racist California state propositions. Over time, through commitment to grassroots organizing one-on-one and small group conversations with parents, students, and teachers, school site by school site, and to organizing among working-class people and in communities of color, CEJ became a much more balanced coalition of teachers, students, and parents. The organization now has representatives and chapters in over thirty schools in LAUSD, and has a democratically elected fifteen member Steering Committee consisting of five high school students, five parents and community members, and five teachers.

CEJ was a key organization in a momentous grassroots victory in 2003, when antiracist groups pressured the LAUSD Board of Education and, eventually, the California State Board of Education to delay implementation of the California High School Exit Exam. As a high-stakes standardized test given across schools that are unequally resourced, the Exit Exam would have resulted in racist and class-biased impacts by stripping mostly working-class students and students of color of diplomas. The author and contributors to this article got involved in CEJ through different aspects of the organization's outreach and recruitment or base building: Alex through a teacher collective that organized against California's Proposition 227, an attack on bilingual education; Frances, through a student CEJ chapter at Crenshaw High School that originated as an antiwar group and eventually merged with CEJ; and Kahllid through a parent organizing collective in South Los Angeles that is focusing on increasing parent power and voice in local school decision-making.

CEJ calls itself antiracist in the spirit of the historic civil rights movements of the past; it sees racism as the central hub of the wider structure of oppression, much as Martin Luther King, Jr. described in his Noble Peace Prize Acceptance speech (King, 1964). Our perspective on civil rights not only includes racism, poverty, and war, the interrelated structures of oppression that King addressed, but also sexism and oppression of gays and lesbians. While some of these forms of oppression are the result of intentional decisions by government and corporate structures, as well as by certain individuals and groups, other forms of oppression occur not by explicit intent but by the continuing impact of earlier acts and decisions, such as slavery and the disenfranchisement of African Americans, genocide of Native Americans, seizure of indigenous land, economic exploitation of workers, and oppression of women.

A key component of CEJ's work, therefore, is encouraging structural analysis of institutionalized and systematic oppression of working-class people, people of color, women, and gays and lesbians. This means building CEJ members' capacity to see different forms of oppression and different policies as specific pieces of a whole, interconnected political-economic structure that benefits some (the disproportionately white middle-class and wealthy) and hurts others (the poor, the working class, women, gays and lesbians, and communities of color).

Teacher participation in CEJ's antiracist organizing opens critical spaces for ongoing and continuous development of what Aronowitz and Giroux (1993) and Finn (1999) have called transformative teachers. Transformative teachers are aware of societal inequities and they see schools as sites of political struggle. In their view, the job of teaching requires them to go far beyond imparting textbook information. They focus on the relationship between knowledge and power, and the relationship between their students' knowledge and their political agency. They understand that student knowledge about their own cultures, and contradictions within those cultures, is key to building their personal and political agency. Their teaching job includes providing spaces for students to connect their knowledge to action, to opportunities for leadership development, and to opportunities to organize and make change.

Transformative teachers understand that parent involvement in working-class schools and schools that serve communities of color has been purposely denied and placed in a subordinate role, often geared only towards having parents provide party items, small fundraising efforts, or supervision on field trips. Transformative teachers create spaces where parents, students, community members, and teachers can become collective actors with the ultimate goal of building powerful social movements that change policy and consciousness.

This social movement building approach to teacher education and professional development takes advantage of the fact that teachers are strategically located in schools, institutions that allow them opportunities to be deeply involved in movement building at the ground level, through authentic relationships with students, parents, and their community. Through the teaching and learning opportunities afforded by their location, transformative teachers are organically connected to working-class communities and communities of color. As these communities undergo continuous attacks, transformative teachers who are engaged with the community can begin to see themselves as learners as well as teachers, and their students as teachers as well as learners.

Transformative teachers also have the opportunity to be organically connected to large, multiracial workplaces. They understand that teachers' unions and collective teacher action hold enormous potential to bring about social change, but remain largely untapped in that regard. Further, teachers are rank-and-file unionists located in the public sector at a time that public services are under the attacks of politicians' austerity plans, and at a time that unions are in need of new direction. Unions represent approximately 13 percent of the U.S. workforce now, down from over 25 percent of the workforce in 1973. Employers continue to use antiunion tactics, such as holding mandatory anti-union meetings for employees, and firing union activists.

Currently within the sectors of the union movement that represent private sector employees, there are interesting strategic and tactical discussions about how to increase the leverage of unions through new approaches to recruitment, alliances, industry analysis, and popular (Freirean) education (Schurman, this volume). Few, however, are discussing the vast potential of public sector unions, such as those representing teachers, to give leverage to the struggle to protect public services and help private sector employees win grueling regional or national fights for union recognition and workplace rights (Bernstein, 2004). Teachers are strategically placed to move this conversation forward.

Groups such as CEJ can coordinate the opening of critical opportunities for teachers to learn structural analysis, organizing, and social movement building, and to teach these skills to their students in their individual and collective self-interest, in classrooms and other organized settings and committees where:

- Classroom curriculum is linked to critical consciousness in young people

- Students, parents, and teachers dialogue and identify common problems

- Students, parents, and teachers develop political demands and strategic organizing plans that form the foundation of pressure campaigns at school sites and at broader levels

- Opportunities are provided to analyze social forces and reflect on actions taken in organizing

- New social theory arises from these actions and reflections.

THE INTERSECTION OF DIALOGUE AND POLITICAL EDUCATION

The cutting edge of this social movement building strategy, with its potential for teacher development, is the intersection between the dialogue that occurs in these social movement spaces, and the overall antiracist analysis that is provided by an organization such as CEJ. Participation in dialogue allows grievances to emerge from the actual experiences of working-class people, women, and people of color. Dialogue that is combined with a broad political education about different forms of oppression allows everyday grievances to be framed within the context of broader structures of oppression.

Dialogue, structural analysis, and political education, and the interplay between them, create an intersection at which demands, campaigns, and classroom curriculum ideas can be developed. In this way, grievances from the everyday experiences of students, parents, and teachers become part of a broad political strategy of working for policy change and for engaging broad sectors of the population in political consciousness raising. In the best tradition of the Civil Rights Movement, the nonviolent, democratic social change tactics include base building, dissemination of flyers, organizing demonstrations, linking to classroom curriculum, meeting with politicians, and engaging people in discussions and forums at schools.

It is this intersection and interplay of dialogue, structural analysis, and political education that sharpens the picture of oppression for progressive activists. Everyday grievances that might otherwise call for simple, quantitative reform are transformed into demands for qualitative, foundational social changes that raise political consciousness. A grassroots request for smaller class sizes becomes a pressure and consciousness raising campaign focused on reducing class size, but within the broader context of a call for:

- Educational reparations for those working-class communities and communities of color that have always been short changed in government provided resources

- An end to the racist practice of tracking youth of color into prison

- The construction of more schools in place of prisons.

For example, what may have started as a history teacher's complaint about student discipline in class may become a student-parent-teacher demand for a more relevant curriculum that engages students by addressing how they can cope with and challenge different forms of oppression in their communities. This process may explore questions of why curricular paens to American democracy do not resonate with immigrant students whose families cannot vote or with African American students who witnessed the Supreme Court disenfranchise voters in the 2000 elections. It may engage the question of how government and corporate structures benefit from a curriculum that does not teach critical media literacy, that does not connect slavery to today's sectors of poverty in the African American community, and that teaches uncritical pledges of allegiance in place of critical literacy about U.S. foreign policy. In this process, which is in fact professional development, teachers are exposed to structural political analysis, the place of schooling within those structures, and the potential for social movements to bring about change.

THE POLITICAL CONTEXT THAT DEMANDS THIS TYPE OF WORK

The political times require that we use a structural analysis-based approach in teacher education to develop skills for teachers in community based curriculum,

culturally relevant pedagogy, organizing, and campaigning, all of which are critical elements in teaching for democracy. Broad systems of oppression can be
challenged most effectively by system-conscious, critical approaches to organizing, campaigning, and consciousness raising. A quick look at the current political
context will help draw this out.

School segregation has increased in the United States for African American students since the 1980s and for Latinos since 1960. Students in the most
racially segregated schools are ten times more likely to be poor than students
in all-white or nearly all-white schools (Colvin, 1999). Their schools are also
more likely to be under-resourced.[3] Schools in communities of color and
working-class communities consistently experience teacher shortages; class and
school sizes in these communities are the highest; and dilapidated facilities are
commonplace. There are chronic textbook and materials shortages. Pedagogy
is often based on nondialogical drill and kill models and Eurocentric materials.
Overwhelmingly white electorates in California and Arizona have passed propositions attacking immigrants' and Native Americans' languages and bilingual
education programs. Other states are moving in the same direction.

Meanwhile, in most inner-city districts serving low-income students of
color, the dropout rates are two to four times as high as the rates in the
surrounding suburbs that serve white and middle-class students (Macias Rojas
& Gordon, 1999). White high school dropouts have a higher employment rate
than African Americans and Latinos with high school diplomas, and white
high school graduates not enrolled in college are employed at twice the rate
of African Americans, and almost triple the rate for Latinos (U.S. Department
of Commerce, 1994). There has been an increase in low-paying service and
light manufacturing jobs, and contracted-out, lower-paying public sector jobs,
where people of color are heavily over-represented.

The U.S. government's responses to these structural school and employment conditions have been criminalization, tracking, blaming the poor and the
public sector, and implementation of racist and class-biased standardized testing
schemes. Many low-income people and people of color have been thrown into
an expanding prison-industrial complex for nonviolent offenses. States are
passing legislation that would allow teenagers to be tried as adults and placed
in jail for longer periods of time (Cooper, 2000; Giroux, 2000). City police
departments regularly violate civic rights.[4] The police presence in inner-city
schools is unprecedented. Zero tolerance discipline policies in schools have a
racially discriminatory impact on students of color, who are suspended at levels
many times that of white students (Ayers & Dohrn, 2000).

The U.S. military concentrates its recruitment in the inner cities, eager to
place working-class youth and youth of color at the front lines of the War
against Terrorism. Part of this recruitment strategy is the Bush Administration's
2001, No Child Left Behind Education Act, which includes a clause that
requires all school districts to give the personal information of all students age
16 or over, including school records and home phone numbers, to the federal

armed services. Working-class students and students of color are receiving many more direct phone calls from recruiters now. Meanwhile, economic prosperity for the middle and upper classes has, as always, relied heavily on profits generated on the backs of Third World workers in a system of global capitalism dominated by the U.S. government.

Within this context, growing student opposition to school-related military recruitment opens opportunities for students and teachers to help a broader sector of educators understand a structural analysis that locates schooling and U.S. imperialism side by side. Recruiters target inner-city youth who have been taught that the military is their only job option and their only way to get to college. This perception is strengthened when students are placed in overcrowded schools with overcrowded classes, making it more difficult for them to learn and for teachers to teach. The handful of academic and college counselors have impossibly heavy workloads, and students unable to master standards under these conditions are likely to fail a high school exit exam or other high-stakes standardized test. For students in this position, who have seen the Junior Reserve Officer Training Corps (JROTC) prominently on their campuses since the sixth grade, the military appears to be the best option to escape the ghetto or help their family. They are tracked into the military.

IMPLICATIONS FOR TEACHER EDUCATION

Teachers have a specific role within this unequal and unjust educational system. If they don't have an understanding of the structure of the system, they inevitably will help to reproduce it through the implementation of curricula that deaden rather than enliven working-class students and the political agency of poor communities. Preparing teachers who seek to challenge rather than reproduce the system requires not only developing skills of structural analysis, political education, and organizing, but also assuring that the critical elements are in place to make this a democratic teacher education. These critical elements include:

A deep exploration, in theory and in practice, of dialogue in which respect, trust, patience, listening, and the development of collective conclusions are core practices in helping campaigns, demands, curricula, and social theories emerge.

A recognition that collective work is of the highest priority, and that the individualistic attitudes of many progressive-minded teachers (e.g., not being accountable to others, and doing their part well but failing to prioritize leadership development within the collective) must be challenged.

Carefully structuring organizational work so that there are many democratic spaces and committees for people to work on, and ensuring that these spaces are based on norms that prioritize the voices of the historically marginalized.

A recognition that, after collective plans and strategies are developed through dialogue and political education, organizing and engaging people around that plan must be constant and must be constantly reflected upon:

- How did teachers react to a particular flyer? To a particular set of demands?

- How did the teacher union react?

- How did the lesson go where students engaged in an "action" to learn about a particular concept?

- How did parents react to a flyer given out at Back to School Night?

- What implications do these questions have for how we are going to organize next month?

Structures and norms that help teachers grapple with their own privilege in regard to their relatively high salaries, their class status, and their access to formal education, and that challenges them not to use these privileges to unfair advantage within organizational work. Teachers also must acknowledge that they may know very little about the lives and experiences of their students and the communities they teach in—and that their privilege and sense of entitlement could blind them to their own limitations in understanding.

A commitment to building multiconstituency and multiracial movements, with majority representation of working-class people, where the goal is true equality between student, parent, and teacher voices. This requires training to help teachers learn the differences in doing political work with parents, students, and teachers. For example:

- In student organizing, a teacher must help to create spaces where discussions center on issues important to youth; they must work with students to create meeting formats that provide support for students in leading meetings and that provide ongoing feedback to students as they develop their leadership skills. Teachers must also build alliances—with other teachers, parents, and administrators—to help protect the student who is organizing from attacks: threats of suspensions, retaliation by teachers who do not like the student's activism, or disapproval from parents who might be fearful of political involvement.

- With parents, teachers need to learn how to break out of the long-standing school practice of marginalizing parents from core school decision making, how to negotiate with existing bodies in which parents participate (e.g., Title One), and how to create independent parent structures where deeper discussion and independent political strategizing can occur.

- With communities, teachers may need to learn how to manage their own class privilege and how to equitably and authentically share leadership with working-class adults.

A commitment to different levels of organizing: combining organizing school-site issues with organizing citywide demands, while assuring that a small progressive victory on a policy at one school is celebrated and pursued with the same intensity as larger victories on more structural district wide demands.

A capacity to critically analyze teachers' own organizations—teacher unions. These typically have been narrowly focused, conservative organizations. Most unions uphold the banking methodology of teaching and mobilize narrowly around pay and benefits. Teachers must develop a political strategy of embedding themselves in independent organizations, like CEJ, that push unions to take on social justice and curriculum issues more aggressively.

A commitment to include social movement building, organization building, dialogue, political education, and activities to develop political agency in classroom curriculum, and to constantly reflect on its implementation.

What we have set out in this article is a still developing and very imperfect model of teacher education that at present resides only in organizations, such as CEJ, that are not affiliated with formal university or teacher education programs. CEJ, however, makes efforts to move fluidly between its own organizing and these formal institutions and programs. For example, CEJ leaders have led LAUSD- and UTLA-approved salary-point classes for teachers on community organizing. Other CEJ organizers have been teaching a formal class on organizing in the Antioch University Los Angeles teacher education program. Still others regularly have made presentations to teacher education classes at the University of California, Los Angeles, California State University-Los Angeles, and California State University-Dominguez Hills. Some CEJ leaders, with the support of teacher union chapters, have built teacher-student-parent alliances that have demanded that progressive themes and CEJ organizers be at the core of district mandated professional development opportunities for teachers. In some of these cases, students and parents have formally taught teachers about teaching, on district time.

CEJ's work is only one small contribution to the larger progressive reform tradition. A quick look at several historical figures provides a summary of where we fit into that tradition. Frederick Douglas said that power concedes nothing without demands. Fannie Lou Hamer and Che Guevara said that only organization will move us toward transformation of oppressive systems. And,

Paulo Freire said that a pedagogy of the oppressed is based not only on dialogue and mutual learning, but also on relating learning to the battle against oppressive systems. Social movements today are at a far weaker point than they were during the times of most of these political leaders, but a synthesis of their thoughts still makes sense today. Building social movements, with their demands, campaigns, connections to curriculum, dialogue, and political education, must be our primary strategy for democratic and liberating education. These same movements provide the laboratories for teachers, and for all of us, to learn and develop.

NOTES

1. For more on this valuable organization, go to www.youthec.org/soul/.

2. To see the Program, go to www.marxists.org/history/usa/workers/black-panthers/1966/10/15.htm.

3. In the 1980s, the ten highest per pupil-spending elementary school districts in Illinois, New York, Ohio, and Texas—vastly white—outspent the ten lowest per pupil spending districts—vastly of color—by more than two and a half times (R. Lowe, 1997). Race, power, and funding: An historical perspective. In *Funding for justice: Money, equity, and the future of public education*. Milwaukee, WI: Rethinking Schools, p. 16).

4. See J. Seeley (2000). Philadelphia story. *LA Weekly*, vol. 22, no. 35, p. 15; T. Hayden (2000). Gato and Alex—No safe place: The human story of the Los Angeles police scandal. *The Nation*, 271(2), 24; J. Getlin (3/20/2000). Despite pressure, NYPD resists call for reforms. *Los Angeles Times*, p. A1.

REFERENCES

Aronowitz, S., & Giroux, H. (1993). *Education still under siege.* Wesport, CT: Bergin & Harvey.

Ayers, W., & Dohrn, B. (2000). Resisting zero tolerance. *Rethinking Schools, 14*(3), 14.

Bernstein, A. (2004, September 13). Can this man save labor? *Business Week.*

Colvin, R. L. (1999, June 12). School segregation is growing, report finds. *Los Angeles Times*, A1.

Cooper, L. (2000). Youth activists fight prop 21. *Against the Current, XV*(2), 12.

Finn, P. (1999). *Literacy with an attitude: Educating working-class children in their own self-interest.* Albany: State University of New York Press.

Getlin, J. (2002). Despite pressure, NYPD resists call for reforms. *Los Angeles Times*, p. A1.

Giroux, H. (2000). At war against the young. *Against the Current, XV*(2), 17.

Hayden, T. (2002). Gato and Alex—No safe place: The human story of the Los Angeles police scandal. *The Nation, 271*(2), 24.

King, Jr. M. L. (1964, December 11). Nonviolence: Cornerstone for a world house. Nobel Peace Prize Lecture delivered in Oslo, Norway.

Lowe, R. (1997). Race, power, and funding: An historical perspective. In *Funding for justice: Money, equity, and the future of public education*. Milwaukee, WI: Rethinking Schools, p. 16.

Macias Rojas, P., & Gordon, R. (1999). Just facts: Racial re-segregation and inequality in the public schools." *ColorLines*, 2(1), 11.

Seeley, J. (2002). Philadelphia story. *LA Weekly*, vol. 22, no. 35, p. 15.

U.S. Department of Commerce. (1994). Bureau of the Census, October Current Population Surveys.

Part II

Social Justice Teacher Education in Undergraduate Courses

4 Developing Critically Reflective Practitioners: Integrating a Practice-Reflection-Theory Cycle of Learning in an Undergraduate Literacy Course

Gillian S. Richardson and Rosemary K. Murray

GILLIAN S. RICHARDSON, ASSISTANT PROFESSOR and Director of the Literacy Center, and Rosemary K. Murray, Associate Professor of Graduate Education and Leadership, Canisius College, describe an action research project designed to assess the impact of integrating critical pedagogical theory, critical reflection, and practice experience into prospective teachers' learning. Surveys, debriefing discussions, focus groups, and reflective logs were used to collect the students' changes in attitude toward their students. Participants shifted from blaming students, to blaming teachers, and finally to an awareness of the structural barriers that impede students' progress.

This chapter is about a course we developed collaboratively to address the needs of our pre-service teachers. The students involved in the project were 22 middle-and upper-middle-class undergraduate adolescence education students completing a required literacy course. In addition to classroom instruction, the students participated in a literacy-tutoring project in a K-8 working-class urban school.[1] The impetus for developing this course was our emerging awareness that our students had no experience with urban schools; they were unaware of the social, cultural, and political contexts of learning, and their teacher preparation coursework typically did not introduce them to the critical reflection that encourages their questioning existing assumptions, values, and perspectives. Our college is a Jesuit institution located in the heart of the inner city, though our students come largely from the surrounding middle-class suburbs. Under the leadership of our college president, we have made a commitment to supporting our neighborhood, its schools, and community.

NEED FOR CRITICAL CONSCIOUSNESS IN TEACHER EDUCATION

Teaching is never a neutral act. Embedded in social, cultural, and political contexts, choices about what, how, and why we teach can be liberating or

dominating. According to Shannon (1992), despite the often negative consequences, "few practicing teachers recognize the political facts about school life
and school literacy. Rather, they consider themselves apolitical in their work"
(p. 2). In part this is the result of what Aronowitz (1973) criticized as the
"methodology madness" in teacher education programs, a criticism that is still
apt 30 years later. By focusing exclusively on teaching methods and behavioral
objectives, "too many courses in these programs are silent about the assumptions embedded in these varied approaches, not to mention the interests they
serve or the ethical consequences of their use" (Giroux, 1980, p. 9). "What is
missing is a theory in which the relational structure of teacher and context,
school, and society, can be explained in terms of possibilities and limitations
that exist in correspondence and tension with each other" (p. 17).

NEED FOR DIRECT EXPERIENCE IN TEACHER EDUCATION

While it is important to include social theories in course content, integrating
direct experience offers learning opportunities not available from instruction
alone. This is particularly valuable in the case of our project because none of
our students had firsthand knowledge of urban schools. They lacked base
knowledge to which they could relate class readings and discussions. By combining classroom instruction with direct experience, "theoretical and practical
learning come together in a dialectical fashion as a means to challenge students
to think critically" (Rhoads, 1997, p. 23).

An integral part of critical consciousness and experiential learning is
critical reflection. Recent attention has been given to reflection and developing reflective practitioners; however, by itself reflection is not necessarily critical: "To engage in critical reflection requires a moving beyond the acquisition
of new knowledge and understanding, into questioning existing assumptions,
values, and perspectives" (Cranton, 1996, p. 76). We encouraged our students
to look at urban education through a new lens by having them explore their
own values and beliefs, as well as the perspectives of others.

> Gillian: I entered higher education with significant awareness of class
> issues that I attribute at least in part to my British background. Both
> of my parents came to the United States as adults raised near Liverpool,
> England, where class issues are much more in the forefront and where
> the denial of the existence of a class system that is so prevalent in the
> United States is much less apparent. My class consciousness was fur-
> ther sharpened by graduate school coursework that focused on issues
> of class and literacy.
>
> My doctoral coursework provided a framework from which to
> make sense of the class-based differences in approaches to literacy and
> education that I had observed personally in my own life. An emerg-
> ing process, my own awareness of the cultural forces that influenced

my educational experiences assisted me in recognizing and addressing the needs of our students.

Rosemary: While my background differs from Gillian's, my experiences as a teacher in an urban magnet school led me to share her confidence in the ability of all children to learn. I learned firsthand that even those from the poorest poverty-stricken homes could achieve at the highest levels if they were provided with the proper preparation. I had the good fortune to be part of an urban public school district's desegregation program which began in 1978 when magnet schools were established city wide. The success of the magnet school that I taught in was influenced by the philosophy of education that promoted multiage student clusters, flexible grouping, team teaching, and individualized instruction, as well as small group and whole group instruction. The resulting learning environment was familial, nurturing, and mutually respectful.

At my school, faculty were told on many occasions by colleagues teaching in other schools that our students weren't "real inner-city poor children," but the fact the students arrived each morning on 31 school busses from all areas of the city refuted that assertion. At least 50 percent of the students were entitled to participate in the federal free breakfast and lunch program. Within the learning environment, students had a voice in choosing academic topics and related activities. They were given responsibility for their own behavior; they were free to travel around the school and at times around the college campus that housed our school. What the faculty were attempting in terms of structure and methodology was consistent with the theories and beliefs of the educational theorists and practitioners I read during this period (1978–1990) as part of my doctoral work in literacy.

Gillian and Rosemary: As we moved from the elementary and middle school classroom to the university classroom we have been given the opportunity to instill our own passion for teaching, and our conviction about the ability of all children to learn, in the young people who we are preparing to become teachers. As we try to truly understand the factors that are inhibiting learning in such a large portion of our population, we also attempt to share these new understandings with our students.

NEED FOR CRITICAL LITERACY IN TEACHER EDUCATION

Critical literacy evolves from the discourse of critical theory (Freire, 1970). Prior understanding of literacy in the United States was seen either from a perspective of training workers for occupational jobs that demand "functional reading and writing, or from a perspective designed to initiate the poor, underprivileged and minorities into an ideology of a unitary dominant cultural tradition" (Giroux, 1988, p. 61). Freire tells us:

> Education either functions as an instrument which is used to facilitate the integration of the younger generation into the logic of the present system and bring about conformity to it or it becomes the Practice of Freedom, the means by which men and women deal critically and creatively with reality and discover how to participate in the transformation of their world. (1970, p. 15)

Giroux (1988) believes that current approaches to providing working-class and minority students with reading and writing skills that will make them functional within the school is theoretically flawed for the following 4 reasons:

1. It fails to view working-class culture as a terrain of struggle and contradiction;

2. It suggests that those educators working with subordinate groups need only to familiarize themselves with the histories and experiences of the students. There is no indication that the culture that such students bring to the schools may need critical interrogation and analysis;

3. It fails to understand that literacy is not just related to the poor or the inability of subordinate groups to read and write adequately; it is also fundamentally related to forms of political and ideological ignorance that function as a refusal to know the limits and political consequences of one's view of the world;

4. There is little focus on the relationship between power and knowledge. (p. 63)

The project we describe here was a convergence of our collective and individual experiences. Our goal was to help students question, challenge, explore, and critique beliefs and practices—to problem solve ways schools can be transformed to meet the needs of all students.

PLAN OF ACTION: PRACTICE-CRITICAL REFLECTION-THEORY-
CYCLE OF LEARNING

In an effort to better prepare prospective teachers to teach in working-class schools, we began a collaborative action research project that resulted in the development of an undergraduate literacy course involving the integration of experiential learning, theoretical readings, and ongoing critical reflection. This course is framed by the critical theory paradigm. A critical perspective focuses on the relationship between knowledge and power. According to Kincheloe and McLaren (1994):

> Critical research can best be understood in the context of the empowerment of individuals. Inquiry that aspires to the name critical must be connected to an attempt to confront the injustice of a particular society or sphere within the society. Research thus becomes a transformative endeavor unembarrassed by the label "political" and unafraid to consummate a relationship with an emancipatory consciousness. (p. 140)

A textbook on literacy methodologies was required reading for the course. We also introduced critical pedagogical theory using *Literacy with an Attitude: Educating Working-Class Students in Their Own Self-Interest* (Finn, 1999), which characterizes knowledge as a construct tied to the social, political, cultural, and economic conditions of society. Central to critical theory are relations of power and control, and the privilege of certain groups in society over others. A critical perspective emphasizes the mutability of sociopolitical constructs and the need for action to confront exploitation, a perspective we hoped to convey to our students.

Students also participated in a middle school literacy tutoring program in a K–8 working-class urban school in an impoverished area of the Northeast. In this school, 95 percent of the students are African American, 88 percent receive free or reduced-price lunch, and only 33 percent of fourth graders and 11 percent of eighth graders met or exceeded grade level standards in English language arts. The literacy classes were held at the school where our students observed and provided one-on-one tutoring in reading and writing each week.

Our students also engaged in continual critical reflection about their experiences and course content. They completed a survey regarding their perceptions prior to the field experience and after completion of the tutoring sessions. In addition, following each literacy tutoring session students engaged in a 20-minute debriefing group discussion. Students also participated in a focus group at the beginning of their field experience and in a second focus group at the conclusion of the tutoring sessions. Reflective logs were also completed.

Framed by a critical perspective, this study set out to determine the impact of integrating critical reflection, critical pedagogical theory, and practical experience on prospective teachers' learning. A model of this learning cycle, adapted from Tooles' (1997) model of the experiential learning cycle, is provided below.

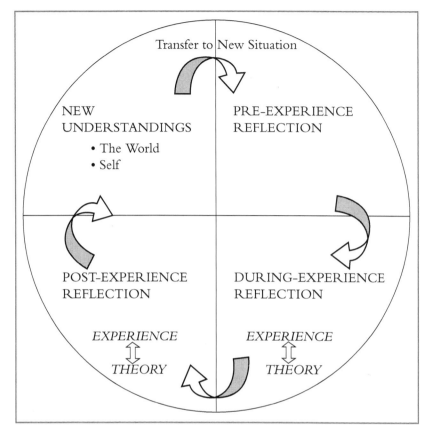

Figure 4.1. *Practice-Critical Reflection-Theory-Cycle of Learning*

LITERACY WITH AN ATTITUDE—FROM THEORY TO PRACTICE

According to Finn (1999), "Our schools liberate and empower children of the gentry and domesticate the children of the working class, and to a large extent the middle class as well" (p. 189). He continues, "But nothing short of dialogue, conscientization, and explicitly teaching school discourse and powerful literacy will give all students a chance at an empowering, liberating education" (p. 190). We felt committed to share these ideas with our own students.

Prior to the current project Gillian taught *Society and Language Arts* at the graduate level and used *Literacy with an Attitude* as her main text. Her students enjoyed reading the book but many doubted its veracity. These students felt that the studies cited were dated and that the attitudes and practices described in the book would no longer be found in public education. Such experiences and our continued interest in and commitment to critical theory provided the impetus to find a way to positively engage our students in these topics through the development of our undergraduate course.

According to Carr and Kemmis (1986), educational reform and the places of institutionalized educational research are increasingly influenced by the development of a critical educational science. From this perspective, educational reform:

> . . . is participatory and collaborative; it envisions a form of educational research which is conducted by those involved in education themselves. It takes a view of educational research as critical analysis directed at the *transformation* of educational practices, the educational understandings and educational values of those involved in the process, and the social and institutional structures which provide frameworks for their action. (p. 156)

We knew, therefore, that it was necessary to actually involve our students in the educational milieu that they were reading about. Students were assigned to read chapters in *Literacy with an Attitude* and to consider practical strategies to promote literacy that were then discussed in the college classroom. On alternate scheduled class days the students met at Tower Middle School to observe and to tutor individual students and small groups of students. During the final 20 to 30 minutes of each session, we met in the school library to debrief the morning's activities. These sessions were tape recorded and later transcribed. As the triangulated data were analyzed, themes and outcomes emerged that are discussed below.

OUTCOMES: NEW UNDERSTANDINGS AND TRANSFORMATIVE LEARNING

Several themes emerged from the data and are discussed here using Alschuler's (1980) theory of problem solving in response to oppressive conditions as a frame. In this section we present our findings in the following categories: (a) school culture, (b) movement towards critical-transforming problem solving, (c) self-development. Student references to Finn's book (direct and indirect) are indicated in italics.

SCHOOL CULTURE

A shift was noted in participants' perceptions of working-class students and the causes of their low academic achievement. Rather than focusing on students' inadequacies, participants began critiquing structural mechanisms in the school that impede their success. One factor noted was the incongruence of students' language and discourse with those required at school. For example, participants noted that despite teachers' assumptions, students had limited familiarity using explicit language, a form of communication upon which school literacy is based:

> Shawana is a perfect example of a student who is unfamiliar with explicit language. Along with her numerous grammatical errors, she also tended to start off paragraphs with the word "he" or "she" never letting the reader know who he or she was. *Just as Finn suggests, she did appear to write as if she was talking to her friends. Finn says that working-class children "need to be introduced into and made to feel welcome in a community where explicit language makes sense, where it's necessary— a community where nonconformity is tolerated and even encouraged"* (p. 90). I definitely found this to be the case at Tower Middle. The students did not seem to know how to express themselves using explicit language, therefore making it difficult for teachers to understand (Lisa, reflective log).

Participants also recognized the classroom as an arena of cultural conflict. Rather than merely a series of skills to be learned, participants became aware of how literacy is tied to social and cultural influences. According to Sara:

> Even when there were a couple of tutors and a couple of students close to each other, the students were much more reluctant to learn the necessary material. It was almost as if they were embarrassed to let any of their peers know that they were smart. *This seems to be directly related to what Finn is talking about when he says that "for involuntary minorities, the dominant group is not only different, it is the enemy. Because cultural differences between them and the mainstream are oppositional rather than simply different, accommodation is difficult if not impossible. Cultural differences become cultural boundaries"* (p. 47). I believe this is very true. The students at Tower Middle do seem to associate speaking proper English and getting good grades as actions that will alienate them from their peers, while at the same time not allow them to be fully included into the group of teachers and tutors either (Sara, reflective log).

Another aspect of the school culture that emerged from this project was low teacher expectations for students. Participants frequently commented on how the potential of students often went unrecognized by teachers. Brian, in particular, found this disconcerting:

> I think in general the teachers there and the administrators made them out to be more dumb than they actually are because the students I'm working with are really smart—even that new boy that

came in. He's really smart—really a good writer. He's well behaved and everything. I think they spend way too much time on discipline and almost making them feel horrible about themselves. They're so uncomfortable in the situation that they just can't do it but when you're one-on-one with them and they actually see that this person wants to help me and not just sit there and correct their behavior and yell at the whole class. You know, in all honesty, I think they're very smart. I think people underestimate what they can do.

Low teacher expectations were often connected to the school's focus on student discipline and control rather than rigorous academics. Participants commented on the cycle of frustration that permeated classrooms as teachers assigned increasingly more busy work in an effort to maintain some semblance of order and learning in response to student resistance to meaningless work:

There was such frustration that I could feel it . . . The teacher knew that the students were out of control. I do not feel that the students gained sufficient knowledge while in her classroom. This was evident when the students were taking tests and quizzes. The teacher and the aide walked around the room literally giving the students answers to problems. This action basically told the students that it was okay to not understand the material or do the work, because there would always be someone there to give them the answer. These students were taught that dittos were instruction. Class time was spent with the students working on dittos the whole time (Ashley, reflective log).

The final aspect of school culture that emerged from the study was the disempowering school environment in the building. Mechanical learning with little room for exploration, creativity, or choice was noted:

. . . When speaking of the teachers in working-class schools Finn stresses the fact that they tend to have a "do it this way or it's wrong" (p. 11) mentality. He also claims that the teachers of working-class children try to control the students' movements rather than open an avenue for discussion. Both of these concepts are displayed at Tower Middle School. The teachers there definitely leave no room for creativity. The students are expected to complete certain assignments in the exact manner that the teacher explains and if it is not done that way then it is automatically wrong. When a student wants to ask the teacher a question, it seems as if the student is bothering him or her and usually gets a rude remark. There is definitely no avenue open for discussion; it is a case where the teacher gives directions and the students listen and do as they are told, end of story (Robin, reflective log).

Another noted the way students in the school were disempowered by the disrespect that teachers directed towards them. Despite the fact that teachers knew that college faculty and students were in the building, several cases of blatant disrespect toward students were observed:

> In the 5th grade classroom the control was no better. I could instantly tell why. The teacher in this room displayed no respect for the students. Here are just two quotes that I recall, "Get your lazy butt off of the floor!" and "I wouldn't wish a student like Autumn [a student in the class] on either of you [Maria and me]." The last statement was announced in front of the whole class. I do not feel that students should be expected to respect someone who does not respect them. I believe that the problems in this classroom were the result of this lack of respect (Ashley, reflective log).

Clearly, the school culture was perceived by our students as inhibiting the academic success of the children in the school. Their analysis of the root causes of this phenomenon went through a series of transitions that are described in the next section.

MOVEMENT TOWARDS CRITICAL-TRANSFORMING PROBLEM SOLVING

Based on the work of Paulo Freire (1970), Alfred Alschuler (1980) developed a three-stage model of responding to oppressive conditions: magical-conforming, naïve-reforming, and critical-transforming. Each of these stages has a distinct way of analyzing a problem:

> *Magical-Conforming:* The situation is seen either as not problematic or as an unchangeable act of existence.

> *Naïve-Reforming:* Individuals who deviate from the rules and roles of the system are blamed for the injustice within a system.

> *Critical-Transforming:* The problem is in conflict-producing, oppressive rules and roles of the system that victimize many individuals.

Using Alschuler's three-stage model of problem solving as an analytic tool, changes in participants' problem solving perspective across the learning cycle were used as an indicator of group transformation in terms of critical consciousness. Initially, participants approached problems in the school mainly from a naïve-reforming perspective. Blame for low student achievement was first placed on students who were viewed as unwilling or unable to learn. Shawna expressed this view on the pretutoring survey:

Some of my concerns would be the behavior of the children and the school atmosphere/environment. I don't know what to expect from the students since I have never been into an urban school. I hope the students are willing to learn.

Lisa also expressed her initial misconceptions about urban students:

I, along with many other people have a prejudice against urban schools. I used to think all the students were gun toting gang members who had no respect for authority and no desire to learn.

Gradually, participants shifted from blaming students to focusing on the role of teachers in the low achievement in the school. For instance, rather than viewing students as unwilling to learn, Ashley singled out the uncomfortable atmosphere created by teachers as a major contributor to students' disengagement from learning:

I would say that it's really surprising how they [students] listen to me as an authority because I'm just a college kid and I'm not a real student teacher. They do listen well and it's really a myth that they're really bad kids. [They] just need positive reinforcement because that's really what the whole school is lacking. Like all that screaming and yelling and not asking things politely and things like that. I was scared at first—I told my mom. My mom was worried. Now that I'm there I'm not scared in the least.

Participants also cited the types of instruction provided by teachers as another factor in their low academic achievement. Brian was particularly disturbed by the incongruence of students' potential with the instruction they were provided:

When I went there my first thought was that the kids would be very hyper and not want to learn. But when I did the "Bio" poem I was kind of surprised because one kid put for "four adjectives that describe you"—he put "smart" in. The other kid copied off of him. They believe, it seems, that they're really smart and I could tell from the reading that they couldn't read. I think if they were given the teaching they need, they could perform well. They seemed much smarter than the test scores would show. If they could just be worked with in small groups instead of large classes, they would probably be up there with all the other students, I think. Because they *are* smart and they seem to want to learn.

Though participants held teachers accountable for the low achievement of their students, they often cushioned this view with an acknowledgement that it was not a purposeful act. In other words, teachers were often viewed as committed professionals who wanted their students to succeed, but simply did not know how to break the cycle of failure that permeated the school. Ashley articulated this perspective in her reflective log:

[*Related to Finn's discussion of low teacher expectations and the tendency to dumb down work, curbing student discussions about schoolwork or controversial topics, and not giving students any power over their own learning*] I found that all these problems were present at Tower Middle School and although the teacher we were working with seemed extremely concerned about the students' learning, her tactics didn't seem helpful to students' understanding of their work. The teacher would lecture the students or give them work to do without telling them what it was for. Then, the students would get restless and feel that they were doing busy work and consequently misbehave or lose concentration. The teacher would get frustrated and yell at the students and would finally assign even more work as a strategy for classroom control. The end result was a cycle that kept repeating itself, creating a classroom mood of frustration and resentment.

Finally, participants began moving towards an analysis of the problems within the school from a critical-transforming stage, noting ways in which both students and teachers were disempowered and critiquing how the system could be changed. According to Kelly:

Probably the most important thing I got out of working at Tower Middle School and from reading Finn's book is a better understanding of the kind of teacher I want to be. I think that students and teachers should both be empowered and classroom activities should be dialogue, not a lecture. Students should be encouraged to ask questions and if their questions happen to be controversial, they should not just be dismissed. The students should be able to relate personally to the material. They should have a stake in their own education.

As the semester ended participants had begun to move into discussions about how the system could be changed. Though our students were just beginning to explore this complex issue, they did begin to critique the political repercussions of institutional change. In one such discussion, Jason took the lead in exploring this topic with his peers:

You see, I don't think he [Finn] meant to blame teachers for the inability [to change] because of the situation we're in as teachers.

We're restricted by our environment. Whereas parents are an outside group and they're able to exert pressure because they don't rely on the school district for their paycheck. They don't have to work in the system. If you're a teacher and you want to have a future in the district, you're not going to go in during the first couple of years and shake things up and become known as a troublemaker. Because you're pretty much shooting yourself in the foot.

Most evident from this study was the fact that participants began to view urban education from a new perspective. Holly articulated this transition in the last focus group:

I became less naïve. And that was really important because . . . I think about how I felt about my school—in high school—and just my whole outlook on things. And it's so different now. You know? I just didn't realize a lot of things about social class and the things we talked about, that I never really thought about before because I never had to.

As the above examples demonstrate, our students had begun to critically analyze the mechanisms that oppress both students and teachers in urban schools. Though this new awareness was in its infancy as the semester ended, it is hoped that the seeds for continued exploration and reflection had been sown.

SELF-DEVELOPMENT

In addition to developing new understandings about working-class schools, the learning cycle also resulted in participants' self-development. A number of students expressed an increased commitment to teaching. According to Ashley: "Overall I feel that being at Tower Middle School was a good experience for me. In all honesty, I was never sure about whether I *really* wanted to teach and I know now that I do." Participants also noted an improvement in their pedagogical knowledge, an important goal for us as instructors of the course. In a humorous story shared in one of the focus groups, Brian expressed learning classroom management skills through trial and error.

Once I tried working with 10 or 20 kids. I tried to . . . at a point where they were all rebelling and I just suddenly raised my voice and said "I have the power here." And that was a BIG mistake because it went exactly the opposite and it turned into where they were screaming and yelling they have the power [all laugh]. And talk about establishing order!

Finally, participation in the learning cycle helped participants develop interpersonal skills. Though building relationships with students is a critical component in any teacher education program, it was particularly important in this case because virtually none of the participants had had any previous interactions with urban students and communities. Jason, who tutored an extremely shy young girl named Tia, spoke about his sense of accomplishment as they learned together.

> One of the changes I noted about myself was being able to open up to a student. When I first meet somebody, I don't tell them my life story. Just being able to open up—to build a relationship and when it got to the point near the end—where Tia would look forward to working with me and she showed me how her writing had improved—how I was able to help her out—I loved that. You know, being able to say—Yeah, I made a difference, no matter how small. I felt, okay, I need to open up. I need to talk to her, to get her to do the same so we can build on that and do something constructive.

In summary, though we did not change the world with this course, positive transformations were noted. Our students began to critique urban education in a new light, calling into question erroneous assumptions. While a number of positive outcomes were noted, perhaps the most rewarding and hopeful was that, across the board, our students loved working with the children and took their side in the learning process.

CONCLUSIONS

The findings of this project suggest that integrating critical pedagogical theory, practical experience in an urban school, and continual critical reflection is an effective instructional strategy to facilitate both critical consciousness and self-development. Each component of the learning cycle built upon and extended learning opportunities provided by the other components. Integrating critical pedagogical theory provided our students with a focus on which to reflect and helped them understand the social, political, and economic forces that converged in their experiences. By looking at their experiences from a wider context, students gained an informed perspective to improve learning and practice.

This study also provides evidence for the importance of integrating practical experience. Working directly with urban students helped dispel a number of misconceptions our students held initially. The field placement also provided a setting in which students could think about and apply the abstract theory and methodologies learned in the classroom.

Finally, the study demonstrated the importance of critical reflection in the learning cycle. Rather than merely acquiring knowledge, our students were able to make sense of their own experiences in light of theory. Students connected course content to their experiences in the school, calling into question held assumptions and beliefs. By integrating all three aspects of learning, our students developed new understandings of the social and political contexts of learning and teaching, as well as increased pedagogical knowledge. The success of this action research project holds promise for other teacher educators searching for ways to develop critically reflective practitioners who understand that educating individuals for participation in a democratic society involves more than transferring knowledge.

NOTE

1. Pre- and post-tutoring surveys, weekly debriefing discussions, focus groups, and reflective logs were used for data collection. The analytic strategy was thematic analysis using inductive reasoning.

REFERENCES

Alschuler, A. S. (1980). *School discipline: A socially literate solution.* New York: McGraw-Hill.

Aronowitz, S. (1973). *False promises.* New York: McGraw-Hill.

Carr, W., & Kemmis, S. (1986). *Becoming critical.* London: Falmer Press.

Cranton, P. (1996). *Professional development as transformative learning: New perspectives for teachers of adults.* San Francisco: Jossey-Bass.

Finn, P. (1999). *Literacy with an attitude: Educating working-class children in their own self-interest.* Albany: State University of New York Press.

Freire, P. (1970). *Pedagogy of the oppressed.* San Francisco: Seabury.

Giroux, H. A. (1980). Teacher education and the ideology of social control. *Journal of Education, 162*(2), 5–27.

Giroux, H. A. (1988). Literacy and the pedagogy of voice and political empowerment. *Educational Theory, 38*(1), 61–75.

Kincheloe, J. L., & McLaren, P. L. (1994). Rethinking critical theory and qualitative research. In N. K. Denzin & Y. S. Lincoln (Eds.), *Handbook of qualitative research* (pp. 138–157). Thousand Oaks, CA: Sage.

Rhoads, A. (1997). *Community service and higher learning: Explorations of the caring self.* Albany: State University of New York Press.

Shannon, P. (1992). Why become political? In P. Shannon (Ed.), *Becoming political: Readings and writings in the politics of literacy education* (pp. 1–11). Portsmouth, NH: Heinemann.

Toole, J., & Toole, P. (1997). Reflection as a tool for turning service experiences into learning experiences. In C. Kinsley & K. McPherson (Eds.), *Enriching the curriculum through service learning* (pp. 99–114). Alexandria, VA: Association for Supervision and Curriculum Development.

5 Teacher Education and Community Organizing

Dennis Shirley

DENNIS SHIRLEY, PROFESSOR OF TEACHER EDUCATION, Special Education, and Curriculum and Instruction at Boston College, addresses contemporary issues of organizing parents and communities around engagement for educational justice. The organizing challenges presented by race and class differences are compounded by high-stakes accountability and standards-based reforms. Yet efforts by teacher educators in seven Boston area schools were more successful in preparing their students to work with parents and communities than their peers who did not provide experiences in community organizing in their teacher preparation program.

Teacher educators with social justice aspirations generally consider some form of positive relationships between schools and communities to be a core component of effective teacher preparatory activities. Anyon (2005), for example, draws upon a variety of sources, from the Civil Rights movement to contemporary community organizing for school improvement, to argue for the importance of strong horizontal ties between parents and teachers in underresourced urban communities. Likewise, Murrell's account (2001) of the community teacher, who is anchored in a stance of political solidarity with urban communities of color presupposes the necessity of preliminary activities that lead teachers to develop their primary loyalty to their pupils and their sending communities rather than bureaucratic mandates or testing regimes.

Noguera (2003) endorsed school choice, not as a formula for escaping from the public schools, but as a means of increasing parent engagement in schools. Oakes, Quartz, Ryan, and Lipton (2000) observed that although virtually all school reform efforts call for the participation of parents and community members, only rarely do they establish the power relationships that would enable parents to realize the potential of participatory democracy. Finally, my own description of the Alliance Schools effort in Texas (1997) provided numerous case studies of strategies for developing conjoint school and community engagement practices—but these are very atypical in the broader school reform landscape, including a congregationally based organizing approach derived from the community organizing tradition of Saul Alinsky (1971).

Each of these approaches differs from mainstream accounts of parent involvement, as articulated by Epstein et al. (1997) in her widely cited six-faceted approach, insofar as they center directly on issues of power, access, and governance. Even if the conceptualizations involve a component of conflict and power shuffling, the researchers cited above all agree that conflict is an essential part of leveling a playing field in which low-income parents of color can conduct advocacy for their children and gain educational opportunities that would otherwise be withheld from them. This is a critical component of what Payne (1995) has described as the organizing tradition; genuine change must involve negotiation and occasional contestation, and not simply assign parents or community stakeholders the role of supporting the preestablished agendas of a school or any other institution that purportedly exists to serve the public good.

The approach thus far is admittedly schematic. Epstein's typology of parent involvement strategies does not preclude negotiation and conflict, and there are important differences, in addition to the similarities, among the educational researchers referred to above. Nonetheless, each approach strives for what I have elsewhere characterized as parent *engagement* as distinct from parent *involvement* (Shirley, 1997, p. 73), namely a conceptualization of school and community relations that seeks to transform schools—particularly urban schools—from outposts of a district bureaucracy to activity settings that promote a wide range of civic and educational enterprises. In the case of the Alliance Schools of Texas, I describe how, in spite of daunting challenges, some of the schools have evolved from low achieving extensions of top-down reforms to high-achieving community centers with preschool and after school programs, parent centers, and liaisons with numerous community-based organizations (Shirley, 1997, 2002).

In spite of the compelling arguments of educators with social justice commitments, however, it is striking just how marginalized low-income communities of color are in contemporary school reform discourse, particularly in terms of latent assets that could be capitalized upon to improve public schools. Although the No Child Left Behind Act (NCLB) (P. L. 107–110) dedicates several sections (111, 114, and 118) to parent involvement, a closer examination reveals that the involvement is primarily defined in terms of enabling parents to withdraw their children from low-achieving public schools, with the option of sending them to schools run by Educational Management Organizations (EMOs) such as have been supported recently with taxpayer dollars in Philadelphia and Chicago (Shirley, forthcoming).

At this historical moment, it is difficult to access any federal or state funding for school improvement without including a role for educational technology in one's grant, but in spite of the pluralistic and democratic promises of technology advocates (Foster, 1996; Sproull & Kiesler, 1996), few of the requests for proposals for the grants include components for promoting community engagement. An older and, ironically, very American, political tradition about the importance of grassroots civic engagement has in many ways been supplanted by newer paradigms of streamlined public management techniques (as in high-stakes testing regimes with sanctions dictated by the federal government and states) and market-based models of reform (as evident in the rise of vouchers, charter schools, and EMOs).

Indeed, viewing the dominant school reform discourse of the opening years of the twenty-first century, it appears that parents' relationship to their children's learning is considered by many to be so insignificant that (aside from implementing school choice models) reformers should emphasize the professional development of their staff and keep parents at a distance from the learning that is to occur in a school. Of course, there are countervailing perspectives. Rothstein (2004), for example, emphasizes the continuing role of social class in education; Henderson and Mapp (2002) have argued that "a new wave of evidence" demonstrates the power of parent involvement; and many urban districts—preserving one of the main school restructuring tenets of the 1990s—still stipulate that parents must serve on a school's instructional leadership team, site-based management team, or local school council (the terms vary from city to city, but the import is largely identical).

Given these divergent points of view, an interrogation of what might be termed the "community-school problematic," with special attention dedicated to community organizing and teacher education, is in order. Hence, in this chapter, I first indicate briefly why community organizing is so difficult; I contend this has little to do with schools, but much to do with larger macroeconomic and social processes. Second, I describe the complex relationship of community organizing with school improvement in an era of standards-based reform and high-stakes accountability. Third, I show that, for a variety of reasons, teacher education is a hotly contested field today and mainstream teacher education does not provided future teachers with opportunities to promote the skills and dispositions they need to work effectively with parents and community-based organizations. Finally, I argue that in spite of these complicated problems, teacher educators can still promote parent and community engagement, and I refer to a coalition I have led for the past five years that has worked with numerous community-based organizations and had some success in this arena.

CHALLENGES TO COMMUNITY ORGANIZING: CLASS AND DIVERSITY

Community organizing, despite its romantic aura of oppressed groups taking on power structures and bending them to serve hitherto disenfranchised publics, is phenomenally demanding work in the current social and economic context. When it comes to participating in the political arena, affluent Americans

are far more experienced, engaged, and savvy than the poor. Political participation is very unevenly distributed in the United States. In 1989, political
scientists conducted research that compared the civic engagement of wealthy
Americans (earning more than $75,000 per annum) with the poor (those
earning under $15,000). They found that not only were the wealthy two-
and-a-half times more likely to be affiliated with a political organization, three
times more likely to be involved in community activities, and four times
more likely to have done campaign work, but they were also more than twice
as likely to have participated in protest activities (Verba, Schlozman, & Brady,
1995, p. 190). Those protest activities could take the form of a referendum
against increased taxes, litigation against affirmative action, or the circulation
of petitions against the provision of low- and moderate-income housing in
affluent communities.

In terms of community organizing for school reform, skewed power relationships routinely undermine the ability of poor and working-class parents
to mobilize effectively for their children. Oakes and Lipton (2002) illustrate
how white middle-class parents easily outmaneuvered the reforms sought by
working-class parents of color in a reforming high school; Wells and Serna
(1996) have shown that detracking reforms in racially mixed schools likewise
can be stalled by elite parents who use their abilities to manipulate school
systems to preserve privileges for their children; Anyon (1997) documents how
white elite parents were able to reverse equity gains of the landmark Abbott
decision in New Jersey; and I (2002) describe how middle school teachers in
Texas were able to undermine changes sought by a community-based organization by emphasizing their professional expertise over largely poor and
working-class Hispanic immigrant parents. The exact issue is less important
than the overarching political import: when one turns to community organizing as a solution to the problems of urban education, one must acknowledge
at the outset that the affluent and the educated have tremendous advantages
over poor and working-class parents in terms of their prior political work and
their extant political networks.

This problem leads to a conundrum. To develop any reasonable clout,
community organizers must do broad-based organizing; they must reach across
race, class, and language barriers to develop a power base that commands the
respect of influential decision makers in urban school systems. In the language
of social capital theory, organizers must move beyond bonding social capital—
which refers to strong social ties among individuals similar to them in terms
of categories such as race, gender, religion, or profession—to develop bridging
social capital (Putnam, 2000, pp. 22–24). Yet to do so is exceptionally difficult.
At the end of a careful review of 40 years of research on diversity in organizations, Williams and O'Reilly (1998) conclude, "The preponderance of
empirical evidence suggests that diversity is most likely to impede group
functioning. Unless steps are taken to actively counteract these effects," they
warn, "diversity is more likely to have negative than positive effects on group

performance" (p. 120). A host of educational analysts confirm that sociocultural dissonance, particularly in terms of relationships between white and black Americans, complicate the work of urban educational reform (Anyon, 1997; Payne & Kabe, 2001; Henig, Hula, Orr, & Pedescleaux, 1999; Orr, 1999).

The point here is not to develop arguments against diversity in American political and social life, for diversity is in many ways one of the richest and most genuinely educational components of the American polity, when elaborated appropriately. Rather, the point is a simple political one: it is easier to organize individuals who can lay claim to a common ethnic or racial identity than it is to organize across group lines. In the second half of the twentieth century, suburbanization transformed American culture to create a new pan-ethnic sense of whiteness which has come to be culturally juxtaposed to the national otherness of people of color, who are concentrated in cities. Overcoming that otherness is a key task for grassroots community organizers who rarely can develop any sustained civic capacity by focusing on a single issue of relevance to a single group.

This second problem with organizing across diversity is not simply a reflection of unfortunate political choices, for it is rooted in a deeper set of structural relationships that have emerged and calcified in the last quarter century. The American power elite has in many ways withdrawn from arenas in which mixed-class encounters were once possible, leading to a phenomenon Reich (1991) characterized as the "secession of the successful." Yet, the economic elite is not the only class to have erected barriers between themselves and their fellow citizens. Middle-class Americans have achieved a high degree of material homogeneity that is juxtaposed to poor and working-class urban dwellers of color who are often spatially removed from new jobs that have been created in "edge cities" in the suburbs (Wilson, 1987; Goode & Maskovsky, 2001). The intensification of class stratification, linked with the movement of new jobs out of traditional manufacturing centers, has made community organizing across economic lines more difficult than in previous eras, although some success has been achieved by Alinsky organizations in this regard (Warren, 2001).

A third problem community organizers must confront has to do with a certain romanticism about what community organizing can realistically accomplish. Community organizations have launched a number of impressive agendas in the last quarter century in the arenas of school reform, crime prevention, health care, job training, and environmental protection, but their net effect has not been substantial when viewing the development of the nation as a whole. The reason for this is relatively straightforward: our current political economy is radically intertwined with increasingly global networks of production, exchange, and distribution. Community-based groups can possess tremendous reservoirs in terms of local knowledge but be relatively powerless to affect economic cycles and the rapid pace of inventions in dynamic arenas like computer technology, telecommunications, and genetic engineering. For this reason, the cautions of sympathetic observers about the limitations of community organizing (Castells, 1983; Halpern, 1995) are well-taken.

These impediments to community organizing for school reform along the lines of nineteenth- or twentieth-century labor unionism or the Civil Rights Movement are daunting. Yet at the same time that one should acknowledge the many barriers to such organizing, it is also important to recognize that countervailing tendencies are at work. Globalization, for example, has widened the gap between the rich and the poor in the United States, but computer technology, the internet, and telecommunications can also expedite the rise of global protest movements, as was evident in the recent peace movement against the invasion of Iraq, which crossed class lines.

By some measures, diversity may impede group functioning, but it also can contribute to a broader understanding of human commonalities, as well as cultural richness that can be profoundly educative. Polleta (2002) has shown that community members derive a wide number of benefits when they become engaged in grassroots civic movements, and Putnam (2000) has shown that social capital has considerable collateral benefits, such as the promotion of social trust and personal self-efficacy. History is inherently unpredictable, cultures are dynamic rather than static, and politics continually provides new opportunities for agency, negotiation, and purposeful coalition building.

CHALLENGES TO EDUCATION ORGANIZING: EXPERIENCES OF THE TEXAS IAF

The rapid transformation of the educational context in the United States in the last 15 years, largely through the ascendance of the accountability movement and high-stakes testing, presents a whole set of new dilemmas for education organizers. Here, the experiences of the Texas Industrial Areas Foundation (IAF), the Lone Star affiliate of the network launched by Saul Alinsky in 1940, are relevant. In the 1990s, it was relatively common for the Texas IAF to inform parents about the nature of the tests and why they were important in gauging their children's academic progress. At Zavala Elementary School—in many ways, the poster child of the Alliance Schools in the 1990s—the drive to improve the school began when an angry father noticed the discrepancy between his child's excellent grades and her poor results on the Texas Assessment of Academic Skills (TAAS) (Shirley, 1997). Texas IAF organizers never endorsed the test as such, but they considered it to be a legitimate assessment tool, even if their own goals for higher-level critical thinking went far beyond the minimum-skills gauged by the TAAS.

In terms of how Texas IAF organizers now view the accountability systems, much changed in the intervening years. "The turning point for many of us came in February 2003 at our annual Alliance School conference," Sister Mignonne Konecny, lead organizer for Austin Interfaith, recalled. She adds:

Teachers and principals were getting lesson plans from their districts dictating what they should teach. They were getting flooded with practice tests and benchmark tests to be given every Friday, and we were really getting the message that the tests had become punitive rather than diagnostic. (Interview with author, June, 2004)

Organizers and leaders now find that the tests drive so many educational practices in Texas that any kind of reflection, analysis, or skill acquisition not measured on the tests is marginalized in the curriculum. "For all intents and purposes, the tests now are the curriculum in Texas," Joe Higgs, an organizer in the Houston area, commented. "Districts are saying more and more that the test is going to be all that we teach, no matter what the cost" (Interview with author, June, 2004).

According to Texas IAF organizers, a host of unethical practices are implemented in schools in which teachers and principals are pressed to raise test scores or face a range of punitive actions such as losing their principals or being taken over by the state. Rene Wizig-Barrios, an education organizer with The Metropolitan Organization (TMO), the IAF affiliate in Houston, described how extreme the new accountability measures have become:

One of our principals was told by her district to make sure that homeless kids in a shelter shouldn't show up on testing day because they would depress the scores. Other principals have abolished free time for kids in first, second, and third grade. Principals tell us that they want to meet with us and work with us but that they're so much under the gun to raise test scores that they just can't make the time. And now we have this new law in Texas which says that if kids don't pass the TAKS [Texas Assessment of Knowledge and Skills] reading test in third grade they can be held back. That kind of pressure seems to us to be way too great to put on kids who are that little, and it's a major source of fear and stressor for the teachers. (Interview with author, June, 2004)

In the climate of fear described by Texas IAF organizers, teachers focus all their efforts on improving test scores, ignoring any subject that is not tested in a given year. Seventh-grade teachers find that their pupils haven't learned writing since the fourth grade, because that is the last grade at which writing was assessed by the TAKS. Fifth-grade teachers discover that their pupils have had little or no science or social studies because they were never assessed before the fifth grade—all of the emphasis was put on reading, writing, and math, to get the annual TAKS scores up. "So all of a sudden the fifth graders are getting social studies and science crammed down their throats, since that is what is tested that year," Konecny remarked.

Ironically, the intense pressure put on principals to raise test scores appears to contribute to a rapid turnover of school leaders, either because principals leave troubled schools as soon as they can, or because districts are continually in search of new principals who they think can raise scores. Principals in many cities in Texas are now hired on one-year contracts; if their school's test scores are low, they are fired, and if the scores are high, they receive generous bonuses. As a result, principals have very real financial incentives to press their teachers to produce high test score results on the TAKS, even when such one-sided emphasis on cognition might undermine the social, physical, and ethical development of children.

In this kind of context, it is almost impossible to sustain community organizing to improve both a school and its immediate environment. "People are so anxious about testing that they try to do everything at once," stated Kevin Courtney, lead organizer with the El Paso Interreligious Sponsoring Organization (EPISO).

> We have testing going on this week in one of our schools that had forty-eight kids in a classroom for the first seven weeks of the school year; there was barely enough space for the kids to even sit on the floor. They finally got them in another class, and now they're testing them for two straight days. It's a disaster, and it isn't just in our Alliance Schools; the paper is filled with letters to the editor from angry teachers every week. (Interview with author, June, 2004)

Community organizers, of course, are used to uphill battles, and it would be disingenuous to suggest that organizing has been entirely eclipsed because of the rise of high-stakes testing. Austin Interfaith is now working with the Austin Independent School District to try to create a cluster of small schools in which teachers can develop and pilot their own assessment instruments, with a component of community accountability built in. Other community-based organizations (CBOs), such as the Association of Communities Organized for Reform Now (ACORN), the Pacific Institute for Community Organizing (PICO), and Direct Action and Research Training (DART) have sought to find ways to use pupil achievement on tests as a kind of winnable issue for developing civic capacity in their communities.

ACORN, for example, has begun its own small schools in inner city neighborhoods, has collaborated with urban districts to improve teacher quality, and has begun a national campaign to support full funding of NCLB. PICO has worked with districts to create new small-school schools in San Francisco and Oakland, and a Denver affiliate has decried budget cuts and highlighted resource disparities in the schools. Some initiatives—such as the endorsement of Direct Instruction (DI) by some DART chapters—are likely to prove disconcerting to educators with social justice aspirations who seek to develop new kinds of critical literacy (Dudling-Marling & Paugh, 2005; Finn,

1999). Nonetheless, the larger point that community organizing for educational reform is continuing, even in the current testing context, is important, so as to not foreclose possibilities for progressive change.

THE TEACHER EDUCATION "PROBLEM"
AND COMMUNITY ORGANIZING

Teacher education as a field in the United States has been contested terrain ever since its inception in Massachusetts in the 1830s, but this contestation has recently escalated to high-intensity policy warfare. The major grounds of debate in recent years have focused on the merit of university-based teacher preparatory programs or alternative routes (or no routes at all) that use data such as improvements on pupils' test scores as the primary indicator of teacher quality. A brief review of each position is relevant here as it is of direct relevance for our understanding of the role community organizing might play in the preparation of future teachers.

On the one hand, teacher educators and their allies in the last dozen years have sought to gather a wealth of evidence proving that traditional certified teachers who have graduated from university-based programs consistently outperform those who are on emergency certificates or have gone through the numerous alternative programs now available in the United States (Darling-Hammond, 2000a; Wayne & Youngs, 2003). This professionalization agenda has been advanced by a range of secondary associations, such as the National Commission on Teaching and America's Future (NCTAF), the National Board for Professional Teaching Standards (NBPTS), and the Interstate New Teacher Assessment and Support Consortium (INTASC). The policy recommendations of these groups have been largely codified in the guidelines of official agencies such as the National Council for Accreditation of Teacher Education (NCATE), the Teacher Education Accreditation Council (TEAC), and state departments of education, which have become increasingly attentive to virtually all facets of teacher preparation in universities and in many ways reinforce the current emphasis on standardized testing that now dominates American education.

On the other hand, a new and major challenge to the professionalizing agenda has emerged from deregulators who contend that there is little or no evidence that traditionally certified teachers are any more effective at promoting pupil achievement than those who have passed through alternative routes (Ballou & Podgursky, 2000; Kanstaroom & Finn, 1999). The deregulators have considerable financial support from conservative policy groups, such as the Heritage Foundation, the Manhattan Institute, and the Fordham Foundation.

More significantly, they have received much uncritical support from the U.S. Department of Education in recent years; since the appointment of President Bush in 2000, the Department has encouraged a wide range of alternative programs with no real standards other than the ability of the preservice teachers to pass the appropriate areas of their states' teacher tests. The Department has also increased its surveillance of traditional, university-based programs through the creation of teacher tests, and new requirements by the federal government that all states have such tests and report their results to the U.S. Department of Education for dissemination, have created heightened visibility for university-based teacher education programs, particularly since programs with low rates of graduates on the tests (generally, below 80 percent), could be closed by the Department (U.S. Department of Education, 2002).

Last but not least, a third group, less mainstream in terms of public discourse but nonetheless contenders in the policy wars, are teacher educators who emphasize social justice commitments more than professionalization or deregulation (Cochran-Smith, 2004a; Ladson-Billings, 2001). These teacher educators generally offer qualified support for the professionalization agenda because they note that virtually all underperforming urban schools have higher percentages of uncertified teachers than their suburban counterparts (Darling-Hammond, 2000b). However, their explicitly political stance of solidarity with students of color in urban schools leads to a nuanced perspective on several issues. For example, given the demographic imperative to prepare more teachers of color in the United States, teacher educators such as myself are strongly in support of alternative programs that prepare indigenous community members to teach in their neighborhood schools. Further, social justice commitments can lead teacher educators to frank criticisms of mainstream professional practices in the field that do not adequately prepare future teachers to engage successfully with culturally and linguistically diverse learners and their communities (Murrell, 2001, 2002; Oakes & Lipton, 2002; Shirley, 1997; Zeichner, 1991).

A profession in many ways under siege and surveillance—one perpetually defined in policy circles as a problem (Cochran-Smith, 2004b)—is not likely to take risks to empower low-income citizens and immigrants of color concentrated in the nation's urban centers. Indeed, Cochran-Smith (2004a) has suggested that a fourth grouping, which goes beyond the professionalization agenda, can be identified in the reform of teacher education today; this grouping promotes an over-regulation of teacher education in universities, micromanaging virtually all aspects of all programs, while allowing alternative programs to devise an endlessly innovative repertoire of offerings with little oversight other than the teacher test.

These considerations elicit a host of questions for our discussion of community organizing and teacher education. ACORN, for example, has made the recruitment and retention of certified teachers a major component of its support for full funding of NCLB, indicating that this rapidly growing community organization, with over 60 chapters in American cities, views at least this strand of the professionalization agenda as congruent with the needs of its poor and working-class stakeholders. At the same time, ACORN is not uncritical of NCLB; along with its push for full funding, the community-based organization has mounted a campaign to "Invest in Schools, Invest in Kids," which calls not only for full funding of the sections of NCLB but also seeks to "refocus its attention on our kids, our schools, and our communities."

In a defensive maneuver, many teacher educators have embraced the professionalization agenda, including that part of it that uses pupil test score data to measure not only teacher quality, but also the quality of the teacher educators who prepared the teachers. This use of pupil test-score data represents a calculated risk, because research indicates that test scores are now being used in a punitive form against educators rather than to diagnose and improve pupil achievement (McNeil, 2000; Orfield & Kornhaber, 2001). As the test scores are deployed as a policy weapon—with no one evidently to be held accountable for decades of unequal funding, the highest rate of child poverty in the developed world, and a long legacy of institutionalized racism—classroom teachers and teacher educators are pressured to both raise pupil achievement on the tests and to devise credible alternative forms of assessment that genuinely demonstrate what their students know and can achieve.

The whole undertaking is problematic because test makers have failed to persuade the teachers who administrate them that the tests are valid and reliable. In one major survey, four out of ten teachers indicate that their school could raise test scores without improving pupil learning; nine of ten teachers disagreed that test scores were an accurate reflection of what their pupils who learned English as a second language knew; and a substantial majority of teachers reported that their state's accountability system led them to teach in ways that were against their personal convictions of best instructional practices (Pedulla, Abrams, Madaus, Russell & Ramos, 2003). Such professional distortions—and the ensuing ethical dilemmas for teachers and teacher educators—are perhaps inevitable for a school improvement approach that from the outset marginalized teachers and community members on key policy making commissions (McNeil, 2000).

Rather than valorize standardized tests uncritically, a number of educators and scholar-activists seek to develop new models of community accountability and empowered participatory governance that promote transparency, civic engagement, and oversight of pupil achievement (Fung, 2004; Mediratta & Fruchter, 2003). While these models are currently works-in-progress, they provide a potential link between community organizing and teacher education that would call on future teachers to understand public engagement around assessment issues to be a core component of teachers' work. Only further experimentation with such models, it would seem, can avoid the apparently unteachable proclivities of policymakers to implement reforms with little input from teachers and community members who will be most heavily impacted by them—a conundrum that Cuban and Usdan (2003) recently captured in the pithy dictum of "powerful reform with shallow roots."

THE MASSACHUSETTS COALITION FOR TEACHER QUALITY AND STUDENT ACHIEVEMENT

Thus far, I have laid out a number of considerable challenges to the promotion of community organizing in society, in schools, and in teacher education. In spite of the challenges and the manner in which many policies militate against education organizing, the existence of competing definitions of teacher quality and teacher education provide multiple venues for such organizing—if teacher educators are willing to take some risks and investigate hitherto unexplored opportunities. Teacher educators can make common cause with parents and community-based organizations to promote the preparation of quality teachers who are predisposed to work effectively with urban communities of color, as the following exposition indicates.

From 1999 to the present, I have been a principal investigator on a $7 million Title II Teacher Quality Enhancement Grant that has funded the "Massachusetts Coalition for Teacher Quality and Student Achievement." The Massachusetts Coalition consists of seven colleges and universities, twenty-one urban schools in the three largest cities of the commonwealth, twelve CBOs, and three business partners. The original purpose of the grant was to support the preparation of highly qualified teachers for urban schools; special emphasis was placed on collaboration with arts and sciences faculty at the higher education level. My grant writing coauthors and I, however, sought to promote a strong awareness of parent and community stakeholders as potential allies for the future teachers in our programs. Hence, we agreed that the second objective of the Massachusetts Coalition should be to enhance the school and community based nature of teacher education, with the goal that future educators would be better prepared to identify and capitalize upon community assets once they enter the classroom as full-time teachers (Massachusetts Coalition for Teacher Quality and Student Achievement, 1999).

Once the Coalition received funding (in September 1999), teachers, parents, and higher education faculty in the Coalition initiated a series of strategies for working with communities to promote culturally responsive critical pedagogies and student achievement. Faculty at Northeastern University broke with the teacher education tradition of school-based placements and placed students in their Introduction to Education class in community settings such as churches, sports facilities, and libraries to teach reading and writing.

The teacher education faculty at the University of Massachusetts at Boston held department meetings at the Dudley Street Neighborhood Initiative in Roxbury; hired the Chair of the Education Committee at Dudley Street to serve as a liaison between the schools, the university, and the community; and developed a substitute teacher induction program in collaboration with activities from the Boston chapter of ACORN. A professor-in-residence from Lesley University hired a parent activist to coordinate communication between teachers and parents in her urban elementary school. Organizers from the Greater Boston Interfaith Organization—the Boston IAF chapter—visited Boston College classes and worked with Coalition partnership schools to acquire additional curricular resources from the Boston Public Schools. Urban schools and universities in Boston, Springfield, and Worcester used Coalition resources to promote stronger ties to Spanish-speaking parents. Coalition conferences and newsletters emphasized the parent engagement thrust of this work, thus overcoming much of the technical emphasis on a narrow definition of teacher professionalism in recent teacher education reform and building on a tradition of democratic activism in the history of American education.

Four years later, the Coalition's Steering Committee and its auxiliary Research Task Force asked our external evaluator, Abt Associates, to develop questions and distribute a survey to cooperating teachers in all of the Coalition schools. Coalition activists wanted to determine if the cooperating teachers considered their preservice teachers to have positive attitudes towards parents and their urban communities; we also wanted to know whether the preservice teachers had been proactive in reaching out to parents and community stakeholders through a variety of activities. The cooperating teachers needed to indicate whether the preservice teachers who worked with them were affiliated with the seven higher education institutions of the Coalition or other colleges and universities. A total of 610 cooperating teachers in 18 urban schools completed the surveys, with a total response rate of 59 percent (Abt Associates, 2003).

The results of the Abt survey were encouraging to the activists of the Massachusetts Coalition. On most measures, there is no difference between preservice teachers prepared at non-Coalition or Coalition institutions, but in the area of community engagement the differences were striking. Forty-four percent of Coalition student teachers versus 34 percent of non-Coalition student teachers took the initiative to communicate frequently with parents; 46 percent of Coalition student teachers versus 23 percent of non-Coalition student teachers were familiar with their pupils' neighborhoods; and 46 percent of Coalition student teachers versus 30 percent of non-Coalition teachers were very effective or effective at working with community members to support school and classroom learning (Abt Associates, 2003, p. 14). Ideally, of course, one would like these numbers to be even higher. Nonetheless, the numbers indicate that teacher educators can have an impact on their student teachers' preparation to work with parents and other community members; we are not so overregulated that we cannot determine our own curricula.

The data indicating that Coalition student teachers are more prepared to work with parents and community stakeholders are both heartening and disheartening. On the one hand, the Coalition worked very hard on this issue for many years, and when one considers that not even half of our student teachers were considered very effective or effective at working with community members to support school and classroom learning, one can easily be discouraged. On the other hand, it is important to remember that student teachers are still very much students, and one should hardly expect that they are accomplished practitioners upon leaving our higher education institutions; skilled teaching is generally acquired through an iterative process over many years of trial and error. Perhaps the wisest message one can take from this experience is that it is very demanding work to prepare student teachers to work well with parents and community members in our nation's large cities—but that this work can be done, and measurable differences can be achieved, if teacher educators are willing to invest in the challenging work of forging coalitions with parents through the demanding, hands-on work of community organizing.

REFERENCES

Abt Associates. (2003). *Results of the survey about expectations for student teachers.* Cambridge, MA: Author.

Alinsky, S. (1971). *Rules for radicals: A pragmatic primer for realistic radicals.* New York: Vintage.

Anyon, J. (1997). *Ghetto schooling: A political economy of urban educational reform.* New York: Teachers College Press.

Anyon, J. (2005). *Radical possibilities: Public policy, urban education, and a new social movement.* New York: Routledge.

Ballou, D., & Podgursky, M. (2000). Reforming teacher preparation and licensing: What is the evidence? *Teachers College Record, 102*(1), 5–27.

Castells, M. (1983). *The city and the grassroots: A cross-cultural theory of urban social movements.* Berkeley: University of California Press.

Cochran-Smith, M. (2004a). *Walking the road: Race, diversity, and social justice in teacher education.* New York: Teachers College Press.

Cochran-Smith, M. (2004b). The problem of teacher education. *Journal of Teacher Education, 55*(4), 295–299.

Cuban, L., & Usdan, M. (2003). *Powerful reforms with shallow roots: Improving America's urban schools.* New York: Teachers College Press.

Darling-Hammond, L. (2000a). Teacher quality and student achievement: A review of state policy evidence. *Education Policy Analysis Archives, 8*(1).

Darling-Hammond, L. (2000b). How teacher education matters. *Journal of Teacher Education, 51*(3), 166–173.

Dudley-Marling, C., & Paugh, P. (2005). The rich get richer; the poor get Direct Instruction. In B. Altwerger (Ed.), *Reading for Profit* (pp. 156–171). Portsmouth, NH: Heinemann.

Epstein, J. L., Sanders, M. G., Simon, B. S., Salinas, K. C., Jansorn, N. R., & Voorhis, F. L. (1997). *School, family, and community partnerships: Your handbook for action.* Thousand Oaks, CA: Corwin.

Finn, P. (1999). *Literacy with an attitude: Educating working-class children in their own self-interest.* Albany: State University of New York Press.

Foster, D. (1996). Community and identity in the electronic village. In D. Porter (Ed.), *Internet culture* (pp. 23–38). New York: Routledge.

Fung, A. (2004). *Empowered participation: Reinventing urban democracy.* Princeton, NJ: Princeton University Press.

Goode, J., & Maskovsky, J. (2001). *The new poverty studies: The ethnology of power, politics, and impoverished people in the United States.* New York: New York University Press.

Halpern, R. (1995). *Rebuilding the inner city: A history of neighborhood initiatives to address poverty in the United States.* New York: Columbia University Press.

Henderson, A., & Mapp, K. (2002). *A new wave of evidence: The impact of school, family, and community connections on student achievement.* Austin, TX: Southwest Educational Development Laboratory.

Henig, J., Hula, R., Orr, M., & Pedescleaux, D. (1999). *The color of school reform: Race, politics, and the challenge of urban education.* Princeton, NJ: Princeton University Press.

Kanstoroom, M., & Finn, C. (1999). *Better teachers, better schools.* Washington, DC: Thomas B. Fordham Foundation.

Ladson-Billings, G. (2001). *Crossing over to Canaan: The journey of new teachers in diverse classrooms.* San Francisco: Jossey-Bass.

Massachusetts Coalition for Teacher Quality and Student Achievement. (1999). Grant Proposal to the Office of Postsecondary Education, U.S. Department of Education.

McNeil, L. M. (2000). *Contradictions of school reform: Educational costs of standardized testing.* New York: Routledge.

Mediratta, K., & Fruchter, N. (2003). *From governance to accountability: Building relationships that make schools work.* New York: Drum Major Institute for Public Policy.

Murrell, P. C. (2001). *The community teacher: A new framework for effective urban teaching.* New York: Teachers College Press.

Murrell, P. C. (2002). *African-centered pedagogy: Building schools of achievement for African-American children.* Albany: State University of New York Press.

Noguera, P. A. (2003). *City schools and the American dream: Reclaiming the promise of public education.* New York: Teachers College.

Oakes, J., Quartz, K. H., Ryan, S., and Lipton, M. (2000). *Becoming good American high schools: The struggle for civic virtue in educational reform.* New York: Free Press.

Oakes, J., & Lipton, M. (2002). Struggling for educational equity in diverse communities: School reform as social movement. *Journal of Educational Change 3*(3–4), 383–405.

Orfield, G., & Kornhaber, M. L. (2001). *Raising standards or raising barriers? Inequality and high-stakes testing in public education.* New York: Century Foundation.

Orr, M. (1999). *Black social capital: The politics of school reform in Baltimore.* Lawrence: University Press of Kansas.

Payne, C. M. (1995). *I've got the light of freedom: The organizing tradition and the Mississippi freedom struggle.* Berkeley: University of California Press.

Payne, C. M., & Kaba, M. (2001). "So much reform, so little change": Building-level obstacles to urban school reform. *Journal of Negro Education* (2), 1–16.

Pedulla, J. J., Abrams, L. M., Madaus, G. F., Russell, M. K., Ramos, M. A., & Miao, J. (2003). *Perceived effects of state-mandated testing programs on teaching and learning: Findings from a national survey of teachers.* Boston College, Chestnut Hill, MA: National Board on Educational Testing and Public Policy.

Poletta, F. (2002). *Freedom is an endless meeting: Democracy in American social movements.* Chicago: University of Chicago Press.

Putnam, R. (2000). *Bowling alone: The collapse and revival of American community.* New York: Simon and Schuster.

Reich, R. (1991). *The work of nations: Preparing ourselves for 21ˢᵗ century capitalism.* New York: Vintage.

Rothstein, R. (2004). *Class and schools: Using social, economic and educational reform to close the black-white achievement gap.* New York: Teachers College Press.

Shirley, D. (1997). *Community organizing for urban school reform.* Austin: University of Texas.

Shirley, D. (2002). *Valley Interfaith and school reform: Organizing for power in south Texas.* Austin: University of Texas.

Shirley, D. (forthcoming). Community organizing and No Child Left Behind. In M. Orr, (Ed.), *The ecology of civic engagement.* Lawrence: University Press of Kansas.

Sproull, L., & Kiesler, S. (1996). Increasing personal connections. In R. Kling, (Ed.), *Computerisation and controversy: Value conflicts and social choices* (pp. 455–475). New York: Academic Press.

U.S. Department of Education. (2002, June). *Meeting the highly qualified teacher challenge: The Secretary's annual report on teacher quality.* Washington, DC: Author.

Verba, S., Schlozman, K. L., & Brady, H. E. (1995). *Voice and equality: Civic voluntarism in American politics.* Cambridge, MA: Harvard University Press.

Warren, M. R. (2001). *Dry bones rattling: Community building to revitalize American democracy.* Princeton, NJ: Princeton University Press.

Wayne, A. J., & Youngs, P. (2003). Teacher characteristics and student achievement gains: A review. *Review of Educational Research, 73,* 89–122.

Wells, A. S., & Serna, I. (1996). The politics of culture: Understanding local political resistance to detracking in racially mixed schools. *Harvard Educational Review, 66*(1), 93–118.

Williams, K. Y., & O'Reilly, C. A. (1998). Demography and diversity in organizations. In B. M. Straw and R. I. Sutton (Eds.), *Research in organizational behavior, 20* (pp. 77–140). Stamford, CT: JAI Press.

Wilson, W. J. (1987). *The truly disadvantaged: The inner city, the underclass, and public policy.* Chicago: University of Chicago Press.

Zeichner, K. M. (1991). Contradictions and tensions in the professionalization of teaching and the democratization of schools. *Teachers College Record 92*(3), 363–379.

6 Learning to Act: Interactive Performance and Preservice Teacher Education

Rosalie M. Romano

ROSALIE M. ROMANO, ASSOCIATE PROFESSOR of Educational Studies, Ohio University, explores the process of building a bridge between poor and working-class students and preservice teachers from middle- and upper-class families through Interactive Performance, an offshoot of August Boal's "Theatre of the Oppressed." The Interactive Performance her students engaged in uncovered many of the issues with which working-class students contend: alcohol abuse, sexism, authority, and control, among others. The theater process enabled these preservice teachers to ask the kind of questions that will lead their future students to act in their individual and collective self-interest. The resulting pedagogy of relations fosters an imagination that helps teachers teach in the interest of their students.

This chapter examines the experiences of a group of preservice teachers who participated in a drama exercise based on the social issues and ethical and moral dilemmas that challenge adolescents. The "Interactive Performance," as this adaptation of August Boal's "Theater of the Oppressed" is called, confronts new teachers with a type of knowledge of their students that is not easily gained in typical classroom interactions. When new teachers interact with adolescents through this structured dramatic technique, a particular critical conversation and attending consciousness emerges. In addition, the difference in social class between the adolescents and the new teachers comes to the fore and presents an interesting opportunity to explore the complexity of what it means to be a teacher in a diverse and democratic society.

Ohio University is nestled in the foothills of Appalachia and is the largest employer in Athens County, which is less than an hour from both West Virginia and Kentucky. Of the approximately 20,000 students who attend Ohio University, the majority are Caucasian and come from more urban areas around the state or from surrounding states. The majority of preservice teachers in the College of Education are from the middle to upper social classes; the small minority of students who come from local communities in southeastern Ohio have working-class backgrounds. The schools where the preservice teachers encounter their first classrooms are, for the most part, poor and working-class.

Within the College of Education classrooms, students' social class background is part of the null curriculum. The focus of the teacher education program is on the future K–12 students their graduates will teach, with social class just one of many issues influencing learning that students read about. New teachers, therefore, may have little opportunity for explicit discussion about or understanding of the role social class plays in their learning to teach.

If socioeconomic status is invisible to teachers, so are the educational issues related to social class. The culture of the surrounding schools and within the college and university looks homogeneous, and it is easy for a prospective teacher to assume that we all think or act in the same way. Without intentional readings, guided questions, and inquiry, learning to teach becomes an instantiation of past school experiences. In short, there is real danger of social reproduction of the status quo in these prospective teachers' future classrooms.

Advocacy and action emerge out of awareness, and if there is any hope of a teacher moving from social reproduction, due to naiveté, into student advocacy and social justice, then consciousness must be raised at the earliest points in a teacher's development; in this case, during their licensure program at the preservice level. Further, awareness is simply the first stage of recognition of social inequities. The aim of awareness should be critical action, action that encourages a particular kind of civic courage and that initiates and sustains awareness and action in youth as well. In *Teaching for Social Justice*, Adams, Bell and Griffin (1997) define the role of social justice teachers and link it with what I mean by critical action:

> Social Justice educators make these connections between awareness and action by helping students recognize various spheres of influence in their daily lives; analyze the relative risk factors in challenging discrimination or oppression in intimate relations, friendship networks, and institutional settings; and identify personal or small group actions for change. (p. 38)[1]

Cultivating a social justice activist disposition within the mechanistic and causal ways that learning and teaching are currently conceptualized is difficult; that the program of study toward licensure is already fully packed deepens the difficulty. In addition, the political climate since the adoption of Goals 2000 and No Child Left Behind legislation has been especially challenging for teacher educators who hold a holistic vision of education's purpose and who want to create time and space in the curriculum to consider social justice advocacy and issues facing youth.

One can see an explicit link between the advent of the No Child Left Behind ideology and the thinking of those who view education primarily as a means of promoting economic growth (Giroux, 2003). When such an instrumental view is operationalized, teacher preparation courses move toward pre-scriptive and teacher proof curricula. The push nationwide is to improve teachers; the assessment tool is the proficiency test. When President Bush lobbied for his No Child Left Behind legislation, for example, one component was that educational programs have to be scientifically based to be eligible to receive federal funding. One program that has become the silver bullet of poor working-class schools in this region of Appalachia is Direct Instruction.

Direct Instruction is introduced in the preservice teachers' university courses in education and also modeled in their fieldwork classrooms. The thrust of Direct Instruction is to build on bites of information that build on previous bites, until a child can recite the concept, what is sometimes referred to as mastery. To achieve this mastery, teachers are required to follow a script. Teacher-made curricula and pedagogical decision-making give way to specific words and actions that Direct Instruction identifies as "prescribed instructional prac-tices" (www.dihome.org).

Throughout the United States, but particularly in poor, working-class districts, the fieldwork classrooms in which preservice teachers are likely to observe will be "packaged curriculum" or Direct Instruction classrooms. They frequently do not see sustained, teacher-developed lessons. Their concept of what teaching is, then, becomes one of classroom management and control, prescriptive methods, and a teacher-proof script. Students enter their profes-sional education program with idealism, but as they progress they dismiss or forget the reason they entered teaching in the first place. As ee cummings (1958) wrote, "down they forgot as up they grew."

How can preservice teachers be taught to get to the root of educational issues, identify the values that are embedded within methods and standards, and step back and ask who is benefiting? What steps might teacher educators take to help new teachers achieve a sense of connectedness with their future students and to broaden their view of the purpose of education as something more than passing tests? These are the sorts of philosophical questions students are taught to pose in their social foundations of education classes. But too often the ideas and concepts of the social foundations courses, which are designed to raise consciousness and critical reflection in new teachers, are not integrated into the rest of the teacher preparation program. In addition, social foundations as a field of study is struggling to maintain a foothold in teacher education.

Butin (2004a, 2004b) argues that students in teacher preparation programs today may be exposed to social foundations ideas and concepts only through secondary sources (textbooks) and "pre-digested perspectives," which fall short of conveying the critical dilemmas and conversations of education. In his survey of more than 2,000 teacher education programs in the United States, Butin (2004a, 2004b) analyzed each program's social foundations syllabi and found an uninspiring lack of questioning, critical inquiry, and discussion of the moral dilemmas and complexities of being a teacher in a democratic society. Historical movements in education were also sparsely represented. He concludes that prospective teachers are prepared to replicate the status quo instead of engaging their students in critical inquiry, debate, and reflection. Where, we might ask, do new teachers acquire the disposition to become aware of their students' sociocultural and economic backgrounds, if not in their teacher preparation program?

As an increasingly diverse population of school age children fill our public school classrooms, teachers, who are not being adequately prepared to critically reflect and make decisions about curriculum and pedagogy that are relevant and responsive to youth, may fall back on how they were taught in their own K–12 experience. Without knowing their students, teachers may replicate the status quo of tracking and categorizing students. If we want to teach our students, we have to know who they are. Paulo Freire (1998) argues that only when a teacher has "ingenuous knowledge" of her students can she increase "methodological rigor" (p. 62). This means that reading about theories of child development is not sufficient to claim ingenuous knowledge; ingenuous knowledge arises out of explicit understanding of the conditions under which students live and "the importance of the knowledge derived from life experiences" (p. 61).

Teaching, by Freire's (1998) definition, is inherently political. As such, a teacher's role is more than teaching, for the very act of teaching entails learning. The reciprocity initiated when teaching becomes learning and learning becomes teaching, transforms the relationship between teacher and student; students become intellectual partners in inquiry, though it is the responsibility of the teacher to organize and set conditions for this engagement. This engagement is neither indifferent nor neutral—from choosing compelling topics to study to encouraging students to develop multiple perspectives of the topic. Freire (1998) urges us to teach with a vision of freedom and a sense of civic courage. As such, teachers must resist methodologies that aim at "silencing constructive diversity, constructive criticism, and, ultimately, freedom" (p. 104). To do this teachers utilize their knowledge of their students.

To acquire ingenuous knowledge of his or her students, a teacher must acquire a consciousness about social issues that affect human lives and public institutions. Each school's local community abounds in relevant subject matter topics from which to design such consciousness-raising curriculum. These relevant topics become compelling ones as students come to understand their import in the life of the community (Romano & Glascock, 2003).[2] John Dewey addresses this intimate connection between school and society:

> [E]ducators need first of all to recognize that the social problems are something of our own; that they, and not simply their consequences, are ours; that we are part of the causes which bring them about in what we have done and have refrained from doing; and that we have a necessary share in finding their solutions." (Dewey, 1933, p. 389)

Dewey's (1933) words still ring true today—over half a century later—when he claims educators need to recognize the community of interest between teachers and their students' families. Our work as teachers is not separate and distinct from the work of those in our community. As such, we should be in alliance with those who struggle against injustice and inequity. Dewey (1933) calls for an "identification of sympathy and thought" and an "alliance in sympathy and in action" (p. 387) to dissolve the gap that too often exists between educators and the rest of the community.

While Dewey was addressing economic conditions during the Depression in 1933, his insight holds true in today's communities, especially in poor, working-class areas where teachers may come from more privileged backgrounds than their students. To foster recognition of a community of interest and sympathy, teacher educators at the university level must introduce prospective teachers firsthand to problems of the community, and, by definition, their students. One approach to building a bridge of connection between preservice teachers and their students is through Interactive Performance.

INTERACTIVE PERFORMANCE

In rural communities such as southeast Ohio, a culture of silence about private problems keeps students and teachers from confronting difficult dilemmas in the lives of youth and thus compounds the distance that exists between schools and the real world lives of students outside of school. Values of the community would also lead many to hesitate to view the school as a place for discussion and exploration of issues, even if those issues are part of a health or social studies class, for example. How then, can issues be explored in safe, meaningful ways?

Dramatic arts can be a dynamic, compelling learning experience leading to an understanding of human complexity and to raising awareness of social issues. Recently, Tony Kushner's "Angels in America" was broadcast over HBO, and viewer responses to this stirring story of people struggling with HIV/AIDS were found in weekly news magazines and daily papers throughout this country. Winston (2002) describes the impact of such dramatic presentations:

> Drama brings a singular coherence to past, present and future action; we see motives, deeds and their consequences with a simultaneity and clarity that is denied us in lived experience. This simplification of life need not render it simplistic; rather . . . it can sharpen the audience's appreciation of the complexity of individual moral lives. (p. 464)

Interactive Performance is an adaptation of Augusto Boal's "Theatre of the Oppressed," (1970) that was established in Brazil and has been practiced around the world since the 1970s. Boal now calls it Forum Theatre and it takes the form of a play that introduces a problem, specifically a problem of inequity. In

Boal's version, the play comes to an end without resolving the problem and the characters remain the oppressed and the oppressor. However, the play begins again, but this time audience members can take the place of one of the characters to try for a more equitable resolution. Improvisation follows as the original actors attempt to keep the ending the same while the new members try to resolve it. Others from the audience can come and take the place of different characters throughout the play. They must improvise to combat oppression. At the end, the audience is asked to determine whether progress was made and if they (the audience) think the resolution is viable (Day, 2001).

Social activist and theatre consultant, Kathy Devecka, (2003) developed Interactive Performance for use with community agencies and schools in southeastern Ohio.[3] In developing short scenes around social and other dilemmas with which youth struggle, Interactive Performance allows issues to be brought forth in ways that seem anonymous, yet relevant; that is, an actor who plays a student who is struggling with a problem is acting, and therefore not breaking the code of silence. Through a series of performances in front of middle and high school youth, prospective teachers are confronted with the moral and ethical social issues that young people grapple with in their daily lives. Both the young adolescents and the prospective teachers are exposed to different ways of looking at and acting on specific issues. The prospective teachers, however, see the situation from a dual point of view: as the adolescent character and as a teacher. One of the interesting outcomes we explore is the difference in social class between the adolescents and the new teachers, which becomes more salient as a result of the experience.

The Interactive Performance process begins with preservice teachers going into local middle and high schools, not to "learn" to teach but to become researchers of the school climate and culture as played out by the students themselves. Through observations and informal interviews, the preservice teachers collect what students tell them are the moral and ethical dilemmas they face on a daily basis. From this, they develop a story line and create the characters under the direction of Devecka. There are no props and the play is not written out. The teacher-actors take the part of middle and high school students grappling with a problem and practice using the story line.

The teacher-actors then present the play in front of middle and high school students, teachers, and administrators in the same school where they collected information about the problem for the story line. After the teacher-actors present a scene, they return to the stage while still in character to answer questions from the audience. This pattern continues throughout all acts of the play. At the end, the teacher-actors "drop" their characters and field questions from the audience about the issues on a more personal level (Owens, 2003).

Using specific issues that arise out of students' lives, taking the role of a student, creating scenes in which the issue is enacted, and then offering this to students for their response and inquiry provides prospective teachers with a window through which to view the very experiences, dilemmas, perspectives, and challenges through which middle and high school students must negotiate their way. Performances are highly relevant to the students, reflecting moral dilemmas that they face as they encounter bias, or sexism, or drugs or alcohol, or abuse, and more. The Interactive Performance gives them an opportunity to try out new ways of thinking about how to act that could potentially be applied to real-life situations (Devecka, 2003).

Within the interactive section of each scene, unpredictable opportunities arise for the preservice teacher-actors to glean new knowledge and understanding of the students, whose questions are direct and frequently judgmental. When provided an opportunity to speak out, it is heartening to hear middle school students do so with a clear strong sense of fairness. The audience and actors together create 75 percent of the performance as the audience interacts with the characters. The play resolves only when audience and actors decide on the resolution.

Devecka works with the preservice teachers and custom designs the story line for each specific audience. In the following example, a class of preservice teachers performed for a class of seventh-grade students in a local school. As the scene opens, the teacher-character sternly calls out the name of each student who is to come forward and pick up his or her assignment. When she calls out the character Toni's name, she also tells the grade she gave Toni's paper so that everyone can hear it. Toni acts embarrassed and leaves the class quickly when the bell rings.

"Just go ask the teacher why you got a low grade on the assignment," the Lisa character tells her classmate Toni who is upset about the "D" on her essay. But Toni has reservations about confronting her English teacher. "She never listens to me, so why should I try to argue about this grade. She won't change it because she doesn't like me." Toni is unsure of why the teacher treats her differently and does not want to make the situation worse by confronting the teacher. Lisa suggests options for action, including going with Toni when she talks to the teacher. What should Lisa do?

Preservice teachers played the parts of Lisa and Toni. During the scene, which takes about five to seven minutes, the actors reveal their character through attitudes, behaviors and responses. This leaves the audience to make their own assumptions about who these characters really are. At the end of the scene, the actors leave the stage but come back in character. "What about the way your teacher treats you makes you believe she does not like you?" asked one middle school student. Toni, in character, tells how the teacher had her brother last year and was always picking on him. Eventually the audience discovers more information about Toni and her family.

The question and answer period becomes intense. The middle school audience asks to speak to the teacher—alone. The Toni and Lisa characters leave the room and only the teacher character remains on stage. The questions are pointed, and one middle school student asks about the teacher's motivation. Another says that the way the teacher treated Toni is unfair: "How would you like to be treated this way?" For almost an hour, the audience of middle school students confronts the characters with their questions. The responses of the preservice teacher-actors are carefully drawn from their thorough development of their character's life history in their preparation for the performance. This makes Interactive Performance a powerful tool for dealing with a variety of issues that challenge middle and high school students. It allows actors and audience to explore issues in their complexity, rather than seek simplistic answers.

The Interactive Performance experience is dynamic, for both the preservice teachers and the middle school audience, because it uses dramatic arts to engage students in multiple perspectives of complex topics. With refreshing honesty, the audience is encouraged to question and investigate social justice topics in real time and in real life. They can see themselves in the situation that is being played out and they are encouraged to think about how to act in their own self-interest by the options the actor-characters pose. The energy and intense interest of the characters and audience provides constructive openings for discussion of conflict and contestation. The teacher character, for example, saw nothing wrong with how she treats Toni. The middle school audience wrestled with how to help the teacher understand that her actions were harmful and unfair to Toni. The dialogue placed ethics at the center of this scene, and the erupting counterpoints between teacher and audience unpacked different perspectives about why people act and react in particular ways.

Interactive Performance helps both characters and audience learn more about themselves as well as the specific social issues that are raised, and strives to move the audience towards critical action. Critical action might be taking the courage to confront the teacher about a perceived injustice. Critical action could be organizing a group to protest against something unfair. Critical action is action in one's self-interest, standing up for what is right. Interactive Performance provides a space for both the characters and the audience to play out different responses to a problem and to recognize the value of advocacy for one's self and others.

Moreover, Interactive Performance provides a chance for students to practice speaking out, speaking their minds to adults. The interaction part of the performance requires those who speak to give reasons and clearly argue their point of view to the character. No matter how unreasonably a character behaves, when the audience poses questions for the character, they must be answered. Devecka leads students in questioning and commenting on the characters and their behaviors, and helps them realize that one can challenge the character through reasoned arguments. Not only do the students learn how to question, comment, and challenge in ways that are productive, but the preservice teacher-actors do as well.

While theater expert activist Devecka facilitates the students' interactions, the preservice teachers learn that they too have a role in teaching the students through their characters' responses and questions, and that they can teach them useful ways to act in their own self-interest. Working-class students will often behave in unproductive ways out of a sense of alienation and the need to resist oppressive authority (Finn, 1999). It is this sense of alienation and resistance that the Interactive Performance often uncovers and to which the preservice teacher-actors must respond. Such resistance is no longer hidden or submerged; and since there can be no one answer or response, the preservice teacher-actors must practice ways to engage the youth in the audience with probing questions that move the dialogue towards action in the self-interest of the youth, a kind of critical action, as opposed to reactive or negative action that does not promote their self-interest individually or as a group.

This process became evident in the Interactive Performance that dealt with the issue of socioeconomic class as identified through interviews and discussions the preservice teachers conducted with the high school students. The subject of this play was the differential treatment students get from teachers, counselors, administrators, and other school personnel. In the southeastern Ohio foothills of Appalachia where Ohio University is located, poor and working-class communities struggle with dwindling resources, the closing of coal and iron mines, and a culture of poverty. Students from poor, working-class homes often attend school with peers whose parents are on the faculty or work within the university and who can be identified as middle- or upper-middle class.

In middle and high school, the divisions between the students are determined largely by socioeconomic class, even more than by race or gender. Students from poor and working-class backgrounds are aware and often vocal about how they are treated by teachers and counselors. This Interactive Performance revolved around a counselor who voluntarily gave a middle-class student an application to a university after a working-class student had asked for a college application and was given one for a local community college instead. This touched a sore spot for the high school audience.

The preservice teacher who played Mrs. Smith, the counselor, in this play was moved by the experience to say:

> Even when the tension in the room began to rise I tried to stay in character. I could almost *feel* (emphasis mine) the angry stares they were giving me. I think the students saw they could do something about Mrs. Smith in their lives. I am glad I played a character who is the complete opposite of myself. It made me think about how other people can think and how they can affect different students in different ways.

The preservice teacher who played Jim, the working-class student, reflected:

> I could *sense* (emphasis mine) the passion in some of the students as they became angry at some of the characters in the performance. I played the role of an average student with a desire to further my

education that was almost sidetracked by a biased guidance counselor. I [felt that] the students were on my side and [that they] quickly discovered the disguised injustice [of the counselor].

In real life, the preservice teacher-actor who played Jim comes from an upper-middle-class background, and during the debriefing after the Interactive Performances he continued to churn over in his mind the vehemence the students expressed as they talked about class issues. He hadn't been aware of his own social class status before, even though he had taken courses in diversity in education and was committed to trying to understand his students who come from poor, working-class, and other backgrounds different from his. The impact of the high school students' passion made a mark on him. He was now aware of what was invisible before, and, because he played the role of a student who was discriminated against, this preservice teacher desired to understand and learn how to relate in supportive ways to students of all classes.

In the same performance, the preservice teacher who played Jane, the privileged student, reflected on her experience:

> I really enjoyed performing. I never imagined that the character I played would be so intense. It was amazing to be able learn about and become another person. Although I was pretty unsure that our skit would come together, I was amazed how we all worked together and how those students seemed to really grasp the message we were trying to get across.

She, too, was able to read the students as a performer in the play.

What makes Interactive Performance such an interesting and potentially powerful parallel to teaching is that the teachers can guide but cannot predict either the reaction or the questions that the students will ask. The discomfort level of the preservice teachers in their characters, regardless of their role, is centered on the unpredictability of the situation. They feel vulnerable in front of students, fearing they will not know what to say or do. This state of vulnerability, even though filtered through their roles in the play, offers a significant opening to foster a need to read the students in the audience. This may have been motivated at first because of the preservice teachers' uncertainty of their ability to handle their role. However, an additional effect results from their playing the part of a student and wondering what reaction or reception they will have from the audience of real students. This is the jolt of imaginative compassion, which leads to feeling and seeing the world from a student's point of view. The upper-middle-class preservice teacher who played Jim wrote:

> Each time that I have done the interactive performance I have thoroughly enjoyed it and learned a lot from the issues we are trying to raise with our students. It's funny how addressing the issues through

our performance not only raises my awareness of them, but also stimulates my thinking about how I would deal with the issues in my own classroom.

The Interactive Performance enabled the preservice teachers to put themselves "in their students' shoes," both the fictional characters they played as well as the actual students they had interviewed just a few weeks before. Teaching became more complex to these new teachers who, on reflection, now had new and different knowledge of their students. By taking the perspective of their students, the new teachers began to think about other aims of education, in general, and their aims for themselves as new teachers, in particular. As the critical reflections collected weekly over the term reveal, a pattern of deepening understanding and compassion for adolescents was clearly developing in the preservice teachers.

The literature of the "pedagogy of relations" (Buber, 1936; Noddings, 1992; Bingham & Sidorkin, 2003) places relationships at the center of the teaching experience, arguing that relationships with students must be cultivated as part of any and all curricula. "Relations are primary; actions are secondary. Human words and actions have no authentic meaning; they acquire meaning only in a context of specific relations" (Bingham & Sidorkin, 2003, p. 7). The barrier between student and teacher can come in many forms: authority and dominance; disrespect for students and their experiences; transmission in the name of achievement. These and other barriers can keep teacher and student separate and ignorant of the potential for relating to and with one another within a classroom that is tolerant, open, democratic, and inquiring.

A complex web of relationships exists in schools that are liberating or oppressing. To complete a teacher education program and not have an understanding of the challenges that students bring into the classroom misses the mark. First-hand experiences, in this case through Interactive Performance and the activities leading up to it, have the potential to foster a particular appreciation for what struggles and challenges students face—and, in fact, will likely bring into the classroom. As a teacher, it is through understanding who your students are, through acquiring ingenuous knowledge, that openings are provided to learn how best to help them learn and to engage in their own self-interest.

The aim is, as Freire states, to "provoke the student into an exploration and refinement" of his or her situation, to understand the difficulty more clearly in terms of his or her own self-interest. The process of learning to listen and using a purposeful response also provokes the preservice teacher into new ways of thinking about relating to students. Preservice teachers developed a newfound respect for these youth of working-class schools through Interactive Performance and came to understand, in some instances, a close connection between the struggles of their students and their work as teachers.

Preservice teacher reflections from these experiences reveal awareness that the issues youth struggle with are actually moral and ethical dilemmas. When issues were cast as dilemmas, preservice teachers acknowledged that they listened to the students in qualitatively different ways, across the insider-outsider chasm. They now saw their students who were contending with alcohol abuse, sexism, authority/control, and more, as people who sought to do the right thing but struggled with competing rights or contradictions of who and what was right. A parent who abused alcohol was at once loved but also feared; a teacher who "picked on" a student constantly was resented and disliked, but the student had to attend that teacher's class each day.

This experience of Interactive Performance can foster an imagination that helps preservice teachers learn to teach in the interest of their students by connecting their academic subjects to the lives of their students. What good is empathetic understanding unless the teacher can use it to set conditions in her classroom that prompt investigation of social justice issues, build community, and infuse the curriculum with a sense of hope and possibility, so that what students know and learn has meaning and value, and teaches them to act in their individual and collective self-interest?

NOTES

1. This is a helpful text in two volumes. The readings include firsthand accounts of social issues, as well as theoretical frameworks for the pre- and in-service teachers.

2. *Hungry Minds* examines a classroom of students who inquired as to whether a local coal mine should be reopened. As the quarter progressed and complex conflicts arose, students became vocal and active in the community, examining how the mine might or might not be in their or their community's self-interest. Along the way, they used academic skills, acquired new knowledge, and constructed deep meaning about the connection between human lives and the land.

3. Kathy Devecka and I collaborated in developing Interactive Performances at Ohio University, College of Education for my Education and Diversity course, which has a Service-Learning requirement. The Interactive Performance becomes the Service Learning for the prospective teachers. Devecka is a theater consultant and director of "Bridging the Diversity Gap," an interactive theater group at Ohio University. She can be reached through United Campus Ministries at Ohio University, 18 North College, Athens, OH 45701. For more information, contact United Campus Ministry at 740.593.7301 or by sending an inquiry to romano@ohio.edu.

REFERENCES

Adams, M., Bell, L. A., & Griffin, P. (1997). *Teaching for diversity and social justice*. New York: Routledge.

Bingham, C., & Sidorkin, A. (2003). *No education without relation*. New York: Peter Lang.

Boal, A. (1970). *Theatre of the oppressed*. New York: Theatre Communications Group.

Buber, M. (1985). *Between man and man*. New York: Collier Books.

Butin, D. W. (2004a). Textbooks and the educational double-bind: Criteria for content in social foundations of education textbooks. Paper presented at AERA, San Diego, CA.

Butin, D. W. (2004b, July 27). The foundations of preparing teachers: Are education schools really 'Intellectually Barren' and Ideological? www.tcrecord.org ID # 11354.

cummings, ee. (1958). "Anyone lived in an any how town." In *Collected Poems of ee cummings*. New York: Random House.

Day, L. (2001). Putting yourselves in other peoples' shoes: The use of Forum theatre to explore refugee and homeless issues in school. *Journal of Moral Education, 31*(1), 21–34.

Devecka, K. (2003). Communities speak out: Interactive theatre as a tool for research and social change. Part I, The performance on campus: Theatre as transformative process. *Journal of Democracy and Education, 14*(4), 58–68.

Dewey, J. (1933). Education and our present social problems. *Educational Method, vxii*(7), 385–390.

Finn, P. (1999). *Literacy with an attitude: Educating working-class children in their own self-interest.* Albany: State University of New York Press.

Freire, P. (1998). *Pedagogy of freedom: Ethics, democracy, and civic courage.* New York: Rowan & Littlefield.

Giroux, H. (2003). *Public spaces, private lives: Democracy beyond 9/11.* New York: Rowan & Littlefield.

Noddings, N. (1992). *The challenge to care in schools: An alternative approach to education.* New York: Teachers College Press.

Owens, K. (2003). Part II: Outreach to schools and communities. In K. Devecka, Communities speak out: Interactive theatre as a tool for research and social change. *Journal of Democracy and Education, 14*(4), 58–68.

Romano, R., & Glascock, C. (2003). *Hungry minds in hard times: Educating for complexity for students of poverty.* New York: Peter Lang.

Winston, J. (2002). *Drama, literacy, and moral education.* London: David Fulton.

Part III

Social Justice Teacher Education in Graduate School

7 New Literacies With an Attitude: Transformative Teacher Education through Digital Video Learning Tools

Suzanne M. Miller and Suzanne Borowicz

SUZANNE M. MILLER, ASSOCIATE PROFESSOR of Learning and Instruction, University at Buffalo, State University of New York, and Suzanne Borowicz, Director of the Western New York Writing Project, Canisius College, investigate ways infusing digital video (DV) technologies into teacher education classes transforms teachers' attitudes towards literacy teaching and learning. Their students learn to infuse DV production into their own classroom curriculum and instruction so their students can draw on multiple modes of learning, an essential aspect of critical (powerful) media literacy. They describe changes in their university students and in their students' students. In both groups, students became more active, inquiring readers and composers, notions of school literacy were broadened, and learning became a social activity.

Over the past decade an emerging line of research has suggested that innovative uses of digital video (DV) arts and communication technologies can provide powerful tools for learning. These new technologies bring multiple forms of "new literacies"[1] for negotiating meaning within and against the backdrop of a digital world (Alvermann, 2002). Understanding and incorporating this broadening of literacy to meaning-making systems beyond printed text is essential for twenty-first century teacher education.

Reality for the "Millennial Generation" (Hagood, Stevens, & Reinking, 2002) includes new literacies embedded in new technologies—such as Internet instant messaging (IM), electronic interactive games, computer dating—and multiple new capacities: copying recorded music, enhancing or changing photo images, immediately accessing digital information once housed only in physical libraries, and creating state of the art films from home video footage. As a significant part of youth culture, these everyday tools and artifacts bind adolescents together in a social culture through communication and meaning making.

Instead of drawing on these literacies in learning, however, the school "preference for print may preclude teachers from even noticing their students' competence with multi- and digital literacies" (King & O'Brien, 2002, p. 41). Print bias, recitation as performance, the structured essay, textbooks, and the student practice of scanning for textbook answers are the elements that constitute restricted school literacy. Its narrow range of opportunities and focus on correctness limits literacy learning for some students. As Finn (1999) argues, it is particularly poor, working-class students who receive such instruction for domesticating literacy rather than empowering literacy with an attitude.

With its many opportunities for symbolic expression, DV production is a tangible and potent meaning making system and mediator for empowering literacy. As students plan and make DV productions of poems, political ads, editorials, and neighborhood inquiries as part of the curriculum, they create images to develop meanings and distill experience into visual concepts, central to what Eisner (1998) calls visual learning—a vital means of making sense of the world, with images often preceding language as a means of coming to understand. Yet most teachers have few opportunities for professional development that prepares them to integrate such twenty-first century technologies effectively into academic classes. Teachers and students in poor urban and working-class school districts, especially, are often arts and technology poor—thereby lacking access to these tools that can promote powerful literacy and level the achievement playing field (Deasy, 2002; Rohde & Shapiro, 2000).

The question addressed in this chapter is, "How, if at all, can a teacher education class expand teachers' notions of literacy and transform their attitudes towards powerful literacy teaching and learning, especially for working-class students?" In what follows, we first provide an overview of a teacher education course devoted to DV authoring, then present a descriptive analysis of the teachers' work in this activity-based professional development experience.

A TEACHER EDUCATION COURSE ON
DIGITAL VIDEO AS LITERACY TOOL

Since 2000, the University at Buffalo's Graduate School of Education has been working in collaboration with the Buffalo Public Schools to help bring new literacies to teachers and students through the "City Voices, City Visions" (CVCV) project.[2] CVCV offers intensive, summer institutes that prepare urban teachers to use DV as a literacy and learning tool for students in grades five through twelve. The project places multimedia and digital technologies in classrooms for ongoing use by teachers and students, and provides teachers with ongoing technical support and professional development activities.

In our research on the CVCV project we found that urban, working-class students became "active designers of meaning" (New London Group, 2000) empowered with DV tools for analytic/visual thinking and understanding that also fostered their school achievement. By combining visualization with composing narratives and identifying thematic music, DV authoring provided a three-in-one mediational tool, a supertool that boosts student attention and conceptual learning, particularly for urban students who were not typically engaged in school (Miller & Borowicz, 2005).

Out of these experiences, we developed the graduate teacher education course—Digital Video as a Literacy Learning Tool—which we have now taught to 36 teachers seeking their master's degree and professional certification. The course explores the uses of specific genres of DV production to meet learning standards in the secondary literacy classroom (grades five through twelve). We are both long-time teachers and teacher-educators who believe that the changing landscape of communication (Kress, 1999) demands that teacher education programs expand and broaden the scope of literacy. This course was our effort to develop new literacy dispositions in teachers who may be in the classroom into the mid-twenty-first century. As coteachers of the course, our project was an inquiry into if and how these teachers might transform their notions of literacy and learn to infuse DV authoring into curriculum and instruction so that their students could draw on multiple, engaging modes of learning.

Specifically, through the mediation of iMovie production in the class, we aimed to expand the notion of literacy by engaging in movie making activities that approached DV as a technological art form that includes textual readings, creative writing, visual arts, performing arts, and music. To these ends, our students worked individually and collaboratively on DV projects related to English and social studies curricula. At the same time, they read relevant theory and practical application literature about new media integration and critical media literacy to examine in discussion and writing their relationships to literacy learning, student achievement, and society (Alvermann, 2002; Goodman, 2003).

Students in this course planned and produced DVs in five progressively more complex genres—iSpeak (visualizing a quotation), poetry videos, uncommercials (selling a concept or idea), video editorials, and multisource DV inquiry. The final project in this first course required teachers to engage in an action-research project in middle and high school classrooms to examine the influence of DV production on teaching and learning. In the second offering of the course, teachers surveyed students to better understand the literacy practices of their millennial generation students. In both courses, teachers wrote reflective pieces aimed at teasing out the complexities of theory and practice and personal beliefs about knowledge and literacy learning. Through our recursive analysis of the written and DV work, we identified key themes that portray how teachers—and then their students—transformed their notions of literacy from reading the printed word to "reading the world" (Freire, 1970)—through technologically afforded multimodality (Miller & Borowicz, 2006). In the following sections we trace the key themes of transformation in the DV classes.

TRANSFORMING NOTIONS OF LITERACY
THROUGH DV TECHNOLOGY

Somewhat surprisingly, many of the twenty-something teachers in both courses were caught in the traditional notion of reading and writing printed text as the only legitimate form of school literacy. Most said they took the class to become more proficient with technology, to keep up with their students' knowledge, or to learn something technologically new. No one spoke of a connection or relationship between technology and empowering literacy. Initially, their interests were in utilitarian benefits: "It's so much better to have students type their papers instead of struggling through their handwriting," or they liked "the ease of finding information for research through the Internet."

From the beginning of each class teachers raised concerns about what should count as English. Cory who was on the job market explained: "As an English teacher a year ago, I thought I would never use multimedia texts to study. After all, is that English? That's not the way I remember it." The idea of print literature as an almost sacred text emerged. Terry, a first-year teacher in a private, all-male, college prep high school, spoke of her worries about technology in her first class reflection:

> The English classroom was, in my eyes, supposed to be a haven devoid of modernity, save the modern relevance of classical literature that we would broach in thoughtful *discussion*, certainly not in any technological forum. I perceived technology to be a degradation and reduction of the sanctity of classical literature and the critical thinking requisite to understanding and enjoying it.

Loss of control as knowledge expert in the classroom was another issue teachers faced. Some, like Dora, an eighth-grade teacher in a suburban school, were afraid. She put up both hands defensively and said, "I can't do this" during the first class and later reflected: "Initially I had to overcome my own neurosis and understand that this facet of my education might cause me to relinquish some of my normally, tightly guarded control . . . Perhaps I was a technophobe."

Roseanne, a first year middle school teacher, wrote: "I truly believe that it is a marvelous tool but at the same time I feel that it is a tool that I do not currently have enough experience using to claim mastery with." As her notions of literacy began to expand, her anxiety to claim mastery began to subside. In creating a visual response for one of our course readings, Roseanne enlisted the help of her seventh graders, who sat her right down and drew her a chart explaining their email shortcuts and definitions. Roseanne was surprised and pleased by her students' eagerness to teach her something about their literacy. She felt that her own questioning of literacy led her to better understand her students' world and accept their role as teachers and her role as student to a younger generation.

In her midterm reflection Roseanne wrote:

> Technology and literacy are intertwined. In fact, I believe that technology improves literacy. Technology, in all forms from the most rudimentary to the most complex, makes literacy more accessible to people. Technology is the human attempt to bridge the gaps that exist in human communication.

Roseanne moved from the anxiety filled teacher who felt she must be a master of anything she brought to her classroom to the teacher-learner, willing and eager to learn with and through her students.

Dora changed, too. As she read, responded, discussed, and created her movies on high-stakes testing, female body images, and sexual pressures in teens, she reframed her vision of possibilities for literacy based in students' experiences and needs. She began to see computers as a social activity responsible for students' shared micro culture, constituted as they talked to each other every night through IM, "using computers and asking questions of digital friends and sources." When she took the newly discovered school digital video camera out of the case, students gathered around, and one said, "Sweet, you have night vision." Then, she reported, they showed her more about the camera than she had learned.

Once her eighth-graders planned, filmed, and edited their own poetry videos, Dora was hooked:

> Expanding the notions of literacy has been the undercurrent of every response journal I've written for this course. . . . Education fails if it is stagnant or silenced . . . I want more than anything to teach my students to think; I have to adjust as they adjust . . . I think we, as teachers, need to invite computers to help us.

As she came to see DV authoring as active, social learning that would keep students thinking, moving, doing, Dora saw it as the means for educators to "teach to the eyes, body, artistic input and digital savvy of our students, not just to their ears—how well they listen."

Cory collaborated with Dora in her eighth-grade class as a coinquirer when her students created poetry videos. The DV process footage from that class shows both of them circulating, teaching at points of need, in an energized DV workshop. Cory's portfolio introduction showed his changing notions of literacy, too:

Why was I so bent on becoming a traditional English, pen and paper instructor to begin with? . . . This digital video story is yet another in a growing library that redefines what we are doing in English classes everywhere, what is possible, and how "perspective" is a term that must be constantly redefined within the society that changes so rapidly.

The potential for DV production as a powerful literacy tool emerged most profoundly as teachers began to see it as a composing activity, similar to but often more engaging than writing text. Dora explained how editing her movie was a very familiar process:

> I needed an introduction, body and conclusion. I had to proofread and spellcheck, speed up some footage, slow down some other. My process of creating a final product, asked me to use a critical lens on myself, scrutinize my work, spatially, musically, socially, emotionally, and technically. . . . [I remember] the absolute rapture, eyes fixated to our computer screens. . . . The process of DV production is the same one we teach year after year in its shadowy paper version.

Through the DV production experiences, novice teachers (and then their students) created new images of themselves and broadened their notions of school literacy from only reading and writing to authoring visual and auditory texts that also incorporated the voices and visions of adolescents' worlds outside of school to address issues ranging from family and friendship to teen pregnancy and violence.

TRANSFORMING NOTIONS OF KNOWING TO/THROUGH KNOWLEDGE-IN-ACTION

A key goal of the DV class was to help create connections between the teachers' newly formed knowledge/beliefs and their pedagogical actions. This was the aim of the teachers' action-research DV project in their classrooms. Findings from the study of our class dynamics and learning were paralleled by the findings of our students' studies of their own teaching: in both sets of contexts, students became more active, inquiring readers and composers as they pursued their own understanding through DV. The notion of knowledge changed from a commodity that students consume and display to knowledge as dynamic, evolving, and composed in context. During DV authoring, curriculum concepts became knowledge-in-action (Applebee, 1996); teachers and their students participating in their own knowledge creation saw purpose and agency in their work. In particular, working-class and minority students, often alienated from academic literacy, frequently appropriated media images for reuse and redesign, connected to the outside world, and redefined themselves not as consumers, but as intense social producers of meaning (Miller & Borowicz, 2006). How does such change happen in DV authoring?

WHEN ACTION AND AWARENESS MERGE

In our courses the teachers engaged in DV production first in teams and then alone, and in the process learned much more than how to use the camera and editing program. Their "intent participation" (Rogoff, 2003) in DV production that Dora mentions above was pervasive among the teachers and, in turn, in their students. We believe that this flow learning experience, focusing on a "coherent future whole" (Csikszentmihalya, 1997), is part of what led to teacher transformations. Bringing their intense attention to making meaning and communicating effectively, DV producers learned deeply—both consciously and through more tacit "incidental learning" which is characteristic of all arts production (Heath, 2004).

For example, Cory described what he calls the authentic practice of composing through DV with a special kind of teacher's attention during weekend editing sessions:

> We became filthy with editing on Saturdays in the computer labs. The garbage can was often times full with empty bags of chips and bottles of Pepsi, evidence of the work being done, the time it took to sculpt our projects into something that would resemble what we saw in our minds. Every step of the way towards a finished—though beautifully imperfect—video production was cause for constant aware- ness of what we were actually *doing*. After all, we were not just training to be users of digital video, but instructors of it, teachers of literacy through the digital video processes.

This sustained visual focus (Heath, 2004) helps to explain how knowledge is created through the mental action of those involved in the highly demanding work of all the arts: its creators engage by "looking and thinking, seeing and planning, viewing and responding . . . they review (often quite literally re- viewing) . . . they also reflect (sometimes trying to re-create what they have seen) on past observations and project ahead to their planned performance or production" (Heath, 2004, p. 339).

The teachers in our classes think into the future in the same way, not only through the DV process of segmenting the project into pieces (shots, scenes) and composing them into the coming whole, but also by developing under- standing (both consciously and tacitly) of the mental and physical habits their students will need to produce their own knowledge-in-action through DV. Their reflective writings about these experiences demonstrated their attention to their thinking in strong active verbs: I decided, I opted, I wanted, images

I chose, control of my project. These phrases and concepts were used repeatedly as the language of their creative thinking process, grounded in the commitment to the end product. As they came to understand the intense attention that DV knowledge production promotes and requires, they examined the strategies and processes to understand what literacies were involved.

Dora captures the metacognitive monitoring that her DV production required from her:

> I was being asked to create a project, operate a camera, import and export using a firewire, be creative, and be analytical and mathematical and cognizant of the entire process as the goal. . . . My video would require planning: I had to draw and sketch, formulate text with pictures and think critically about the stages of development that my project would demand. . . . *I would have to think like someone was watching!* I would have to understand how images often have their own appeal and do not need to be drowned out by the music or audio clips I originally thought I needed.

Notice her awareness of audience, visuals, sounds—of her thinking/action moving the project forward toward a future, personally meaningful communication. We believe teacher education classes must provide this kind of powerful literacy experience and opportunities for reflection so that teachers can acquire this kind of felt knowledge-in-action (Applebee, 1996) and draw on it to make powerful literacy part of their pedagogy.

For instance, based on her DV experiences, Dora was able to communicate effectively to parents in writing about how students producing digital videos fits into English class:

> As an educator, the merits of this program are exciting and inspiring to me. I have already spent hours and weekends working on my own projects, enthralled that upon completion of planning, writing, scripting, selecting footage and images, applying soundtracks and editing, I have a final piece to show for myself. My students, I am certain, would share this sentiment.

All of her 120 students returned signed parental permissions; some of the parents came to help out, and students did share her sentiment. Her student Emily reenvisioned poetry: "I learned a lot from this project. It further developed my knowledge of poetry terms. I learned how to make a movie. . . . Poetry doesn't have to be boring. It is everywhere." Dora created such a buzz in her school that, as a second-year teacher, she was asked to give the faculty a presentation on using DV authoring as a multimedia learning tool in the classroom. We believe that engaging in the collaborative, flow experience of DV authoring, and recursive reflection on its processes promote a professional attitude in teachers—a possible step to creating "transformative intellectuals" (Giroux, 1988) in millennial schools.

SHIFTING ROLES AND STANCES

The degree of involvement of teachers and students varied throughout their class experiences, but in every class evidence of "meaningful role shifts" (Heath, 2004) occurred. As they saw themselves as members of a learning community—as film makers creating meaning—they engaged with peers and with the DV tools in order to communicate to others. First, in our DV class with its production team process, the teachers evolved a collaborative stance. Dora noted the impact: "We were reconfiguring how it felt to be part of a group, in charge of a common product." Jackson, an urban high school English teacher with some DV experience in the class, found it empowering to assist other students [teachers] in their time of need. Learning directly through collaboration led all of the teachers to take that stance when they attempted to integrate DV into their own teaching and curriculum. All appropriated the idea of creating production teams for use in their own grade five through twelve classes.

Once in their classrooms, teachers also shifted to a more collaborative instructional role. In video shot during their own students' DV production for their teacher inquiry projects, the teachers' changing role was striking. After teachers planned and set the task and production teams, their classes unfolded in a studio atmosphere where some students edited, some went out to film, others fine-tuned storyboards. Teachers assisted where needed; Dora "circulated the room offering advice and camera angles." In his senior class, Jackson acted as a "technical troubleshooter, [and] on the producer side, I traveled throughout the groups and questioned aspects of their projects in order to push them towards more sophisticated thinking."

In the study of her classroom, Dora found that, "These students had flourished in their new roles. They were cinematographers, planners and directors." As we found in our prior research (Miller & Borowicz, 2005, 2006), these teachers found that students who were "not your typical good students find a voice with video production because there are many roles to fill . . . [DV can] turn kids into archeologists, have them figure out what their peers want." One of Dora's students had been floundering all year, but DV sparked a change: "What I saw happen to Justin was transformational. He was involved, initiated direction and wrote the entire script for his group's movie."

Manny, a fifth-year urban high school social studies teacher, concluded in his teacher research that "integration of digital video validates the often marginalized 'voice' of the student, particularly and especially the urban student. . . . As a tool of validation, DV allows students to be both creative and reflective in what they are producing." For example, his students used artifacts and images to answer the question, "What is culture?" The complexity of the question became apparent as students narrated their diverse visual answers and aggregated them on DV: a Muslim girl sets down a prayer rug; an African-American boy has the camera circle his braids; a girl shows a picture of her baby as each also explains his or her view of culture.

Traditional notions of schooling for domesticating literacy do not portray students as active, creative, reflective members of a community of learners. In their classroom inquiries our teachers found that through DV authoring students shifted to active engagement in production teams and developed a sense of agency and community. Dora explained why:

> Kids have decision-making, footage-finding, sound and filming capabilities. . . . They need to edit and reap the rewards of seeing a project through to completion. [DV production can] make students directors of their own learning.

This agency happened in groups, in most cases, and that was what made the difference, according to Manny:

> DV is a true community builder within the classroom. . . . To complete this project, the students had to be *committed* to the task; they had to *trust* the advice of others; they had to be *accepting* of each other's strengths and weaknesses; and, most of all, they had to be *mindful* of each others' contributions. As a tool to bring students together for a common purpose, to have an entire class work as one organism, DV passes the test. What this project accomplished in the end, was simple but profound—"Yes, we do exist, and yes, our contributions matter."

To orchestrate such a learning environment in schools, teachers must have these experiences themselves in their teacher education classes.

Remarkably, once in their schools, teachers approached DV production as a completely social activity—whether they had approached teaching this way beforehand or not—*from* planning, searching out equipment, asking parents' permission and support *to* seeking assistance from other people in the building who were more technically savvy, satisfying the curiosities of other teachers and administrators about the excitement in the building, sharing and changing roles with students, and culminating with the social pleasure of joint viewing and commentary. In all, through powerful literacy experiences in this teacher education class, these teachers learned what could not be directly taught, but had to be learned through reflection on direct experience—the felt, the tacit knowledge-in-action of the importance of community, collaboration, of flow and agency, of new roles and stances, of the validation from "seeing a project through to completion."

EMPOWERING TEACHERS AND STUDENTS WITH
DV ATTENTION CREATION

DV production allows communicating self/community/cultural perspectives in an attention getting form that has rich cultural capital among all youth and in the world at large. The need for DV publication (primarily screenings in a group) emerged repeatedly in our classes and in the classes our students taught. Jackson said he never shares his academic papers with friends who stop over for a beer, but frequently shares his movies with his friends—including his video poem about homelessness and his video editorial about the senselessness of SUVs. Another teacher noted the unusual intimacy of sharing her vision of the limited views of females in high-school literature through her multigenre video inquiry. The desire to share their DV inquiries, spotlighting their voices and visions, was a profound motivator.

ATTENTION TO VOICES AND VISIONS

When struggling students produce DVs in their school contexts, they are sometimes repositioned as experts—those whose attention is needed by other students and teachers to solve problems—thus challenging their school positioning as failures. Typically schools withhold all of these forms of attention seeking in favor of compliant behaviors of showing up and paying attention. Dora saw empowerment of her students as providing opportunity for adolescents to focus on their readings of the world and have others pay attention. Among her students she found that DV production helps:

> . . . develop a better link between a kid's life and his education. . . . For the first time, the struggles they face on a day to day basis were suddenly commentaries that adults wanted to pay attention to. . . . [As] students make meaning and create understanding on their own, they turn the cameras on themselves. They tell their own stories, bear witness to other stories, talk to strangers and learn how to research.

With a hand-sized minidigital video camera and movie-making computer software, and the support of their teacher and their peers, youth voices and visions become part of school. As Dora put it, they "feel like experts in the process."

ATTENTION TO INQUIRY

A key genre in literacy education is persuasion, which in DV production (e.g., video editorials, uncommercials, political commercials) becomes a socially powerful practice from which attention flows and from which student producers feel repositioned as competent. The experience of Jackson's urban vocational class illustrates the DV hook. He started with a problem among his working-class students: "I have trouble getting them to be persuasive and authentic. . . . Persuasive essays written by students reflect the fact-starved news reports of twenty-four hour cable news stations. They are more style than substance." For his final project in our DV class he chose to introduce the "Uncommercial" to his students in order to address what he saw as two neglected and "essential elements of savvy citizenry—media literacy and political/social awareness." The senior class read short stories, studied the film *Bowling for Columbine*, and discussed issues and problems in society. They analyzed commercials, attending to a unifying concept, persuasive techniques, and characteristics of the genre. Jackson also shared his own powerful Uncommercial on the negative impacts of ads on female body image.

In production teams, his students brainstormed, storyboarded, and pitched their concept to their teacher as producer. He was very pleased with the results: "I have never seen the level of involvement that I saw with this project." He analyzed what had happened:

> Simply put, students work harder and are more engaged working with iMovie than when working with a more traditional literacy medium. . . . This increased motivation manifests itself in such a way that only can be described as inquiry. Both their time commitment and their resourcefulness in their quest to capture their point of view become critical attributes in this quest of inquiry.

Jackson noted, too, that while "writing was individual, iMovie was community oriented." The DV inquiry required students to become collaborative problem solvers for "how best to get the point across," including conceptualizing their theme. They used "advanced problem solving methods of meaning making," such as montage, skits, and statistics.

> [One] group dealing with the issue of suicide took the beginning of a music video, cut it up, and interspersed somber paintings by Salvador Dali and bleak lines from poems found in a poetry anthology. . . . Another group used toy army figures and positioned them to represent gang violence.

These visually persuasive methods took students way beyond "their standard five paragraph essays." Students dissatisfied with shots they could take in school, met outside of school and filmed gravesites and streets signs in Buffalo's most violent neighborhoods. In school, they recruited students from other classes who were dressed in black and white and filmed them standing up against the wall:

> In the first shot, there were roughly fifteen students. In the second shot, there were eight. In the third, there were four. In the fourth shot, only one male student remained. When they got this footage

back on the computer, they juxtaposed the shots of the decreasing male population with shots of the street signs and shots of the graves. The final product is somber, mesmerizing, and thought-provoking.

The grade average of the working-class students in the group that produced this digital video had been 52 percent the previous quarter. During the DV unit though, "They were the hardest working group in all of my classes. They developed and pitched a solid concept, kept a tight film schedule, and feverishly edited their product together. After two weeks, they had produced a superbly performed *Stop the Violence* commercial."

As Jackson exported the films, he had a moment of doubt, wondering why violence was so pervasive in their DV products—why not pollution or drug abuse? He knew why: "They see violence all over. Our country invades Iraq. A former student is killed in action. A cousin is killed as a result of gang warfare. So is a brother. So is a friend." And he knows that he succeeded in his goal of helping "give students the power to express themselves in a powerful medium about a societal issue *that was important to them.*" (Emphasis mine). In the end, he saw that students used DV inquiry just as he had hoped:

> I wanted to have them manipulate the power utilized by corporations and government and raise their voice about something that concerned them. And that's what democracy is about. It's about raising your voice when you see something is wrong. It's about having the power and means to do so.

This reenvisioning of literacy as powerful and political would not have been possible without the teachers' experiences of knowledge creation through their own DV inquiries.

The following year Jackson introduced a social issues unit on Heroes to his eleventh-graders, again mostly working-class students, following the same path of literature and films and DV production. In this sequence he introduced the notion that heroes are often common folk who act to change the world. This reenvisioning of the concept was vivid in the "video quilt" that his students produced. In black and white, each student in a close-up intoned a startling fact about the world their I-Search paper inquiries revealed. In response to the overwhelming amassing of these problems, the final message filled the screen, white on black, "ACT!"

In these unit explorations, we believe Jackson was expanding student perspectives in a critical way: helping them disrupt the commonplace, interrogate multiple viewpoints, identify and understand sociopolitical issues, and take action to promote social and civic change. In their writing and DV inquiries, they were drawing on literacy practices with purchase for adolescents to make sense of world issues, and were encouraged by their teacher to "make connections with academic literacies and to work toward empowered identity development and social transformation" (Morrell, 2005, p. 313). This kind of integration of new multimodal literacies into the life and life worlds of adolescents has a tremendous potential to develop critical consciousness among working-class—and all—students.

CONCLUSION

We believe it is our task as teacher educators to provide embodied multimodal literacy experiences and professionalizing tools that all teachers need so that they can become agents of change not only in their classrooms but also in their schools and larger educational communities. Moreover, we have argued here that DV authoring can play a key role in those professional experiences and in transformations of literacy learning for working-class students (*see also* Miller & Borowicz, 2006). If we are to teach with an eye on the future—a highly wired and visually sophisticated world—we must understand the growing need for new stances toward knowledge as designed, and we must reconceptualize teacher education to promote deep understanding and uses of these new multimodal literacies as knowledge-production tools in schools.

The eloquence of the teachers quoted here demonstrates the possibilities for creating such transformative intellectuals who use DV authoring to create an alternative learning space *inside* of school, but also, potentially, as an intervention for civic and social change. DV authoring in teacher education and in the schools can be a tool for critique. It can transform working-class students' sense of who they are in the world and how they relate to other people and to media, institutions, and other world shaping instruments. With DV multimodal authoring, teacher education potentially puts powerful tools of inquiry and attention getting communication into the hands of teachers and their students. Such approaches can change significantly the educational ecology of schools and help prepare teachers and all students to participate critically in an increasingly digital democracy.

NOTES

1. The concept of "New Literacies" represents a critical broadening of the term literacies to include multiple forms of representation (e.g., poem, painting, play, piano concerto, political ad) (Eisner, 1997, p. 353; Kist, 2002)—that is, the "performative, visual, aural, and semiotic understandings necessary for constructing and reconstructing print and non-print-based texts" in the context of social, institutional, and cultural discourses, relationships, and inquiries (Alvermann, 2002, viii).

2. http://www.gse.buffalo.edu/org/cityvoices/home.html.

REFERENCES

Alvermann, D. E. (Ed.). (2002). *Adolescents and literacies in a digital world.* New York: Peter Lang.

Applebee, A. (1996). *Curriculum as conversation: Transforming traditions of teaching and learning.* Chicago: NCTE & University of Chicago Press.

Csikzentmihalyi, M. (1997). *Finding flow.* New York: Basic Books.

Deasy, R. L. (2002). *Critical links: Learning in the arts and student academic and social development.* Washington, DC: Arts Education Partnership.

Eisner, W. E. (1998). *The kind of schools we need: Personal essays.* Portsmouth, NH: Heinemann.

Finn, P. (1999). *Literacy with an attitude: Educating working-class children in their own self-interest.* Albany: State University of New York Press.

Friere, P. (1970). *Pedagogy of the oppressed.* New York: New Seabury Press.

Giroux, H. (1988). *Teacher as intellectual: Toward a critical pedagogy of learning.* Westport, CT: Bergin & Garvey.

Goodman, S. (2003). *Teaching youth media: A critical guide to literacy, video production.* New York: Teachers College Press.

Hagood, M. C., Stevens, L. P., & Reinking, D. (2002). What do THEY have to teach US? Talkin' 'cross generations! In D. E. Alvermann (Ed.), *Adolescents and literacies in a digital world* (pp. 68–83). New York: Peter Lang.

Heath, S. B. (2004). Learning language and strategic thinking through the arts. *Reading Research Quarterly, 39*(3), 338–342.

King, J. R., & O'Brien, D. G. (2002). Adolescents' multiliteracies and their teachers' needs to know: Toward a digital détente. In D. E. Alvermann (Ed.), *Adolescents and literacies in a digital world* (pp. 40–50). New York: Peter Lang.

Kist, W. (2002). Finding "new literacy" in action: An interdisciplinary high school western civilization class. *Journal of Adolescent & Adult Literacy, 45*(5), 368–377.

Kress, G. (1999). "English" at the crossroads: Rethinking curricula of communication in the context of the turn to the visual. In G. E. Hawisher & C. L. Selfe (Eds.), *Passions, pedagogies & 21st century technologies* (pp. 66–88). Urbana-Champaign, IL: NCTE.

Lankshear, C., & Knobel, M. (2003). *New Literacies: Changing knowledge and classroom learning.* Berkshire, UK: Open University Press.

Miller, S. M., & Borowicz, S. (2005). City Voices, City Visions: Digital Video as Literacy/ Learning Supertool in Urban Classrooms. In L. Johnson, M. Finn, & R. Lewis (Eds.), *Urban education with an attitude* (pp. 87–108). Albany: State University of New York Press.

Miller, S. M., & Borowicz, S. (2006). *Why multimodal literacies? Designing digital bridges to 21st century teaching and learning.* Graduate School of Education Publications (Imprint of State University of New York Press).

Morell, E. (2005). Critical English education: *English Education, 37*(4), 312–321.

New London Group. (2000). A pedagogy of multiliteracies: Designing social futures. In B. Cope & M. Kalantzis (Eds.), *Multiliteracies: Literacy learning and the design of social futures.* London: Routledge.

Rogoff, B. (2003). *The cultural nature of human development.* New York: Oxford University Press.

Rohde, G. L., Shapiro, R. J. (2000, October). *Falling through the net: Toward digital inclusion.* A Report on Americans' Access to Technology Tools by the U.S. Department of Commerce, Economics and Statistics Administration, & National Telecommunications and Information Administration. [Available on line at: http://www.ntia.doc.gov/ntiahome/fttn00/contents00.html.]

8 The Journey to Justice: Inquiry as a Framework for Teaching Powerful Literacy

Diane Zigo

DIANE ZIGO, ASSISTANT PROFESSOR OF LITERACY Education at LeMoyne College, traces the development of the English education courses that she taught through a framework of inquiry. The inquiry framework is designed to move students through three stages of growth in becoming teachers for justice: increasing awareness of justice issues that are related to teaching contexts, becoming advocates for justice in education, and developing strategies for implementing education for justice in their own classrooms and schools settings. Students are profiled who were initially resistant, confused, or frustrated and who now have moved into or chosen to remain in the profession with new hope and energy for teaching that promotes deep critical thinking in students normally denied such experiences.

I have been a language arts teacher educator for the past six years, following fourteen years as a middle and secondary school English teacher. I pursued advanced graduate studies in English education because of my inadequacies in providing access to what Finn (1999) calls "powerful literacy" (p. 124) to my students who were experiencing difficulties in reading and writing as they entered high school. As I worked with increasing numbers of students identified as having learning disabilities, who came from households facing downward economic mobility, or who were English language learners trying to fit into an unfamiliar environment, my repertoire of teaching strategies was only intermittently effective.

Unfortunately, struggling students tend to receive approaches to literacy education that emphasize the "performative level" of sounding out words and constructing simple written sentences, the "functional level" of meeting the narrow literacy demands of entry-level working life, or at best, the "informational level" of comprehending and producing the kinds of limited factual knowledge expected in standard school assignments and assessments (Finn, 1999; Wells, 1987). In contrast, Finn explains, "Powerful literacy involves creativity and reason—the ability to evaluate, analyze, and synthesize what is read" (p. 124). Students apprenticed into powerful literacies are consciously able to understand, create, critique, and control information in ways that give them agency within their sociopolitical worlds.

Even though I did not yet have a clear professional understanding of the distinctions among levels of literacy, I knew that providing students with only functional or informational literacies was not good enough. I am a member of a Catholic women's religious community, the Sisters of St. Joseph of Carondelet. As Kathleen Casey (1993) observes in her research on women teachers working for social change, religious women tend to organize their beliefs, behaviors, and uses of language around particular, commonly understood discourses and practices. Membership involves years of socialization into the history, documents, and "charism" or "spirit" of an order. For service-oriented apostolic communities, that often includes both a strong identification with the poor and an imperative to act on behalf of the poor, either in providing direct assistance as needed or in promoting systemic change that addresses the economic, political, and social conditions that create and sustain inequities and injustices.

Such a stance can manifest itself as charity—an individual or collective "doing for" that sustains power differentials—or it can lead to inner transformation and commitment to systemic action such as that undertaken by Dorothy Day (1952), founder of the Catholic Worker Movement, after she came to recognize how traditional Catholic institutional systems promoted "plenty of charity but too little justice" (p. 150). As a teacher, then, how could I move beyond giving my students the educational equivalent of charity—skills that would allow them to graduate and enter the work force—to promoting educational justice and critical literacy by providing them with the tools and experiences for understanding and using information in ways that would give them access to greater sociopolitical power (Shor, 1999)?

My studies led to the professional development I sought; instead of returning to my ninth-grade classroom, however, I entered the field of teacher education. While undertaking research in urban schools, I became even more convinced that one committed teacher in one classroom can make a significant contribution to a child's opportunities for meaningful learning. As an instructor in courses for preservice and early career teachers, I also recognized the challenges these students were facing, and perceived an urgent need to support them during their first critical classroom experiences. They wanted to be effective teachers who could make a difference, especially within schools challenged by socioeconomic inequities. Given their predominately middle-class backgrounds, however, many of them had little experience of diversity or were reluctant to question the curriculum and structures that had served them well in their own lives (Sleeter, 1995).

From my perspective, I saw a need for them to stretch beyond their own memories of school that too often fell into the stratified patterns that Anyon (1981) identified and described so many years earlier. In addition, those who became most interested in critical literacy theory frequently asked for more concrete examples of critical pedagogy in practice to see how such ideas could take shape in real school contexts, how to facilitate discussions of potentially controversial ideas, and how to stand up to intimidating systems.

In addition to locating such examples for my students, I was also working my way through figuring out how to apply these very same strategies within my own teaching. As I look back over my first four semesters of teaching at my previous institution, I see patterns emerging in my courses and in my students' responses to those courses that suggest that we are, in fact, making progress together in how we make sense of and engage in powerful literacy in multiple academic settings.

A CONCEPTUAL FRAMEWORK GROUNDED IN INQUIRY

This chapter discusses my development of course work designed to move students through stages of growth in becoming educators of and for powerful literacy. Of course, the ways the students make sense of course content are not linear but reflect recursive and highly individual processes. Nonetheless, I am aware of a general progression of their learning, manifest in their responses to assignments, the nature of their participation in class discussions, and the directions of their eventual course projects. In addition, while it is possible to identify examples of student growth through a single semester, it appears that when students have the chance to extend their thinking through a series of courses taught from a consistent conceptual framework, they continue exploring and internalizing ideas, picking up where they left off on earlier projects and moving toward richer, more articulate insights and thoughtful applications. I have come to see an underlying framework of "inquiry" as a component around which to shape course content and assignments as well as a fundamental, underlying pedagogical principal designed to promote powerful literacy, both within my own students' experiences and as an extension into their own actual teaching.

My understanding of inquiry has been influenced by Fecho's (2004) thinking in *"Is This English?" Race, Language, and Culture in the Classroom.* For Fecho, an inquiry-driven classroom is one in which the teacher and the students are mutually engaged in the process of meaning-making, beginning with authentic questions that grow from their lived experiences in relation to ideas, theories, and information that they encounter and seek to integrate into their continually evolving understandings.

Similarly, Cochran-Smith and Lytle (1999) encourage teachers and teacher educators to assume an orientation of *"inquiry as stance"* (p. 288) as a fundamental conceptualization underlying their identities and roles as educators, educational researchers, and members of communities of learning and practice. They explain:

> *Inquiry as stance* is distinct from the more common notion of inquiry as time-bounded project or discrete activity within a teacher education

course or professional development workshop. Teachers and student teachers who take an inquiry stance work within inquiry communities to generate local knowledge, envision and theorize their practice, and interpret and interrogate the theory and research of others. Fundamental to this notion is the idea that the work of inquiry communities is both social and political; that is, it involves making problematic the current arrangements of schooling; the ways knowledge is constructed, evaluated, and used; and teachers' individual and collective roles in bringing about change. (p. 289)

My goal is to help beginning teachers develop a stance of inquiry as their own guiding intellectual and professional orientation. As Cochran-Smith and Lytle (1999) point out, inquiry should not be regarded as an alternate label for traditional, isolated course projects or research assignments. Instead, such a stance should prepare teachers to assume the identity of lifelong learner and gain increasing familiarity with the intellectual and practical resources that make such explorations possible. Further, they argue that because *inquiry as stance* is more concerned with generating questions, exploring uncertainties, acknowledging multiple perspectives and problematizing "norms" than with finding definitive answers, it can lead to the kind of broad thinking and creative initiatives more typically associated with "democratic schooling and to the formation of a more just society" (p. 294).

I integrate the concept of inquiry into course work in various ways. First, I frame the entire syllabus for each course, no matter what topics are to be covered, around inquiry, whereby class members or working groups develop their own authentic questions and then develop projects that help them explore issues of personal interest. I am conscious that I am nudging them toward an appreciation of a more socially just and powerful literacy by the nature of course readings and assignments, so what unfolds is a facilitated, scaffolded approach to internalizing social justice course content. But I also provide students with space to make their own choices and formulate their own questions, arising from their individual experiences and teaching contexts.

I see this as a necessary way to introduce students to issues of powerful literacy that have political and social connotations which may not have been apparent to them from their previous educational experiences. By embracing a stance of inquiry together we learn to examine our underlying assumptions and to remind each other to refrain from declaring that we have found universal answers or "truths." One student reflected, at the end of a course, that she felt students were coming to understand and internalize concepts at their own pace, through their own discoveries, without feeling that I was "pounding them over the head" with my own agenda. Although they knew I had an agenda and could certainly identify what it was, they felt that they were allowed to come to their own conclusions through their research, as opposed to having to voice back an instructor's opinions to play an academic game for a good grade.

A second level of inquiry emerges as the students gain not only a richer understanding of the theoretical basis for inquiry as an approach to learning, but also as they gain experience in research strategies for their own investigations. As they become more confident in using research methodologies and intrigued by what they are learning, they also become convinced that authentic inquiry is an approach to use with their own students. This insight is an epiphany for many. It is often their first experience of coming to internalize what Finn (1999) means by "powerful literacy" and recognizing that all students can and must be given opportunities to strengthen their literacy skills by conducting critical explorations of issues of consequence.

Finally, as they gain confidence in methods of inquiry, analyzing and interpreting data, crafting a variety of papers and teaching materials based on their discoveries, and communicating their learning within their school contexts, they often express new respect for formal inquiry and teacher research. In addition to valuing the meaning-making process itself, they also value their inquiries as immediately useful tools for documenting their teaching and their students' learning, improving their professional credibility within their school settings, and confidently advocating for their beliefs within their districts (Zigo, 2001).

INQUIRY WITHIN COURSE WORK

While each of the courses I teach fosters inquiry, the nature of class assignments and topics differs. I will focus on three courses I taught in an Ed.M. program in English education. I have had a small number of students who have enrolled in all three courses and a larger number in two. It is easiest for me to describe the progression of both my own and my students' experiences of these courses by describing them in the chronological order in which I developed and taught them and my students experienced them. I believe we were mutually influencing one another: As they responded to my instruction, I attended to those responses and continued to revise the courses further.

The first course I taught with an orientation toward inquiry focused specifically on literacy and social class. Two of the required texts were *Literacy with an Attitude* (Finn, 1999) and *Reading, Writing, and Rising Up* (Christensen, 2000). In this course, however, I experienced some of the tensions commonly noted when aiming to move students toward critical social understandings. Some students were resistant to the readings, insisting that the content just "wasn't true." Others admitted, after the course was over, that they were reluctant to speak up in class for fear of being challenged by more self-assured students.

I allowed students to develop their own project ideas, however, and while many admitted that this was initially difficult, most came to see it positively. One student, Karen (all student names are pseudonyms), decided to write an article suitable for the op-ed section of the local newspaper. Instead of writing a concise article, however, she realized that she had much more to learn and say about a number of topics relevant to her work in an urban high school. Her final paper was a hybrid: while still written for a public audience, it became a lengthy essay filled with her emerging understandings of socioeconomic influences on language arts education. It was not quite a finished paper because Karen was deeply immersed in inquiry. She was hooked on the process itself, and knew that this was a topic she needed to continue investigating. At the same time, however, she still felt frustrated; she was learning so much, but did not yet feel that she knew how to apply it to her teaching.

My experience of teaching Karen felt incomplete, as well; she was delving into complex ideas, but as an early career teacher, she was still unsure of the best ways to translate these ideas into instruction that would support and challenge her students. I had not yet helped her put her emerging ideas about powerful literacies into practice. Karen herself was still engaging in informational rather than powerful literacy. I realized it is not enough to introduce critical and powerful literacies as theories to learn "about." That just repeats the pattern of providing students with limited levels of literacy and reduces inquiry to a euphemism for traditional academic research.

In the meantime, I developed an Advanced Composition course grounded in a framework of inquiry using Sunstein and Chiseri-Strater's (2002) *Fieldworking: Reading and Writing Research*, which encourages students to assume an anthropological approach to researching culture by "talking, listening, recording, observing, participating, and sometimes even living in a particular place . . . to help you become more conscious as you observe, participate in, read, and write about your own world and the world of others" (p. 1).

My goal was to help students gain experience in composition and research that was probably different from, yet complementary to what most of them had experienced as English teachers and as students of literature and writing. In addition, I hoped that by their own experience of this kind of writing process, they would see ways to apply such a generative, inquiry-oriented approach to writing for discovery and understanding in their own classrooms. I was especially motivated by the urgent need for students to experience and reflect on a writing process that was a far cry from the strictly formulaic approaches they were feeling pressured to use in their classes to prepare their students for the state English language arts assessments. I also saw this as a promising way to help students understand the difference between functional/informational and more authentically powerful approaches to composition.

Most of these students understood academic research as "the ability to read and absorb the kind of knowledge that is associated with the school and to write examinations and reports based on such knowledge" (Finn, 1999, p.

124). The fieldworking approach, however, extends such an understanding into more creative, knowledge-making realms of inquiry and writing, whereby students are allowed to explore a wider range of genres, voices, and purposes for their developing texts. While this course did not explicitly claim a justice orientation, I saw my underlying pedagogical goals as providing teachers with tools to counter the injustice of reductionist school literacy curricula. Such a pedagogy of inquiry helps provide all children with greater agency and flexibility in developing ways of understanding, manipulating, and participating in the multiple discourses utilized by those who hold sociopolitical power (Hicks, 1997).

I believe that this course led to an even greater acceptance of the principles of inquiry than my earlier, more overtly justice-oriented class. Students chose a wide range of cultural groups to explore: online gamers, skydivers, bingo players, a bicycle advocacy group, Goth culture, triathletes, Quakers, spiritualists, and volunteer firemen, to name a few. As students began to gather information through traditional ethnographic methods, they were also required to explore in writing their own identities in relation to the cultures they were examining. This first paper was pivotal in transforming their sense of research from simply gathering information to composing a sustained, reflective dialogue between the information they discovered and their personal processes for constructing meaning from such information.

Although this course did not specifically address powerful literacy as a topic of study, the underlying theme of deep cultural understanding moved students toward the stance necessary for understanding and enacting powerful literacy in ways that just reading and talking about it could not have done. One student who wrote about people bearing full-body art tattoos, for instance, was initially puzzled by such individuals. The student came to respect them, however, as people deeply invested in a quest for identity and living out of a passionate spirit of nonconformity. In addition, because a significant amount of class time was dedicated to writing groups, a genuine spirit of community developed. The writing groups became safe places for sharing and trusting each other's words and responses. As students became invested in and respectful of the cultures they were studying and writing about, they also became invested in and respectful of each other.

This time, students had moved beyond an informational approach to composition. Through my pedagogical decisions and practices, and their experiences of the many stages of gathering data, reflecting, drafting, revising, and sharing, we were now experiencing and understanding the power of powerful literacy as a pedagogical goal. In addition, students who had already mastered the conventions of academic discourses and possessed the most cultural capital came to understand why narrow understandings of academic informational literacy could be pedagogically and politically insufficient for the needs of less experienced students.

Evan, for example, had already abandoned the course mapped out for him by his family, that of following an upwardly mobile track culminating in a successful business career. In his mid-twenties, he struggled with the disappointment of being rejected by a prestigious literature Ph.D. program. At the same time, he felt that it would be worthwhile to obtain certification as an English teacher. He chose to explore the subculture of open-microphone night at a well-known local music club for his inquiry project. Open-mike night was different because it was on a weeknight—not the usual younger, weekend crowd coming to hear edgy, up-and-coming bands. Evan's paper became notably different from his classmates' papers. Inspired by Jack Kerouac, Evan began to integrate his restless search for identity and meaning with the stories of the patrons drawn week after week to Monday night at the club. It was here that we learned of Evan's passions, worries, and ambivalences, as well as his skills as a writer.

Evan was one of the first to volunteer to share his draft to the entire class, seeking their feedback. As Evan read his multilayered, stream-of-consciousness draft, a few classmates were confused. "Did he follow directions?" they wondered. "Is this research?" Others, however, were mesmerized. Evan had opened the door to reconceptualizing research and expository writing as a hybrid genre of fact, fiction, and sheer language play. We also became the trusted audience for Evan's unfolding quest. How and why did Evan's upbringing influence his desire to spend time in a late night bar listening to older men and women share their stories of hardship and heartache? Why did he feel so drawn to this place? That was the question he was trying to answer for himself, and in sharing his questions and quest with his classmates, he helped them understand how expository writing can also become a powerful medium for personal exploration and transformation.

I next taught a course entitled Language Diversity and Literacy, designed to give teachers a critical understanding of the principles of sociolinguistics, particularly in relation to how language is conceptualized and taught in schools. Once again, I set up a class where students would focus on their own questions and develop their own exploratory projects. I gave careful thought to the order of texts. We began with Kutz' (1997) *Language and Literacy: Studying Discourse in Communities and Classrooms* that provided a solid overview of principles and practices of a sociocultural, sociolinguistic understanding of language, grammar, and discourse.

I followed that with Fecho's (2004) *"Is This English?" Race, Language, and Culture in the Classroom.* I knew that my students would grow annoyed if I did not provide the examples they craved, and Fecho's text is ideal for a number of reasons. He locates himself within his urban classroom and is refreshingly honest about who he is and why he teaches as he does; he provides stories of his students' work as they become inquirers into issues of language and culture; he provides a convincing rationale for why potentially controversial issues must be dealt with rather than avoided; and he models a true inquiry stance in that questions and processes are more important than arriving at conclusive answers. It was in this course that I first began to hear students claiming "inquiry" as their preferred mode for engaging in graduate class work and for their own teaching, citing Fecho (2004) as their model and inspiration.

I was particularly interested in the course projects initiated by the students who had already taken my earlier courses. What could I learn about their developing understandings and the cumulative influence of my pedagogical decisions? Karen, for example, was still concerned about her effectiveness in teaching her predominantly African American urban students. Her inquiry project in this third course focused on strengthening her professional knowledge base for clarifying what she meant by "effectiveness" as an urban teacher. She came to see that in the vocational high school setting where she worked, some colleagues understood effective teaching to mean classroom management, satisfactory test scores, and basic skills instruction. "Powerful literacy" was never identified as a curricular goal for these students.

After reading the work of Ladson-Billings (1994), Perry and Delpit (1998), and Tatum (1997), Karen redefined effective teaching to mean facilitating an education that is sociopolitically empowering and culturally relevant to students' needs, identities, and experiences. Karen's final paper in the earlier course had been a lengthy, honest attempt to synthesize her content knowledge, her understanding of critical pedagogy, her reflective insights, and her ideas for ways to reform the resource-starved district in which she worked. At the same time, she was frustrated by her lack of experience with methods for teaching powerful literacy and her insecurity about communicating her views to influential building and district personnel.

In this course, Karen now felt ready to revisit the topic of her first paper. This time, instead of studying other educators' examples of teaching for powerful literacy, she was determined to develop and inquire into her own efforts at teaching from this stance. She wrote,

> I would like my instruction to encompass social issues that are prevalent in society, giving students the opportunity to critically analyze language, our society, and the world. I believed that teaching Lorraine Hansberry's *A Raisin in the Sun* would open up worlds of opportunity to discuss issues of language and race.

As Karen attended to the ways her students were responding to this text, she gained new insights similar to those Fecho (2004) describes in his earliest efforts at creating a classroom space open to critical dialogues. Karen realized that her prior history of providing informational knowledge, and her reluctance to allow student-centered critical conversations, was holding her back from allowing her students to explore the questions and comments they were initiating while reading the play.

As she analyzed her unit, she also realized that the mere content of the play would not be enough to promote rich, thoughtful discussions of race and class. She also realized that her own European cultural background might prevent her from interpreting the play in ways her students might. Nonetheless, she resolved to keep teaching this play because she still believed that it could invite her students to draw upon their own rich background knowledge in embarking on an inquiry stance, possibly more so than texts from the traditional literary canon.

Karen also realized that she incorrectly assumed that her students would respond to the play out of an awareness of the sociopolitical context in which it was originally written. Instead, her students approached the play from their own contemporary experiences. Some argued that the Younger family would have been outsmarting the white Clybourne Park residents if the Youngers accepted the money intended to keep them from moving into the all-white neighborhood, coming out ahead with even more money to apply toward their goals. Others were appalled at Ruth Younger's reluctance to stand up to her husband, Walter Lee. They insisted that a strong black woman would never allow a man to treat her with such disrespect. Still others found the dialect of the written text confusing.

Karen recognized that in a truly dialogic classroom, her role was not to teach students the "correct" interpretation of the play but to allow readers to take risks in developing their own interpretations. She also speculated on reasons why her students may have responded to the text as they did. Regarding students' discomfort with the spoken dialects of characters, she considered possible explanations: "Stories told through the use of dialect may be troublesome in some respects; it seems that students are often confused by the differences in how they are taught to write with grammatical correctness and texts that offer English in dialectical forms."

After describing a variety of student responses to the text in terms of language, characterization, and themes, Karen's final section of her course paper was entitled, "A Teacher Learns." In her conclusion, she wrote,

> At one point I decided that I would not teach this play again. I felt that there were too many problems ready to bubble up over the surface, problems I wasn't prepared to deal with . . . I didn't feel I could teach this unit effectively. Further reflection brought me to a different point . . . This play will now become a staple of my teaching . . . I feel prepared to design ways that students can study language and history.

Over two years Karen moved toward greater self-confidence in both articulating her understanding of powerful literacy and in developing actual classroom instruction to put such principles into practice. Initially dismayed by what she felt were unsuccessful results, she was inspired by Fecho's (2004) descriptions of his own 20-year-long journey towards an inquiry-based classroom.

Another student, Linda, carried the ideas developed from her bingo-players study in Advanced Composition into a more personal exploration of her own teaching identity and pedagogy within an urban setting. What began in one class as a study of a culture that she admitted was completely foreign to her, evolved into a profoundly personal analysis of her own attitudes, assumptions, and behaviors as a middle-aged white substitute teacher working with African American urban middle schoolers. While Linda enjoyed writing her study of the bingo culture in the Advanced Composition class, it was her participation in the third course that truly moved her into a stance of critical inquiry. Her ideas began to take shape when she realized that she could integrate her emerging question exploring "how to make the classroom environment less confrontational between students and teachers" with the research strategies she had learned in constructing her paper on the culture of elderly suburban bingo players.

She realized that she needed to spend time in her students' neighborhoods and out-of-school social settings to gain a deeper understanding of potential disconnections between home and family cultures and the school culture to which these children were expected to conform. Because she already felt comfortable as a qualitative researcher in a community bingo setting, she gathered data in an urban parish center whose bingo games drew predominantly African American players who brought their children and grandchildren along. She extended her explorations into additional church and community centers and quickly saw a troubling contrast between the happy, friendly, enthusiastic, well-behaved children in the community settings and the unhappy, seemingly resistant children in neighborhood school settings.

Linda considered how the school setting and teachers' attitudes, including her own, could be directly contributing to the children's perceptions of school as a hostile, unsafe place, leading to the conflicts and tensions that concerned her as a teacher. As a result, she revised her initial question into one of a more reflective and critical nature:

> I started asking myself what it is about the school environment that brings out the negative in students. More specifically, I decided that I needed to take a look at myself as a teacher, and my question became, "How, as a person and a teacher, do I create situations that result in hostility and conflict within the classroom and school environment at large?"

As Linda gained her students' trust, she learned that they felt their teachers were too quick to discipline and make demands on them, without making efforts to establish warm, personal relationships with them. One student explained to Linda why students sometimes think she is mad at them: "Ms. Wallace, no offense, 'cause you know I like you, but sometimes you go down the hallway, look right at me, and you don't smile or say hello or nothing." Linda realized that this was, in fact, true, and that it had a definite impact on how her students perceived their relationship with her and their other teachers.

She gained insights into her own identity and behaviors as a teacher and, by the end of the course, she was also more comfortable in recognizing inquiry as a method for addressing concerns and a process that would inevitably lead to more questions:

> My research is open-ended in that it has created new questions for me that I feel will not be answered until I become a full-time teacher. Having the same students every day will hopefully build up a trust that makes our classroom an environment for open discussion.

RECOMMENDATIONS FOR TEACHER EDUCATION

Just as Fecho (2000) argues that adolescents need "authentic means and circumstances for inquiry," I believe that teachers also need similar "support and structures that facilitate such learning" (p. 391). My work with students such as Evan, Karen, and Linda has helped me identify factors that help teachers move toward more just and equitable orientations and practices in their own literacy instruction. First, teachers must be given opportunities to learn about, personally experience, and debrief experiences of powerful literacies. For me, this means providing students with readings that present clear definitions and examples from practice of both powerful literacy and inquiry. Then, as students undertake their own inquiry projects, they can recognize that the reading and writing in which they are now engaging reflects a literacy that encompasses more than merely functional or informational uses of language.

Such metacognitive awareness is essential in helping teachers begin to develop authentic inquiry projects within their own classrooms as a way to help their students gain access to powerful literacies. In addition, we must be patient together. Inquiry takes time; transformation takes time. The ability to articulate deeper understandings may not happen according to the artificial academic timetable of sixteen weeks of weekly class meetings. Evolving levels of awareness are more likely to emerge and take shape within extended course work designed around a consistent conceptual framework, such as the one I have described in this chapter.

Finally, educators need to be provided with research strategies and tools that allow them to engage in inquiry not only for personal growth and insight, but also for professional development with immediate practical value within their schools. An ultimate goal of critical inquiry is concrete action leading to systemic change. Such an undertaking empowers both teachers and their students on two levels: They are enacting powerful literacy together by the very act of purposeful inquiry, and if they are formally documenting their findings, they are also gathering the evidence they need to advocate for authentic change within their school, their neighborhood communities, and, ideally, beyond.

REFERENCES

Anyon, J. (1981). Social class and school knowledge. *Curriculum Inquiry 11*, 3–42.

Casey, K. (1993). *I answer with my life: Life histories of women teachers working for social change*. New York: Routledge.

Christensen, L. (2000). *Reading, writing, and rising up: Teaching about social justice and the power of the written word*. Milwaukee, WI: Rethinking Schools.

Cochran-Smith, M., & Lytle, S. L. (1999). Relationships of knowledge and practice: Teacher learning in communities. In A. Iran-Nejad & P. D. Pearson (Eds.), *Review of research in education: 24* (pp. 249–305). Washington, DC: American Educational Research Association.

Day, D. (1952). *The long loneliness: The autobiography of Dorothy Day*. New York: Harper & Row.

Fecho, B. (2000). Critical inquiries into language in an urban classroom. *Research in the Teaching of English 34*, 368–395.

Fecho, B. (2004). *"Is this English?": Race, language, and culture in the classroom*. New York: Teachers College Press.

Finn, P. J. (1999). *Literacy with an attitude: Educating working-class children in their own self-interest*. Albany: State University of New York Press.

Hicks, D. (1997). Working *through* discourse genres in school. *Research in the Teaching of English 31*, 459–485.

Kutz, E. (1997). *Language and literacy: Studying discourse in communities and classrooms*. Portsmouth, NH: Heinemann.

Ladson-Billings, G. (1994). *The dreamkeepers: Successful teachers of African American children*. San Francisco: Jossey-Bass.

Perry, T., & Delpit, L. (Eds.). (1998). *The real Ebonics debate: Power, language, and the education of African-American children*. Boston: Beacon Press.

Shor, I. (1999). What is critical literacy? In I. Shor & C. Pari (Eds.), *Critical literacy in action: Writing words, changing worlds* (pp. 1–30). Portsmouth, NH: Heinemann.

Sleeter, C. E. (1995). Reflections on my use of multicultural and critical pedagogy when students are white. In C. E. Sleeter & P. L. McLaren (Eds.), *Multicultural education, critical pedagogy, and the politics of difference* (pp. 415–437). Albany: State University of New York Press.

Sunstein, B. S., & Chiseri-Strater, E. (2002). *Fieldworking: Reading and writing research*. Boston: Bedford/St. Martin's.

Tatum, B. D. (1997). *"Why are all the black kids sitting together in the cafeteria?" And other conversations about race*. New York: Basic Books.

Wells, G. (1987). Apprenticeship in literacy. *Interchange 18*, 109–123.

Zigo, D. (2001). Constructing firebreaks against high-stakes testing. *English Education 33*, 214–232.

9 Accessing Praxis: Practicing Theory, Theorizing Practice in Social Justice Teachers' First Year of Teaching

Peter Hoffman-Kipp and Brad Olsen

PETER HOFFMAN-KIPP, ASSISTANT PROFESSOR of Education at Sonoma State University, and Brad Olsen, Assistant Professor of Education, University of California, Santa Cruz, describe the UCLA Center X teacher education program, where students have a Novice year of study and student teaching followed by a second Resident year as employed, full-time teachers in urban public schools. During the Resident teacher year, students meet weekly in a seminar to engage in praxis—to plan action in light of theory and examine theory in light of practice. This chapter details the ways that new teachers perceive the transition to teaching for social justice and suggests that teacher preparation may end too soon, leaving students with a body of theory but too few skills to put it into practice.

Teacher education programs, both preservice and in-service, introduce theoretical concepts that practitioners must translate for use in their classrooms. But articulating and communicating a theoretical foundation that practitioners find consistently meaningful enough to engage with, and utilize in their work, has long been a challenge. Too often, teacher preparation programs do not provide the necessary space or opportunity for new teachers to develop the agency required to translate theory into practice. In addition, teacher education rarely values comments and vignettes about practitioners' concrete experiences in schools as a doorway into conversation about how a theoretical concept might be translated for use in a classroom.

In this chapter, we argue that theory can, in fact, be considered inside of practice—as praxis. Freire (1972) defines praxis as the dialectical union of reflection and action; it is the notion that theory and practice are inseparable. Interpretation, understanding, and application are in constant interplay as one pursues thoughtful action.[1] The study that gives rise to this chapter demonstrated that, if given the opportunity through their teacher education program, teachers in the first year of teaching can develop a praxis which includes two different notions of how theory functions within practice.

That is, beginning teachers can develop a praxis that both informs their practice with theory and, that leads them to realize a new understanding of theory as a result of engaging in their practice. In the first instance, the teacher begins with theory and moves to practice; in the second, the teacher begins with practice and comes to more fully understand theory. In both cases, the emphasis is on making continual moves (Hedegaard, 1990, 1998) between theory and practice through reflection (Hoffman-Kipp, Artiles, & Lopez-Torres, 2003) and action, the key components of praxis.

A first year teacher's view of the relationship of theory to practice reveals that many new teachers believe they ought to be perfect at the teaching performance from the start. The disjointed nature of their thinking about and reflecting on their teaching suggests to them that they are not good performers. Praxis solves that problem as it offers a reflection/action dialectic that incorporates the notion of "beginnings"; you learn to teach through practice,[2] and learning to teach should be envisioned as occurring over time, as practice and theory meet in teacher reflection.

Research suggests that praxis can also act as a tool for teacher educators who hope to affect teacher beliefs and practices, not just in the first years of teaching, but over the professional career of their graduates. Within teacher education programs, structures that offer chances for dialogue that encompasses both theory and practice appear to offer the most opportunities to develop moments of praxis. Most often, these structures appear during a graduate seminar or other small, weekly setting where new social justice teachers can return to the theoretical base established in their teacher preparation coursework. This chapter focuses on just such a setting in order to explore these moments of praxis within the UCLA TEP. Of particular importance in our study is a two-year social justice teacher education program, UCLA's Center X, where students begin teaching full time in the second year.[3]

TEACHER EDUCATION AT UCLA: CENTER X

The Teacher Education Program (TEP) at UCLA—part of Center X—provides urban teacher preparation in the form of a two-year, intensive, M.Ed. program in teaching for social justice in urban communities. During the first year students (who are called Novices) engage in inquiry-based courses, projects, and dialogues on what it means to be a social justice educator in urban Los Angeles. The curriculum stresses theoretical views of social and economic inequity in the U.S. social structure. Social and educational activism are seen as necessary to effect social change, and multiculturalism and the critical study of race are viewed as crucial in the role of social justice teachers.

TEP rejects purely technical, social efficiency models of teaching and learning in favor of culturally relevant pedagogy, sociocultural learning approaches, and acknowledgement of the moral-political dimensions of teaching. Students join small learning teams that meet regularly during both years, engaging around notions of social learning (Lave & Wenger, 1991; Oakes & Lipton, 2003; Vygotsky, 1978); funds of knowledge (Moll, 1988, 1998); second language acquisition (Cummins, 1996, 2000); and cultural identity (Tatum, 1997). During this Novice year, students carry out their student teaching at one of the participating urban schools. During the second year, the TEP students (now called Residents) become paid, full-time teachers in local schools while they continue their university participation by meeting weekly with their seminar group to talk through their teaching experiences and complete their master's projects. After the two years, they are awarded a M.Ed. and a California state teaching credential.

The authors of this paper were part of a team[4] that conducted a year long qualitative study examining how Novices shift out of their roles as university students and into their new roles as full-time teachers (Residents) partnering with TEP. The study attempted to select a sample that reflected the larger TEP population but because of logistical difficulties, missed interviews, and uncompleted data analysis we can write conclusively only about the six teachers we studied. Our results are better understood as heuristics, issues, and themes rather than findings generalizable to larger populations. Table 9.1 represents the demographics of our sample.

Three rounds of audio-taped interviews were conducted with each teacher—one in winter, spring, and summer.[5] Corresponding analysis was employed to investigate ways the six teachers conceived of and made use of the four parts of the TEP program that were intended to prepare and support them in their transition from Novice to Resident: (1) courses in methods of teaching; (2) program-wide emphasis on selected social and educational theories;

Table 9.1. *Demographics of the Study Sample of Teachers*

Total N = 6[a]			
	Male		Female	
Gender			
	1		5	

	Asian	Latino/a	White	Other
Race or ethnicity				
	1	1	4	0

[a] 4 elementary and 2 secondary

(3) cohort/teams; and (4) faculty advisor support.[6] In addition, Residents conduct an Inquiry Project in which they identify an area of their practice that they want to focus on for most of their Resident year. This project fulfills the M.Ed. thesis requirement. Our analysis also focused on the preparation and support structures the teachers reported as missing from the TEP program; we report how the teachers conceived of their first year as teachers against the backdrop of ways they believed TEP did or did not adequately prepare them. In particular, we focus on TEP's theoretical foundation around social justice and its impact on the Residents' first year of teaching.

FINDINGS—DOES PRAXIS BEGIN WITH THEORY OR PRACTICE?

Our findings help to illuminate types of experiences Residents had when moments of praxis arose for them. For the most part, these experiences can be classified as to whether they first arose out of theory or out of practice. Was a Resident attempting to enact a theory in his or her practice, or was a Resident attempting to better understand a theory through the lens of his or her practice? Due to the circular, iterative nature of praxis, however, no matter where the process began, it continued as an oscillation back and forth between theory and practice, and thus maintained a connection between the two.

BEGINNING AND ENDING THE THEORY/PRACTICE DIALECTIC WITH THEORY

For several of the Residents, theory was the starting point for the praxis dialectic. Theory was helpful to these Residents when they could easily use it to generate social justice pedagogy (Gay, 2000; Ladson-Billings, 1995, 2000). Examples of activities that reflected theory to which they had been exposed included: creating a sense of classroom community or encouraging student collaboration; partnering across cultural, linguistic, and ability lines; classroom management that sponsors intrinsic motivation and moral development; and creating lessons engaging higher order thinking skills for "sheltered" students.

Residents reported using "a lot of [theory] by people who were teachers, by people who had been teachers, or by people who were doing research in classrooms." One Resident said this helped "develop my own [practices], based on what [theorists] said you needed to do." Residents also reported that practice enhanced their understanding of the theories to which they had been exposed, creating a dialectic that began and ended with theory.

BEGINNING WITH THEORY: THEORY GENERATES PRACTICE

Residents often initiated a praxis experience by reflecting on theory. They understand what researchers might consider to be a good practice, but felt they had no idea of how to translate it in their classrooms. One Resident commented:

It's great to talk about theory, and it's great to talk about "How do we create a community? How do we scaffold [students] so they feel validated in their home culture? How do we bridge the gap between home and school?" That's all great theoretical stuff, and has practical uses, but how do we turn it into practical activities? How do we still do that but also cover the standards that we're responsible for in the real world?

For most, the issue was how one can turn theory into practice. We found that teacher research was considered helpful, especially if it led to specific programmatic suggestions:

As a first-year teacher I think it's important to look back at what other teachers—and some of the theories I've read, a lot of it, actually, was by people who were teachers. . . . And you know, a lot of the books, they'll tell you the theory, but then they'll tell you, they'll give you practical uses of it.

Translating theory into practices was important for Residents because of their philosophical and political commitment to the social justice tenets of TEP and its theoretical framework. This social justice framework often stood in direct opposition to the district-mandated programs that require teacher scripting, certain seating arrangements, and culturally mismatched curriculum. Reconciling this tension fit into the theory-practice split: "Theoretically, what is our purpose as social justice educators? And how do we teach practically within an environment where social justice is not at the forefront of our school system?"

Often the student population itself challenged a Resident to translate a theory for his or her particular classroom dynamic:

We've done all this reading on social justice, and I feel like a lot of it is focused more on a higher level, maybe. Like, it will say, "Oh, the students," [and] my idea is like, "What does social justice look like [with students] in an ESL 1B classroom?" Because I remember, a lot of the articles we read talk about ways of essay writing, critical thinking, and, the Socratic seminar. And I'm like, "I can't have a Socratic seminar right now," and so my [question] is, "How do we define 'social justice,' how do we define 'rigor,' how do we define all these things that we talk about all the time?"

For this Resident, defining theory is a translation process and therefore reveals a praxis interaction between theory and field practice, though the starting point appears to be the theory.

Many Residents began the praxis dialectic with a theory, engaged in practice, and returned again to the theory to understand it better in light of their new experience with the practice. For example, one Resident described the problem of best practices that do not engage the agency of the teacher. It is the teacher, ultimately, who must decide whether and how a theory fits his or her experience and needs:

> [Practice] is like a test. [The theories] I was studying were based in research in classrooms and on kids and the way kids learn, but I don't think there's this one theory on how kids learn, so, you know, it's just an idea, and you have to use it in order to know if that theory works for your students.

Practice itself made the theory clear to one Resident: "I mean, a lot of theory really is practical, but until you have teaching experience, you're not going to get what they're talking about." The same Resident also stated: "So theory is just the ideas, the big ideas behind why things work. So I need to see the results, or the actuality, the practice, to be able to understand the theory better." And, "I don't take a lot of theory and am able to easily apply it until I've seen it, or until I have a practical application of it, and then I'm like, 'Oh, that makes sense, how the theory actually applies.'" Another Resident simply stated: "now that I have the experience I really realize how valuable [theory] is."

Although their practical experiences often shed light on their understanding of theory, Residents' perceptions of how theory changed their practice were vague. Often, Residents did not know the exact way in which their practice was different, although their deepening understanding of theory suggested to them a shift in practice was occurring. For example, one Resident remarked on her enriched understanding of theory:

> But really, I didn't have a lot to connect [theory] to, and I realized this [second] year [in the TEP], when I started to go back, both in the fall semester Resident readings, and also through the Inquiry [Project] process, and some of it I would re-read for a second time, or whatever, and I feel like, 'Yeah, yeah,' it kind of clicked. . . . And so in that respect, my own views of theory changed this year, because now it just made a lot more sense to have something to sort of base it on, or something to apply it to.

However, this same Resident could not pinpoint how her practice reflected her improved understanding of theory:

Although, I don't really know that I can say, that like, theory guides my every day practice, I don't know that it does. Maybe in a way that I'm not aware of, it sort of trickles down and I'm not even aware of it. But I don't consciously think, "Well, what would Bourdieu say?"— you know, it's not like that, but I definitely appreciate it more now, and I can see where it does apply to what I'm doing.

Whether or not her practices were affected immediately may be secondary to the Resident's perception that she does understand the theory itself better, an important first step in accessing praxis. As the connection between teacher beliefs and practices is well established, we believe a better understanding of theory, filtered and generated through a teacher's practice, will lead to changed practices.

Another Resident defined the praxis experience a little more explicitly:

. . . when I see something in practice I can think back to where the theory matches, because now I'm doing things and I'm like, "Oh, yeah, there is that theory, where is that piece?" And now go back and I find it, and I'll do something and I'll think, "Well, that sounds a little bit like Bourdieu or somebody like that," and I look back and I'm like, "Oh, that's what [a theorist] meant by all of that," because all of a sudden it makes sense. . . . Then when you see a student actually use a [meta-cognitive] strategy, and it increases their understanding, it's like, "Oh! it makes so much more sense." It makes sense for the student and it makes sense for you. So the theory helps me reflect on my practice, but it didn't help perform my practice.

The praxis dialectic is quite evident here; however, it is interesting to note her final line. This Resident is aware that a change is occurring in her thinking and reflection about her work. However, she suggests that the enactment of that work—her performance—is unaffected by her understanding of theory. Similar to the Resident quoted above, the specific application of theory in her practice appears vague, even though she feels confident identifying a scenario in which the theory made sense: "when you see a student actually use a [meta-cognitive] strategy." Theory in this case is a tool for recognizing why good pedagogy works.

BEGINNING AND ENDING THE THEORY-PRACTICE DIALECTIC WITH PRACTICE

Some Residents reported another avenue into the theory-practice intersection. They suggested that instead of finding theory's meaning in practice, theory helped them to organize their already existent practices into a consistent philosophy which could be shared and in turn help them to revise their practice. In other words, rather than finding that praxis begins with theory, moves into practice and then returns to theory, these beginning teachers reported that theory was a way for them to better identify, examine, and articulate their practices as part of a coherent philosophy.

BEGINNING WITH PRACTICE: ORGANIZING THE CONCRETE
INTO A PHILOSOPHY AND SHARING IT

Seeking a way to organize what they were observing in schools and constantly being forced (by the TEP program) to revisit the theories they had studied the previous year, Residents found that theory helped organize their understandings of practice.

For example, one Resident describes her practice of starting with a pacing plan,[7] finding the most important concept, creating activities that could be done with partner pairs, and then actually beginning the lesson with a large group discussion of what a good partner is. What differentiates this rather traditional approach from what is commonly seen in schools is apparent in the Resident's next comment:

> I really saw them sharing strategies, you know, learning from each other. You know, one has a little bit of knowledge, one has a little bit more, and they put it together, it's like, Vygotsky—it's like a Vygotskyian classroom—and it was really cool. I mean, it didn't work perfectly every day but it made it so much better than what it was before, which was, I don't even know what.

This Resident organizes an organic, commonsense approach with minor alterations (partnering) into a reflective moment that connects what she sees to Vygotskian theory. This is similar to Hedegaard's double move in teaching:

> Teaching within the ZPD can be characterized as a *double move* between the students' experience and their exposure to theoretical concepts (Hedegaard, 1998, pp. 120–121) . . . by relating scientific concepts to everyday concepts, teaching provides . . . new skills and possibilities for action. (Hedegaard, 1990, p. 355)

Theory prompted a new way for this Resident to understand practice rather than relying on experience: "It helps me understand things I see happening, and make connections between them, rather than just going on instinct or what I did in school."

As we examined the data, we found that this process was not simply a way for Residents to better conceptualize their teaching to themselves, it also helped them access, evaluate, and articulate other teachers' practices and professional identities. It enabled Residents to better relate to colleagues since it gave them a means by which to understand and discuss what others believe about education and learning. One said:

> . . . we were talking about something in our grade level meeting, and one of my teachers was saying something. I was like, "You're so sociocultural sometimes," and she said, "What?" And I told her, "Here you go, here's this learning theory [for you]" and I outlined for her [my view of what she was doing]. She said, "Oh, I never knew that." She's like a 10-year veteran in teaching, but she said, "We never learned that stuff in [our] teaching program." It's interesting because, the way she deals with her children, we are pretty similar, but she just does it from a different angle than I do, and now that I noticed that and where she fits in [to the theories], I know how to interact with her better.

Of importance here is the way that theory enabled the Resident to connect her practices with a colleague's through the use of theory. Theory provided a common language. This vocabulary also enabled Residents to speak about their work with administrators—an important social justice process for change within schools, and an integral part of the Residents' professional development as well. For some it was a persuasion device employed to convince administrators of something, or to sound educated so administrators would listen when they argue for a certain social justice or student-centered approach.

> And so, [my Faculty Advisor and Residents in the seminar] talked about how to stand up to an administrator, how to stick to your guns. . . . We got a lot of strength that night from [our Faculty Advisor], and that gave us the confidence to meet with the principal, because then we went in and said what we needed to say. And she saw that we knew what we were talking about. So I think that's part of why she defended us, took our side and said, "you're doing a good job"— it was because we sounded educated in the way we approached it.

Whether teachers were learning to name their practices, dialogue about practice with colleagues, or convince administrators of socially just practices, theory gave them a language of practice that connected their practices to their beliefs and therefore widened the circles of understanding and influence.

ENDING WITH PRACTICE: THEORY REVISES PRACTICE
THROUGH THE INQUIRY PROJECT

Learning to name their practices was an important phase in praxis; however, this was not the end. Residents then took this process and turned back to their practices with new lenses through which to understand and change how they conduct their work. In other words, new theoretical understandings revised their practice.

A major source for the revision of practice in their first year of teaching was the Residents' Inquiry Projects. The Inquiry Project allowed these beginning teachers to focus on a topic in their work that they wanted to better understand through a data-based study of their classroom. Utilizing a standard research design and project outline, Residents selected a topic, reviewed the literature, designed and implemented the study, collected data, analyzed the data, and wrote a 25- to 50-page research report on their findings. Seminar meetings focused on the development of this document throughout winter and spring quarters. The Inquiry Project returned them to a praxis dialectic that begins with their current immersion in practice, then engages theory, and brings them to a conscious revision, implementation, and evaluation of their practice. What began with the cognitive organization of their experience using theory became a chance to revise practice with their new theoretical understanding. This occurred in several ways.

First, it was clear that the Residents, as practitioners, felt a need to see or understand theory's impact on their practice. "I just think, as a teacher, it's important to know the theory, because that's why it's there, to help the actual practitioners. I mean, people don't do research for no reason." In fact, although some initially resented the process of writing the Inquiry Project itself, there seemed to be a consensus that "you have to do your theory research to do your practice."

Second, theory mapped out Residents' practices for them. Residents found that their practices required theoretical organization, then, in turn, their newfound organization resulted in a practical map for new practices to occur. Two quotes by the same Resident clarify this point:

> [Theory is] harder to implement than it really seems. I mean, it's easier to sit there and write about it, but to really do it. And so, yeah, I have changed some, and I've sort of mapped out ways that I want to continue slowly changing, more to fit what I write about in my Inquiry [Project]. . . . And so, I think that, like I have these goals, that this is what I want to do, but it will take time, I think, to get myself there. And that's what I mean by 'mapping out,' like how I want to change. I've done some of the things, but some of it is still a little over my head.

Important to note here is the Resident's focus on the beginning phases of change in her practice and the fact that certain theories and their practical expressions are "still a little over my head." Mentally mapping the future captures our notion of praxis that includes elements of practice and planning for the future as a form of theoretical reorganization.

Third, Residents reported confronting the gap between theory's portrayal of perfect practices and Residents' need to undergo a process of change in order to come anywhere close to enacting the practices that the theories called for. Thinking about this gap (Hoffman-Kipp, Artiles, & Lopez-Torres, 2003) became an important way for Residents to engage theory and practice. In other words, Residents, at best, saw themselves moving in the direction suggested by a theory rather than feeling the theory and practice are incompatible. For example, one Resident, when attempting to build a classroom community, posted a bonus point chart for good behavior. This fell into what she saw as an extrinsic motivator and therefore destructive to the very community she wished to build, but it seemed like a necessary halfway measure:

> These are still kids; they need something concrete and visual to see that they're moving, that they're improving so that they can, you know, maybe they won't understand abstractly what is community, at first. But I started that off this year, but then over time, it's kind of symbolic, [the bonus point chart] actually kind of fell down by itself, because our walls are hard to put tape on, so it started to fall down physically, the posters started to fall down. And I was like, kids were kind of running into it accidentally, it was starting to get really tattered, so I just took it down and threw it away. Nobody said anything about it, because at that point we had started to really build community, so it was no longer necessary.

The initial practice was not congruent with the theory, but the practice grew in the direction of the theory. Later, the same Resident reported needing to acknowledge the past experiences of the students in measuring one's practice against the theory:

> So it is trying to build their sense of teamwork, but I feel like they need, especially these kids who have never had community building, these kids who've always been taught in a very behavioristic manner, they need a little bit of something to get them moving in the right direction.

It is the process of reflection and action, both on the part of the teacher and students, that grows the practice in the direction of the theory. This growth is part of our definition of praxis.

Fourth, theory provided the impetus and organization to return to one's practices and systematize them. Understanding their practices through the lens of theory brought accountability. "It just really forced me to hold myself accountable for what I was doing in my classroom." Praxis held Residents' practices under the microscope so that they couldn't maintain a pedagogical practice without conscious inspection. One Resident remarked:

Well, my Inquiry Project was on instruction and motivation, and so it influenced the whole way I teach. Like, it forced me to not get lazy and just do Open Court. Like, it forced me to actually be intentional with planning and implementing things in my classroom, and so as a result, I was doing better teaching. So hopefully I'll keep that up for next year, but you know, it kind of just was like a mandatory way of making me actually do good teaching.

Often, Residents had to confront the gap between their hopes for a social justice classroom based in the theory they had studied, and the reality of their beginnings. Throughout the Inquiry Projects, Residents learned to engage their urban realities by bringing theory to bear on practice so they might reenvision this reality. Rather than perceiving the theoretical world of the university as disconnected, Residents, at times, were able to bring their worlds together and realize a praxis-oriented approach to their work.

CONCLUSIONS

We believe that beginnings in themselves can lead to praxis. Beginning teaching will always be hard; a novice is supposed to be learning how to think about and talk about practice. Encouraging Residents to acknowledge their beginning-ness and work inside those frames of beginning practice precedes successful uses of theory. If teacher educators and Residents view new teaching success as unfolding over several years, and see praxis as the mechanism that produces the unfolding, then we believe it will become easier for Residents (and instructors) to accept the inextricability of theory and practice and choose to stay engaged in the praxis struggle.

Explicit praxis conversations, discussions that weave studies of theory with the teachers' daily experiences in the classroom, are not hard to place within a teacher education program, though to do so requires conscious and constant reflection and reinforcement on the part of faculty and students. Preserving the faculty member's and the students' moments of praxis or theory-practice intersection is often more difficult. Following, are five programmatic suggestions to deepen these praxis moments and to increase their occurrence and expand the dialogue:

1. Teacher educators bring biases to their work that can privilege theory or practice. We suggest that these biases be made as explicit as possible, and a commitment to a praxis-oriented reflection be maintained, or developed where necessary. This can occur in several ways: bringing theory into conversations about practice, and never allowing theory to remain defined outside of the concrete experiences students are having in schools.

2. To programmatically ensure that a praxis dialectic remains possible for new teachers, teacher education programs should develop bridges from the university to the school that continue the connection through the first years of teaching. At UCLA, this bridge takes the form of the Urban Educator Network, where students continue to dialogue both in person and through an online journal *Teaching to Change Los Angeles* (www.tcla.gseis.ucla.edu).

3. Forging relationships with veteran teachers, administrators, and other school constituents is an important part of a teacher educator's work in helping to make schools into the kinds of places where their graduates can effectively work. UCLA has enacted such a program through its Circle Groups that meet once each quarter at a school site. Surrounding schools participate, usually in school families that include elementary and middle school feeders to one or more high schools. These groups discuss the philosophy of UCLA's TEP and ways schools can support new teachers in their efforts to implement that philosophy.

4. Praxis is most accessible through practice. Case studies and case analysis of actual practices have been used effectively in the medical and business fields, both areas of study that have a theoretical foundation that interacts with a large practitioner base. Case studies can provide new teachers with opportunities to examine actual moments of praxis.

5. Teacher education programs must help students see schools as sites within a community, so that their interactions with the theory–practice dialectic are not purely pedagogic, but encourage them to find a similar dialectic in school-community. One way UCLA has accomplished this task is through the Community Project, in which students research a school's surrounding community, interview community members, map community resources, and develop an action plan based on this knowledge that they might enact to connect their classroom curriculum and their school to the community

Through this study, we found that praxis can be accessed either through theory or through practice. In either case, the praxis dialectic returns the practitioners to their source for reflection, and in this way leads to a deepened understanding of both theory and practice. At this point in our research, we cannot say whether it is more productive to begin with theory or with practice. Our main conclusion has been that praxis itself is a vitally important vehicle for teacher educators interested in understanding and bridging the historic gap between theory and practice as perceived by new practitioners.

NOTES

1. The term praxis is often associated with Freire (e.g., 1972) and is commonly linked to thoughtful action. Praxis is not merely about theory and practice but about attempts to reveal the world as a site of political and cultural struggle and to use education to transform the status quo. For those of us at Center X, this is a programmatic priority.

2. Gloria Ladson-Billings suggested this concept to the authors when discussing this paper at the Urban Teacher Educator Net2work Conference, 2004.

3. Applicants to UCLA's TEP are evaluated based on academic factors and their desire to teach in urban schools. Students are expected to find a job at the end of their first TEP year in one of the Los Angeles school districts with which UCLA works. Students also commit to the "Partner Policy," which means they must go to a school where an alumnus is already placed, or go with a partner who is a current student.

4. The authors wish to thank the UCLA Center X TEP Student Development Committee for conducting the larger study from which the data in this chapter are drawn. Committee members include Leslie Dwyer, Michelle Guire, Peter Hoffman-Kipp, Sheila Lane, Leandra Marin, Brad Olsen, Mario Perez, Deanna Staake, Irene Swanson.

5. Protocols for the first and second interviews were open-ended so we could identify the sources of support Residents found valuable, and how they were understood. For the third interview we used a more pointed protocol with questions shaped by preliminary analysis so that Residents could voice specific feelings about issues of practicality, theory, and support within TEP.

6. We employed ethnographic and sociolinguistic analytical methods to examine the meaning systems the Residents relied on as they talked about their experiences (Becker, 1998; Miles & Huberman, 1984).

7. A textbook or district provided teaching plan that provides amounts of time in which a concept ought to be taught. These plans are often accompanied by standardized testing schedules to match the teaching.

REFERENCES

Becker, H. (1998). *Tricks of the trade*. Chicago: University of Chicago Press.

Cummins, J. (1996). *Negotiating identities: Education for empowerment in a diverse- society*. Los Angeles: California Alliance for Bilingual Education.

Cummins, J. (2000). *Language, power and pedagogy: Bilingual children in the crossfire*. Clevedon, England: Multilingual Matters.

Freire, P. (1972). *Pedagogy of the oppressed*. Harmondsworth: Penguin.

Gay, G. (2000). *Culturally responsive teaching: Theory, research and practice*. New York: Teachers College Press.

Hedegaard, M. (1990). The zone of proximal development as basis for instruction. In L. Moll (Ed.), *Vygotsky and education: Instructional implications and applications of sociohistorical psychology* (pp. 349–371). Cambridge, UK: Cambridge University Press.

Hedegaard, M. (1998). Situated learning and cognition: Theoretical learning and cognition. *Mind, Culture, and Activity, 5*(2), 114–126.

Hoffman-Kipp, P., Artiles, A. J., & López-Torres, L. (2003). Beyond reflection: Teacher learning as praxis. *Theory into Practice, 42*(3), 248–254.

Ladson-Billings, G. (1995). Toward a theory of culturally relevant pedagogy. *American Education Research Journal, 35,* 465–491.

Ladson-Billings, G. (2000). Fighting for our lives: Preparing teachers to teach African American students. *Journal of Teacher Education, 51*(3), 206–214.

Lave, J., & Wenger, E. (1991). *Situated learning.* Cambridge, UK: Cambridge University Press.

Miles, M., & Huberman, M. (1984). *Qualitative data analysis: A sourcebook of new methods.* Beverly Hills, CA: Sage Publications.

Moll, L. (1988). Some key issues in teaching Latino students. *Language Arts, 64*(5), 465–472.

Moll, L. (1998). Funds of knowledge for teaching: A new approach in education. Keynote address: Illinois State Board of Education, February 5, 1998.

Oakes, J., & Lipton, M. (2003). *Teaching to change the world.* 2nd Ed. Boston: McGraw-Hill.

Tatum, B. (1997). *Why are all the black kids sitting together in the cafeteria? And other conversations about race.* New York: Basic Books.

Vygotsky, L. (1978). *Mind in society.* Cambridge, MA: Harvard University Press.

10 Russian Children in American Schools: Towards Intercultural Dialogue in Diverse Classrooms and Teacher Preparation Programs

Vladimir Ageyev

VLADIMIR AGEYEV, CLINICAL PROFESSOR of Educational Studies, University at Buffalo, State University of New York, addresses the problem of communication across cultures between teachers and students using a cross-cultural and sociocultural theoretical framework to describe the situation of American teachers and Russian-speaking immigrant students. He argues that intercultural education should be an important part of all teacher preparation programs.

This chapter, based on ethnographical research, provides some theoretical insights and practical advice on ways to help Russian-speaking immigrant students adjust to American schools. I first address teachers, such as those who work with students who recently emigrated from the former Soviet Union, who may be totally unfamiliar with their students' home culture. Such teachers need intercultural education skills to bridge important cultural differences and insure the academic success of immigrant children, as well as those children whose homegrown cultures clash with the dominant culture of U.S. schools. In addition, I argue that intercultural dialogue is an important and too often neglected component of multicultural education, so I am also addressing all who seek to improve teacher education programs by improving teachers' ability to educate all culturally diverse students, including both recent immigrants and native born students from diverse racial, ethnic, and social class backgrounds.

NEW DEMOGRAPHICS, NEW EDUCATIONAL CHALLENGES

The number of families with school-aged children emigrating to the United States from the former Soviet Union and Eastern European countries does not show any sign of decline; instead, it is steadily growing due to political instability, religious controversies, economic turmoil, civil unrest, war, and terrorism. These changing demographics go along with changing educational challenges. The previous wave of immigration from the former Soviet Union, from roughly the late sixties to the early nineties, was a rather homogeneous one that consisted mostly of Jewish middle- and upper middle-class professionals. The current wave of immigration, which started in the early nineties, is more diverse and includes a variety of ethnic and racial groups, as well as fundamentalist religious groups such as Baptists and Pentecostals. Among the new immigrants from the former Soviet Union and Eastern Europe are many low socioeconomic status (SES) families who come from working-class and rural communities.

The previous wave of immigration from the former Soviet Union was without doubt an educational success; Russian students from this earlier period are sometimes called a "second model minority" (the first "model minority" being Asian Americans), however flawed the concept of model minority itself may be (Li, 2002). The situation is quite different with the current wave of immigration. While some Russian-speaking students are still quite successful in U.S. schools, a significant number of them are having serious difficulties. In many cases, these children demonstrate low test scores and low motivation to learn; they remain isolated and find it difficult to establish normal relationships with their U.S. peers. The high school dropout rates of these students, especially among males, is higher than average. This is especially prevalent for students coming from families of working-class backgrounds with strong religious associations.

The general attitude of these students toward school and learning is, in many ways, similar to American students coming from low SES and working-class backgrounds. It is common for those students not to have any plans for continuing education on the college level after graduating from the high school; typically, boys look for accessible manual labor, and girls look for swift marriage and raising children.

The whole situation, however, is aggravated by cultural differences and language barriers. Unlike their American peers, even those who come from the similar working-class backgrounds, Russian-speaking immigrant children have additional difficulties associated with the needs of a broad cultural and linguistic adaptation, as well as adaptation specifically to U.S. school culture. While some research exists concerning Soviet-era immigrant students (Harrington-Lueker, 1991; Hoot & Bonkareva, 1992), research addressing more than a decade of post-Soviet immigrant students is all but lacking. Especially lacking is research that thoroughly examines Russian-American cultural differences and the implications for students' academic and social success. This is explained in part by the fact that the sheer number of students from the former Soviet Union and Eastern Europe remains relatively small when compared with the major U.S. minorities, such as African Americans, Asian Americans, Latino-Americans and Native Americans, who remain the main focus of research in multicultural education.

What is even more striking than the shortage of research on the educational aspects of Russian immigration is the almost total lack of knowledge of Russian and Eastern European culture in teacher preparation programs. Even in classes on diversity and multicultural education, Russian and East European cultures are hardly ever mentioned, let alone more seriously analyzed. Meanwhile, teachers and counselors who work with Russian and Eastern European students whose number in some school districts may grow very rapidly, as is the case in the high school where we conducted our research, might need help right away.[1]

The purpose of this chapter is to provide U.S. educators with some insights into major differences between U.S. and Russian cultures in general, and between some U.S. and Russian educational practices in particular. I strongly believe that the cultural awareness that results from these insights can facilitate more effective academic achievement and promote more successful social adjustment among immigrant students from the former Soviet Union, as well as provide ideas for teacher educators preparing students to teach all populations of students whose home culture differs from the dominant, white, middle-class culture of U.S. society and most teachers. I also argue in my conclusions that this sort of cultural awareness is neglected in mainstream multicultural education courses in teacher preparation programs.

I will base my narrative on three main sources: Ongoing ethnographic research on Russian-speaking students in one high school in the northeastern United States (Ageyev & Goulah, 2003); content analyses of written reflections by teachers enrolled in my graduate teacher education courses on multicultural, intercultural, and sociocultural education; and my personal experience teaching at the university level in both Russia and the United States.

ISSUES OF IDENTITY

When families, adults and children alike, move from one country to another, especially when the countries are so drastically different as is the case with Russia and the United States, their identity is profoundly changed and they face many challenges in the process of constructing their new identity. The major challenge for U.S. teachers is to recognize the enormous ethnic diversity of students who emigrate nowadays from the former Soviet Union. The mere task of remembering all the names of the diverse ethnicities and nationalities can be a problem in itself. As one student in my class put it:

> It is just not possible to remember all the names of all these nationalities coming from the former Soviet Union. You'd never know where the next national conflict will occur, and folks from there would come here, and nobody has ever heard about this nationality before, let alone the knowledge of their culture. How am I supposed

to be sensitive to and knowledgeable of this particular culture that I've never heard before and nobody ever taught me about?

Another student wrote:

> I'm totally confused. All these kids seem to be quite fluent in Russian, and tend to congregate together using predominantly Russian language. But on my question about their background some of them would say, Yes, I'm Russian, while others would say, No, actually I'm Ukrainian (Byelorussian, Moldavian, Kazak, etc.). This I can understand. The confusing part is that sometimes the very same student identifies himself/herself as Russian in one situation, while denying being Russian in others—strongly insisting, for example, on his/her Ukrainian or Belarusian identity.

This kind of multiple, complex, or confused identity is the rule rather than an exception when it comes to an ethnically diverse population of students from the former Soviet Union (as well for many other immigrants from elsewhere). For many of them, especially for those not ethnically Russian, the major challenge is to accept the Russian identity that is imposed on them by their new social environment, including their teachers and peers, an identity that they often are quite unwilling to accept. It is true that most of them are truly bilingual and can use Russian language as fluently as their native language, often with little or no accent whatsoever. (This situation may change in the future due to the loss of status, popularity, and prestige of the Russian language in some parts of the former Soviet Union that have become independent republics.) Yet, the challenge of negotiating and reconstructing one's new identity remains.

This confusion between Russian and Russian-speaking presents a real challenge for many non-Russian teachers, as the following example illustrates. Boris, a 15-year-old Ukrainian said, in quite an emotional manner:

> You Americans never learn who is who. Something might be wrong with your brain. No matter how many times I had said I was Ukrainian, not Russian, nobody remembered it. Every teacher keeps calling me Russian. And eventually I gave up. And nowadays I do not object when they call me Russian and do not correct them any longer. Personally, I'm fine with this. My best friends are Russians. But if you'd ever try to call my old folks, especially, my grandfather Russian, you'd be in big trouble. My folks, they all hate Russians for what they did to Ukrainians during revolution.

Clearly, not all cases are as dramatic, or anti-Russian feelings as strong as in the case of this family. But even if there is no any hostility, or negative feelings toward Russians, the necessity of accepting this new Russian identity for Russian-speaking, but not ethnically Russian students, can be quite challenging. We all want to be taken for what we really are. And immigration, as with some other major changes in life, makes our search for identity even more salient and intense. Here are some things U.S. teachers can do to facilitate their immigrant students' process of reconstructing their identity.

First, recognize that immigrants take their identity quite seriously. It is different from the rather indulgent attitude prevalent in white, middle-class U.S. culture, where people are easily excused for not remembering one's exact combination and ratio of different ethnic backgrounds. But forgetting who was Serbian, and who was Bosnian, for example, could have cost one one's life during the war in Bosnia in the mid-1990s. Teachers need to be aware of these aspects of identity and take steps to fully understand the country of origin, language, and ethnicity for each student. We also recommend practices used by some teachers in our study, like the art teacher who said, "I'm getting better. I have them take me to the map over in Mr. Brown's room next door and point out where they are from. It's easier for me to get a visual."

INTERPERSONAL RELATIONSHIPS

Another challenge the Russian-speaking students face is the difficulty of interacting with their U.S. peers. Both immigrant students and their parents often cited fights in the cafeteria and social ostracism as problems the students faced. As Olga, put it, "Why do they [U.S. students] hate us? They ignore us. They just joke, make fun of us." One father said it is so bad that his son "never leaves the house; he has no friends." Analysis of Russian-American cultural differences is needed in order to understand the deep roots of these difficulties in communication and interpersonal relationships. What follows is my attempt to bring modern advances in the field of cross-cultural psychology into the field of mainstream multicultural education through an examination of some important dimensions of cultural differences.

INDIVIDUALISM VERSUS COLLECTIVISM

There is a rare consensus among researchers in defining white, middle-class U.S. culture as highly individualistic and Russian culture as much more collectivistic (Triandis, 1995; Alexander, 2000; Ageyev, 2003). A famous study of more than 50 countries and regions on all five continents by Hofstede (1997) ranked the United States as the number one individualistic country on the continuum of Individualism versus Collectivism. Differences between individualist and collectivist cultures are numerous, profound, and encompassing.

According to Hofstede, in collectivist cultures: "People are born into extended families or other ingroups which continue to protect them in exchange for loyalty . . . identity is based in the social network to which one belongs . . . children learn to think in terms of 'we' . . . relationship prevails over task," while in individualist cultures: "Everyone grows up to look after him/herself and his/her immediate (nuclear) family only . . . identity is based in the individual . . . children learn to think in terms of 'I' . . . and task prevails over relationship" (1997, p. 67).

Other researchers have added many other important distinctions between collectivist and individualist cultures. For instance, in individualist cultures, goals of an individual prevail over the goals of a group; independence, self-reliance, and privacy are highly valued. In collectivist cultures, on the contrary, goals of the group prevail over the goals of an individual; interdependence is highly valued and privacy is downplayed (Brislin & Yoshida, 1994). Interpersonal relationships seem to be more numerous and diverse in individualistic cultures, yet tend to be short-term oriented, while in collectivist culture interpersonal relationships, though not as multiple and diverse, tend to be long-term oriented (Cushner & Brislin, 1997). In sum, collectivists tend to overemphasize the personal, or interpersonal component of any social interaction, including teacher-student interactions, while individualists tend to de-emphasize it.

LOW-CONTEXT VERSUS HIGH-CONTEXT OF COMMUNICATION

United States culture is often defined as a Low-Context Communication Culture, or Direct Communication Culture (Hall, 1976). "Say, what you mean! Don't beat around bush! Don't make me guess!" Maxims like these can be seen as the true communicative logos of U.S. culture. The opposite is true in many other countries and cultures, including Russia, where communication patterns are often defined as high-context or indirect communication.

A high-context communicative pattern is one in which "most of the information is either in the physical context or internalized in the person, while very little is in the coded, explicit, transmitted part of the message" (Hall, 1976, p. 79). Thus, while "low-context communication tends to be direct, precise, and clear, high-context communication tends to be indirect and ambiguous" (Gudykunst, 2004, p. 57). There are many perfectly logical reasons for being indirect in high-context communication cultures, including specific cultural conventions, like a generalized attitude of conflict avoidance and "saving face," for example. The differences between high- and low-context styles of communication have a huge impact on interpersonal interaction and are believed to be among the most frequent sources of intercultural misunderstandings, cultural blunders, culture clashes, and mutual frustration in interpersonal relationships (Hofstede, 1997; Fry & Bjorkquist, 1997).

MASCULINITY VERSUS FEMININITY

It is a little more difficult to compare the United States and Russia from the point of view of this third dimension, masculinity versus femininity, and the conclusions that follow from the limited research data available may seem counterintuitive and even contradictive, especially when considered in the light of achievements by women's liberation and gender equality movements in the U.S. during past half century. That is why one should pay special attention to the criteria upon which the classification of masculine and feminine cultures is based in the field of cross-cultural psychology (i.e., assertiveness versus modesty).

According to Hofstede (1997), the United States ranked 15th on the assertiveness dimension, while the former Yugoslavia ranked 46th, which means that American culture seems to be rather masculine, while Yugoslavian culture seems to be quite feminine. Russia was not included in Hofstede's first sample, but by all accounts, Russian and Serbian cultures have much in common. We do not know of any recent research focusing specifically on the feminine nature of Russian culture or directly comparing American masculinity with Russian femininity. However, a century-long tradition in Russian history, philosophy, and literature, portraying Russia as a feminine culture, as well as some indirect data that can be drawn from recent empirical research, including our own research on Russian-American stereotypes (Stephan, Ageyev, Coates-Shrider, Stephan & Abalakina, 1994), seem to corroborate Hofstede's conclusions (Alexander, 2000). In short, the more masculine a given culture is, the more emphasis is put on assertiveness as a basic cultural value and a desirable societal and educational goal for all, and especially for men. The more feminine a given culture is, the more emphasis is put on modesty (as the opposite of assertiveness) as a basic cultural value for both men and women.

These three examples of cultural differences may have a direct impact on the problems Russian-speaking students have interacting with their American peers. For instance, for a student who has just arrived in the United States from a highly collectivist, high-context communication, and feminine culture, the culturally familiar way to interact with others (friends, peers, and teachers) is to be indirect, interdependent, collaborative, noncompetitive, nonassertive, personal, and modest. Can we predict what would happen to a student with such a communicative attitude in a typical U.S. classroom?

The age of adolescence is characterized by the search for identity. It is the age when the first deep friendships based on similarity of values, manners, tastes, and behaviors are being developed. It is clear that even very subtle differences, including those just described, can become a reason for exclusion, isolation, and ostracism. To aggravate the situation, many of the recent immigrants from the former Soviet Union are deeply religious and follow a rather restrictive dress code. In addition, some immigrant students might not be aware, at least at first, of the rigorous norms of hygiene in the United States, which can be very different from what they were accustomed to in their home countries. All these differences create a fertile ground for cultural clash, and may preclude Russian-speaking immigrant students from establishing normal relationships with their American peers.

Although the opportunity for teachers to regulate interpersonal relationships among culturally diverse students is limited, some initiatives can be
helpful. For instance, as some teachers in our study took steps to include the
immigrant students' language and culture in class, nonimmigrant students became
more familiar with their immigrant peers and barriers began to fall. Measures
such as those taken in the advanced English as a Second Language (ESL) class
we observed, where immigrant and nonimmigrant students are brought together for open dialogue on cultural perceptions of each other, and where
immigrant students present aspects of their culture to their U.S. peers, are very
useful in bridging communication gaps between the two populations. A math
teacher and a biology teacher stated that they encouraged students to teach the
entire class a couple of Russian words each day. The class repeats the words
and tries to use them with the students. This not only validates the immigrant
students' language, but also cultivates communication between them and their
nonimmigrant peers. Another math teacher began using words like *kniga* (book)
and *domashiniya rabota* (homework) in class and allowed students to work in
pairs or groups if they desired.

SCHOOL-PARENT CONNECTIONS

Yet another challenge for Russian immigrants is poor communication between
the school and the parents. This is perhaps the most culturally rooted aspect
of the immigrants' experience with U.S. schools and it manifests itself in a
number of areas. Russian immigrants coming from a collectivist culture find
themselves in an unfamiliar individualistic environment, which creates many
gaps in communication. Among the important differences between individualistic and collectivistic cultures mentioned above, the distinction between long-
term and short-term orientation in personal relationship is especially relevant.
Russian parents seek long-term types of communication and relationship formation with American teachers, as they used to do in their home country.

Another dimension of intercultural variability, the distinction between
large and *small power distance cultures*, is also relevant. According to Hofstede
(1997), the major criterion of defining culture as possessing relatively large, or
relatively small power distance, is the way the society at large deals with
inequality. That is, the more willingly people accept inequality, the larger the
power distance of the society is. Of the 53 countries and regions of the world
in Hofstede's sample, the former Yugoslavia ranked 12th, which means a relatively large power distance, and the U.S. ranked 38th, which means a relatively
small power distance. Our task here is not to describe all the potential consequences, manifestations, and complications of these profound cultural differences, but to indicate simply that in cultures with large power distance, of
which Russia is clearly an example, schools, school administrations, and teachers are still seen much more as authority figures than in small power distance
cultures such as the United States.

This means that parents in large power distance cultures hardly ever contest any of the teachers' decisions, including curriculum issues, pedagogical strategies, or students' grades, for example. In the rare case of conflict between teachers and students, parents hardly ever take sides with their children, and any kind of legal action against the school or individual teachers is almost unheard of. As democratic reform progresses in Russia, people's awareness of their rights grows, and the prestige of the educational professions declines, things are likely to change. But for now, the large power distance view of schools and teachers as authority figures still remains pretty much intact in the minds of people emigrating from the former Soviet Union.

Large versus small power distance differences also play an important role in communication breaches between U.S. schools and teachers and Russian parents. For example, parents in our study repeatedly stated that they have no means of knowing their children's homework. "In Russia," parents informed us, "there were daily or weekly journals in which teachers wrote assignments, student behavior, and progress. Parents must write their initial beside each entry so the teacher knows they have seen it." The journals also act as a way for parents to help their children with homework. Clearly, those parents were referring to what is called "Dynamic Assessment," a practice still common in the former Soviet Union and now considered a cutting edge innovation in U.S. educational theory (Kozulin, Gindis, Ageyev & Miller, 2003).

The parents also stated that they never receive phone calls regarding their children, which many teachers validated saying they never *have* to call home, as the immigrant students usually do not have discipline-related problems. Other teachers stated they were apprehensive calling the home because they did not know if the parents spoke English. Lastly, parents stated they had no idea what curricular and extracurricular activities were available to them and their children through the school, because nobody ever told them. When asked why they did not contact the school to find out, they stated they had no way of knowing what to call about or who to address their questions to. Over and over again, we could see the repetition of the same pattern of miscommunication, with Russian parents complaining to U.S. teachers "Why did you not tell us this and that?" And U.S. teachers complaining to Russian parents "Why did you not ask us about this and that?"

Teachers often claim that they did send parents a letter at the very beginning of the semester that contained a lot of information they would need. But one has to ask, what would be the value of these letters for people whose English is limited or nonexistent? Besides, in many collectivistic and high-context communication cultures, the power of interpersonal communication is far greater than the written text. Therefore, it is crucial that the American schools take the initiative in establishing relationships with families that have immigrated from large power distance cultures. Many parents stated that repeated contact was necessary to make them knowledgeable enough about U.S. school matters to be able to look after the progress of their child and establish more long-term relationships. Such initiative by U.S. schools could alleviate unneeded anxiety and isolation felt by the immigrant families.

FROM MULTICULTURAL TO INTERCULTURAL EDUCATION: THE NEED FOR INTERCULTURAL DIALOGUE

No one would contest the necessity of courses on educational and developmental psychology in teacher education. And for almost a century, these courses have been firmly embedded in teacher preparation programs in the United States. The situation is different with multicultural education, which varies greatly from one educational institution to another and is as diverse as diversity itself. Multicultural education is a relatively new addition to the field of educational studies and there has not been enough time for the subject to be solidly embedded into teacher education programs. Even more importantly, it is generally not connected with the academic disciplines for which studying cultures itself is a paramount concern, including cultural anthropology, cross-cultural psychology, or intercultural communication.

I strongly believe that what the modern generation of U.S. teachers need first and foremost, in the face of ever growing diversity of learners in U.S. schools, is the willingness, readiness, and skill to engage in "authentic intercultural dialogue" with their diverse students who come from nondominant cultures, native and immigrant, and to be able to help their students do the same. The following example illustrates what I mean by authentic intercultural dialogue. It is a simple and quite concrete and operational concept, but it does require some fundamental changes in the teacher's attitude and behavior. As one math teacher reports:

> I had a rather obnoxious Russian kid in my 7th grade. He'd always bring some arrogant comparative remarks in class, like "What kind of math is this, in Russia we used to solve this problem when I was yet in the 5th grade," or when I'd bring a deck of card for some math game, that consisted, as usual of 52 cards, he would argue that this is a wrong number, and that, back in Russia, the right number of cards in the deck was always 36, not 52. Or else, he would get engaged in an argument on how much better the metric system is, compared with all this stupid inches and pounds. At first I'd find it to be very annoying and even disruptive, and quite honestly tried simply shut him up. But after taking your class, I realized that I could use it more productive way. I took a risk, and once, instead of shutting him up, I simply asked him, using the above mentioned examples, if it is really better to start studying more complex math problem in earlier grades, rather than later, and why, or could the game I had in mind be played by using 36 cards, not 52, etc. To my surprise, other kids in class got interested in his answers, and everything else he had to tell about

Russia, and we all had an amazing conversation on many issues I'd never imagined they were interested in.

This example illustrates the enormous educational potential of intercultural dialogue in the classroom, and beyond, when addressing issues raised by resistant students with an attitude, be they working-class American students, or Russian-speaking immigrant students. The simple fact is that immigrant children, and culturally diverse learners in general, have trouble making their points articulate and interesting for their peers by themselves. They need help from their teachers. The good news is that to provide this much needed help, U.S. teachers do not have to study Russian language, nor do they have to do an extensive in-depth study of Russian culture, an apprehension many teachers have while working with immigrant students. Certainly, all kinds of knowledge about immigrant students' home culture is highly beneficial, but what U.S. teachers really need to have is the ability to hear their students' different cultural voices (as well as their own) and to facilitate dialogue between these voices.

It is clear that the teacher's ability to hear these sometimes vague and inarticulate cultural voices is not an innate capacity. It is a skill that, as with most other social skills, is socially constructed (Vygotsky, 1978) and gained, for instance, through extensive personal intercultural experience, such as a sojourn in a foreign country, or a carefully designed intercultural teacher education course. Can teachers develop such important skills within the traditional format of teacher preparation programs? I believe they can and should, but conscious effort must be made to direct their development to new attitudes of cultural awareness.

The typical attitude of the white, middle-class teachers, who constitute a majority of students in a typical teacher education program, can be described by a question that I am often asked at the beginning of my class: "Could you teach me all I need to know about other cultures so I can become more culturally sensitive and skillful as a teacher, and more successfully meet some the educational needs of my culturally diverse learners?" At first glance this question seems to reflect the best possible pedagogical attitude. In fact, it does not because if I ask, as I usually do, "How about your own culture? Do you want to learn about it?" I usually get one of the two following answers, plus some laughs: "Are you kidding, professor? I know all I need to know about my culture," or even better, "Are you kidding, professor? We don't have a culture; we're just normal."

It is imperative that this attitude, this unrecognized condescendence, be acknowledged and changed. Authentic intercultural dialogue is possible only between equals. Any, even the slightest, condescendence may jeopardize it. Authentic intercultural dialogue presupposes an attitude which can be best described as: "Let us compare in what ways, small and big, my culture and yours are different from each other, so we can think together how to bridge, to overcome, these differences in a nonjudgmental and creative manner." How can teacher education programs prepare teachers to conduct such authentic intercultural dialogue?

Intercultural dialogue is possible in each grade, in each subject matter, in each curriculum, with all sorts of culturally diverse students. As soon as there are culturally diverse learners in the classroom, the major conditions for initiating intercultural dialogue are present. The thing that remains is the teacher's awareness, willingness, readiness, and skill in initiating it. How can teacher preparation programs help to develop this awareness, willingness, readiness, and skill? How can novice teachers without extensive intercultural experience learn how to use intercultural dialogue in their own classroom? These questions forced me think deeply about how classes on multicultural education are traditionally taught and led me to recognize the need for change. The following are but a few strategies that consistently prove to be successful in my classes on intercultural education.

1. Exploring cultural differences. Students in my classes usually spend a lot of time exploring all kinds of cultural differences, big and small, some of them highly relevant to educational issues, others seemingly mundane. It is crucial that this kind of exploration take place simultaneously on two levels and combine together two different discourses: academic (theory, research data) and personal (narrative, individual stories). Neither of these two discourses alone seems to be able to promote a capacity to go beyond one's own cultural convention and to break through one's own cultural encapsulation.

   It is also crucial that this exploration of cultural differences take place as dialogical, some important features of which are: active listening, continual perception checking, co-construction of meaning, and constant comparison of analytical/theoretical information taken from textbooks with students' personal experience. Using the Bakhtinian framework (1981), a successful multicultural education classroom will have at least five types of dialogue going on: students in dialogue with the teacher; students in dialogue with each other; students in dialogue with their own culture; students in dialogue with other students' culture; and last, a personal-narrative discourse in dialogue with an analytical-theoretical discourse.

2. Embracing controversial topics and themes, including such sensitive matters as cultural stereotypes and prejudices, and not shying away from discussing these issues. Embracing negative cultural attitudes does not mean condoning, or justifying them. It simply means an honest attempt to understand the real causes of prejudice, stereotypes, or any other form of culturally biased and preconceived ideas individuals have about each other.

3. Exposing teachers to a variety of educational theories and practices that have originated outside the U.S. educational mainstream. The following works discuss theories and practices that may work better with, and correspond more properly to, the skills, expectations, and attitudes of culturally diverse learners: Vygotsky's sociocultural perspective on child development and learning (Vygotsky, 1978; Kozulin, et al., 2003); Bakhtin's (1981) dialogical perspective on culture, literacy, and learning (Ball & Freedman, 2004); Freire's (1994) *Pedagogy of the Oppressed*, and Finn's (1999) approach to educating working-class students in their own self-interest.

CONCLUSION

I have given but a few examples of how authentic intercultural dialogue can bring much positive change, empower both U.S. teachers and Russian-speaking students, and help the latter adjust to realities of U.S. schools. In order to offer opportunities for U.S. teachers to develop awareness of their own culture, and to consider the impact of cultural differences on their teaching and on their students' learning, teacher education programs need to include information on the ways U.S. culture differs from that of other countries, in general, and in school culture, educational theories, and pedagogies, in particular. With this information and understanding well in hand, teachers can begin to develop a pedagogy based in intercultural dialogue and thus take the first steps toward establishing authentic multicultural classrooms.

NOTE

1. This study is based on data collected at a primarily Caucasian, middle- and working-class suburban high school in upstate New York. Data consists of audiotaped interviews, observations, informal discussions, field notes, and reflective journaling. Interview data came from three students (two Belarussian females and one Kazak female), four parents (two Russian; two Bellarussian), seven teachers (one English as a Second Language (ESL); two social studies; two math; one biology; one art) and two reading paraprofessionals. Interviews and discussions occurred in English with simultaneous Russian translation when needed and ranged from thirty minutes to two hours. Observational data, informal discussions and field notes were taken from an advanced ESL class. Also present in the ESL class, in addition to the three students described above, were students from Russia, Ukraine, Kosovo, Finland, and Thailand.

REFERENCES

Ageyev, V. S. (2003). Lev Vygotsky in the mirror of cultural interpretations. In A. Kozulin, B. Gindis, V. S. Ageyev, & S. Miller (Eds.), *Vygotsky's educational theory in cultural context*. Cambridge, UK: Cambridge University Press, 432–449.

Ageyev, V. S., & Goulah, J. (2003, June 15–18). Teaching American educators about Russian and East European culture. Paper presented at the UNESCO Conference on Intercultural Education, Jyvaskyla, Finland. The paper is published in the Conference Proceedings.

Alexander, R. J. (2000). *Culture and pedagogy: International comparisons in primary education.* Malden MA: Blackwell.

Bakhtin, M. M. (1981). *Dialogic imagination.* Austin: University of Texas Press.

Ball, A. F., & Freedman, S. W. (Eds.). (2004). *Bakhtinian perspective on language, literacy, and learning.* Cambridge, UK: Cambridge University Press.

Brislin, R., & Yoshida, T. (Eds.). (1994). *Improving intercultural interactions: Modules for cross-cultural training programs, Vol. 1.* Thousand Oaks, CA: Sage.

Cushner, K., & Brislin, R. (Eds.). (1997). *Improving intercultural interactions: Modules for cross-cultural training programs. Vol. 2.* Thousand Oaks, CA: Sage.

Gudykunst, W. B. (2004). *Bridging differences: Effective intergroup communication* (4th Ed.). Thousand Oaks, CA: Sage.

Finn, P. (1999). *Literacy with an attitude: Educating working-class children in their own self-interest.* Albany: State University of New York Press.

Freire, P. (1994). *Pedagogy of the oppressed.* New York: Continuum Publishing.

Fry, D., & Bjorkqvist, K. (Eds.). (1997). *Cultural variations in conflict resolution: Alternatives to violence.* Mahwah, NJ: Lawrence Elrbaum.

Hall, E. T. (1976). *Beyond culture.* New York: Doubleday.

Harrington-Lueker, D. (1991, January). Demography as destiny: Immigration and schools. *The Education Digest,* 4–6.

Hofstede, G. (1997). *Cultures and organizations: Software of the mind.* 2nd Ed. London: McGraw-Hill.

Hoot, J. L., & Bonkareva, E. (1992). Understanding the special needs of former soviet children. *Childhood Education* 69(2), 82–85.

Kozulin, A., Gindis, B., Ageyev, V. S., & Miller, S. M. (Eds.). (2003). *Vygotsky's educational theory in cultural context.* Cambridge, UK: Cambridge University Press.

Li, G. (2002). *"East is east, west is west"? Home literacy, culture, and schooling.* New York: Peter Lang.

Stephan, W. G., Ageyev, V. S., Coates-Shrider, L., Stephan, C. W., & Abalakina, M. (1994). On the relationship between stereotypes and prejudice: An international study. *Personality and Social Psychology Bulletin, 2,* 277–284.

Triandis, H. (1995). *Individualism and collectivism.* Boulder, CO: Westview Press.

Vygotsky, L. S. (1978). *Mind in society.* Cambridge, MA: Harvard University Press.

Part IV

Social Justice Teacher Education through Professional Development

11 Urban Teacher Development That Changes Classrooms, Curriculum, and Achievement

Jeffrey M. R. Duncan-Andrade

JEFFREY M. R. DUNCAN-ANDRADE, ASSISTANT PROFESSOR of Education and Codirector of the Cesar Chavez Institute, San Francisco State University, examines the potential of critical teacher inquiry groups to promote urban teacher retention, professional support, and development. Drawing on analysis of data gathered from a group of South Central Los Angeles elementary teachers who used critical inquiry to support each other in tackling multiple forms of inequity, he recommends inquiry groups as critical professional development to support teachers confronting the challenges of urban schools.

"The Voice of the New Teacher" (Public Education Network, 2003) lists peer interaction (formal and informal) as two of the five most positive influences on teachers' early careers. The report also lists the absence of resources and the "lack of a strong professional community" and positive school culture as the biggest concerns for new urban teachers (p. 20). In response to these and other reports that express concerns over poor retention and professional development plans for urban teachers, an increasing number of researchers are calling for professional development that emphasizes teacher dialogue and collaboration. This has led to a series of studies examining the use of inquiry groups as a site for teacher development that provides a more collaborative professional environment.

The narrative about the working conditions in urban schools is hardly ever positive. Typically, one of two extremes is described. The first is the school out of control, completely dysfunctional, often with absentee school leadership, and a school culture with little support and few opportunities for collaboration for teachers and students. The other is the "Joe Clark reform school" model, where teachers and students alike are under constant surveillance and threat of punitive measures, reducing teacher collaboration to shared grumblings over meaningless staff meetings and excessive rules and regulations. While these types of school environments do exist, a more accurate narrative of urban school climates describes schools that are searching for answers. Historically, these answers have been offered by outsiders with outdated or limited insight into the rapidly changing conditions of urban teaching.

A growing number of teacher education researchers suggest that the solution to this de-professionalization of teachers lies with teachers themselves. Their research investigates what it is that teachers want and need to remain in urban classrooms and to be successful there (Hunter-Quartz, Olsen, & Duncan-Andrade, in press; Nieto, 2003). One of the key findings of this research is evidence of the power of teacher dialogue, mentorship, and collaboration as ways to stimulate professional engagement and growth.

INQUIRY GROUPS AS PROFESSIONAL DEVELOPMENT

The use of teacher inquiry groups, which is also commonly referred to as teacher research, has gained momentum as a response to literature that suggests the importance of teacher dialogue and self-study (Cochran-Smith & Lytle, 1993, 1999; Goswami & Stillman, 1987). This approach to professional development is guided by the principle that teachers are capable professionals, able to engage in meaningful self-improvement when given the proper intellectual and professional space. This belief, although commonsensical to those of us who have taught, remains contested in the field of teacher education. Nowhere is this more true than in urban schools, where rampant failure serves to justify the continuation of deskilling approaches to teacher work and professional development.

Part of the dispute over the capacity of teachers to control their own professional development can be traced to the historical marginalization of the profession of teaching. The history of teaching as semiprofessional, and one of the only viable professional employment options for women, has meant that control of the profession has been in the hands of outsiders (mostly white men) (Lortie, 1975). This resistance to teacher inquiry and research is also due, in part, to the false notion that if teachers engage in self-study, by default they are not using professional developers' services. The combination of these two approaches, where teachers draw from their own context specific expertise to discuss problem areas and explore solutions, while also identifying areas where they need additional support from outside sources, is a more sensible option, but one that is rarely employed.

This is precisely the approach to professional growth that good teacher inquiry recommends. Broadly defined, teacher inquiry brings together a group of teachers from a school to discuss pertinent issues in their classroom practice. The ways that these groups are developed can vary widely, ranging from grade level teams in elementary schools to subject matter teams in secondary schools. Some schools prefer to use a model where teachers are placed in mixed groups, based on teaching assignment and/or level of experience. Although group size can vary, the fact that the inquiry process is meant to be dialogic suggests that groups benefit from being small enough to allow full participation from members and large enough to permit a range of perspectives (generally somewhere between five and seven teachers).

INQUIRY GROUP ACTIVITY SYSTEMS

The most common and the most comprehensive activity strategy used in inquiry groups is a self-study of teacher-defined research questions. In this activity, teachers identify research questions that investigate core issues in their classroom, collect data (student interviews, student work, video of lessons, field notes), and review the literature to situate their analysis in a theoretical framework. The inquiry groups meet regularly to discuss their research, reading, and data analysis, and to provide support as each teacher produces a written analysis of their questions and shares that information with the group.

However, inquiry groups can also employ a variety of separate activities that drive group conversations, as well as broader self-studies that are not necessarily tied to research questions. Some of the other common activity systems are: shared readings, video lesson study, student work sampling, best practices, and theme driven meetings. The shared readings approach presents teachers with a set of readings on a topic of interest that they then come together to discuss, focusing on the relevance of the readings to their own practice and growth. The video lesson study approach has one teacher videotape a lesson in his or her class that the inquiry group watches and gives the teacher feedback, emphasizing what is being done well and suggesting concrete strategies that might improve weaker parts of the pedagogy.

Student work sampling has teachers select work examples from a set of focal students that capture the full range of academic performance in their classroom. The inquiry group's examination of this work allows teachers to study closely, dialogue, and receive concrete action strategies for maintaining growth across the achievement span. In the best practices strategy, participants bring in their best curriculum unit, activity system, or other teaching tool to share with the group. Like the other activity systems, the sharing of best practices opens dialogue about the undergirding philosophy of education that guides a teacher's practice and creates the opportunity for teachers to be experts and learners among their colleagues.

Theme driven inquiry meetings are used to respond to a particular topic of interest identified by the group, such as the most pressing concerns in their classrooms or larger professional experience. Here, teachers receive the type of focused support that is most pertinent to improving their practice, rather than the more traditional school-wide professional development model that is generally unresponsive to specific needs of individual teachers.

DO INQUIRY GROUPS WORK?

There is a growing body of literature that suggests inquiry groups are a powerful form of professional development (Cochran-Smith & Lytle, 1993; Dana & Yendol-Silva, 2003; Richardson, 1994) that does improve teacher learning and collaboration. This growth can be attributed largely to the fact that the inquiry comes from "real-world observations and dilemmas" (Hubbard

& Power, 2003), and investigates issues grounded in participants' immediate practice, which is more likely to develop into improved classroom teaching and learning. It is also more likely to produce a sense of professionalism and to develop the internal capacity of teachers to address pressing issues in classrooms.

This call for more teacher control over their professional environment is echoed by Ingersoll (2003), who found that "increasing the control wielded by teachers has a positive effect on relations between teachers and administrators." His analysis of the perspectives of over 5,000 teachers reveals that school culture and, ergo, student achievement, are deeply shaped by the amount of control that is given to teachers. Teachers want input into the social culture of the school, not just the curricular decisions they are more often invited to help make. In short, Ingersoll (2003) reveals that teachers want an autonomous inquiry type of professional development, one that allows them to research, collaborate, and address cultural and disciplinary issues in their class and in the school (pp. 245–246).

It is important to note that some researchers caution teacher-inquiry participants to remember that this increasingly popular form of professional development has roots in a long history of Freirean, praxis-based, critical-philosophical inquiry. Without this perspective, teacher inquiry could become just another out of the box type of professional development. Fox & Fleishcher (2001, p. 188) argue:

> . . . in order for [teacher inquiry] to continue to have an impact, its practitioners must continue to be self critical. We must be vigilant about our work as we ask difficult questions about our role as class-room inquirers: What are our responsibilities and relationships toward the students with whom we research? toward their parents? toward our administrators? toward the larger community?

Nieto (2003) has made a similar argument about the need for teacher inquiry to be increasingly more intellectually critical. Her most recent research into what keeps teachers going reveals that veteran and new urban teachers alike want teacher development that advances "the model of teacher-as-intellectual . . . providing *time and support* for teachers to meet and work together." This, she contends, is a major challenge in most urban schools, where the professional development model "is defined as bringing in experts to do a workshop" (p. 126).

CRITICAL INQUIRY AT POWER ELEMENTARY

While much of the literature on teacher inquiry suggests that it is an effective tool for teacher development and increased professionalism, too little attention has been paid to the use of this professional development model to promote teaching for social justice. With that in mind, the remainder of this chapter will focus on a social justice oriented teacher-inquiry group in a South Central Los Angeles public elementary school. After briefly introducing the origins of the group and its participants, the chapter will examine the impact of teacher inquiry with a social justice agenda, focusing on four key questions: (1) What were the philosophical underpinnings of the group? (2) What were the readings that guided group discussions? (3) What sorts of dialogue was generated from those readings? (4) How did those readings and discussions impact the classroom practice and student achievement of participants?

THE PARTICIPANTS

The principal at Power Elementary was in his second year at the start of this program. In his first year he had worked hard to develop the reputation that the school welcomed partnerships with universities. Based on this reputation, I approached him about the development of a teacher-inquiry group that would gather teachers at the school committed to developing as social justice educators (Oakes & Lipton, 2001). In keeping with his reputation, the principal invited all interested teachers to an informational meeting. Seven teachers (see Table 11.1), several of whom were already working together on various projects, and all of whom were familiar with each other's commitments to social justice education, volunteered to participate in the program for three years. In exchange for their participation, teachers received annual university extension credits, copies of the selected readings, and dinner at each meeting.

THE ROLE OF THE RESEARCHER

I am a researcher directing a three-year UCLA Graduate School of Education research project examining the impact of critical teacher inquiry on teacher development, retention, and efficacy. My role in the Power Elementary inquiry

Table 11.1. *Power Elementary Critical Inquiry Participants (2003–2004)*

Name	Ethnicity	Gender	Yrs teaching	Grade level
Ms. Grant	Black	F	7	4th
Mr. Ballesteros	Philippino-Chinese	M	3	4th
Mr. Truong	Philippino-Chinese	M	3	5th
Ms. Kim	Korean-American	F	3	3rd
Mr. Kinsman	Assyrian	M	6	1st/2nd
Ms. O'Reilly	Scots-Irish	F	4	2nd
Mr. Vasquez	Chicano	M	5	3rd

group was to help teachers locate readings that address topics that they designated and to facilitate the group's discussion of these readings and their relevance to their school and classroom. These discussions were videotaped and transcribed for data collection. Additionally, I made myself available for individual meetings, phone conversations, and electronic exchanges to extend the dialogue and to provide additional support. Immediately prior to beginning this research project, I finished my tenth year teaching in the Oakland, California, public secondary schools. I did not know any of the participants personally before our first meeting; however, my teaching experience allowed me to sympathize closely with the group's struggles, which made it easier for us to bond quickly.

The remainder of this chapter is an analysis of activities that took place in the second year of the group's meetings. The culmination of this second year was a set of self-study research papers that the participants presented at the American Educational Research Association's (AERA) national conference in San Diego, California.

A PHILOSOPHY OF CRITICAL TEACHER INQUIRY
FOR SOCIAL JUSTICE

To better understand the guiding principles of the Power Elementary inquiry group, it is important to briefly attend to the term "critical," which has quickly become the quintessential modifier for progressive practices in urban schools (i.e., critical literacy, critical inquiry, critical reflection). The modern use of the term critical in educational discourse is often linked to Freire's notion of critical pedagogy and its relationship to liberatory pedagogy. In his seminal work, *Pedagogy of the Oppressed* (1970), Freire relies on a Marxist dialectic framework to define the three-stage process of being critical.

For Freire, the first stage of being critical is the attainment of an awareness of the existence of oppressive conditions and recognition of the causes of those conditions (Stage A). This awareness generates a desire to pursue a "fuller humanity . . . the authentic struggle to transform the situation" through action (Stage B). But, this transformative action is critical only when "it is not merely an occupation but also a preoccupation, that is, when it is not dichotomized from reflection" (Stage C). This process of awareness, transformative action, and reflection is what Freire refers to as praxis: "reflection and action upon the world in order to transform it" (pp. 29–35). This process is ultimately a dialectical one, each stage informing the other and returning one to the first stage to begin again the critical dialogue that leads to action (see Figure 11.1).

For the group at Power Elementary, teacher inquiry began with critical dialogue about issues facing their students, their school, and the surrounding community. This dialogue was sparked by teacher-led discussions of readings they selected to address issues of social and economic inequality in schools and the larger society. These discussions spawned a cycle of teacher praxis that

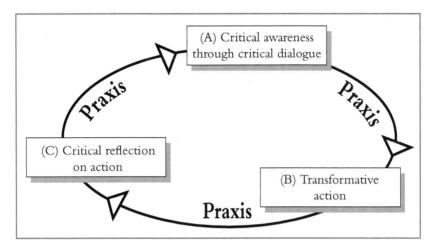

Figure 11.1. *Freirean framework of critical teacher inquiry.*

began with raising the teachers' critical awareness and led to the design and implementation of social justice curriculum and pedagogy as a transformative action. Teachers then studied and reflected on this curriculum and transformative pedagogy, which returned them to a critical dialogue with a new awareness, restarting the cycle of their praxis.

In the second year of the inquiry group, this praxis took shape in five-week cycles of two-hour weekly meetings focused on the work going on in their classrooms, issues of social justice, and a cycle of activities that were designed to support the teachers in the study of their own classroom practices. The activity cycle was as follows:

- Week 1: Teacher-led dialogue on shared readings.
- Week 2: Large-group discussion of curriculum planning.
- Week 3: Partnered discussion of student work.
- Week 4: Video lesson study of selected group member.
- Week 5: Writing and reflection time on self-study research.

This chapter focuses specifically on the impact of teacher-led dialogue and shared readings, the pursuant research conference presentations, and evaluations of student achievement.

READINGS TO GUIDE SOCIAL JUSTICE INQUIRY GROUPS

Each teacher was paired with the other group member teaching at the same grade level, except Mr. Truong, who worked by himself as the only fifth-grade teacher. Each pair was assigned to lead a five-week cycle of activities that began with selecting and leading a discussion of a set of shared readings around a theme they identified as important to their practice. Participants made selections from various readings on social and educational theory from their preservice programs, professional development experiences, personal readings, and the first year of the inquiry group project. They also frequently asked me to help them select pertinent texts for the topics they chose to discuss. Typically, teachers chose sociotheoretical texts that would lead to discussions of broader social justice themes. The readings focused largely on issues of social reproduction and the role of school as a complicit institution. Readings chosen included Jay MacLeod's (1995) *Aint No Makin' It*, Patrick Finn's (1999) *Literacy with an Attitude*, and Paulo Freire's (1970) *Pedagogy of the Oppressed*.

URBAN TEACHER DIALOGUE FOR SOCIAL JUSTICE TEACHING

Teachers used the readings to situate their mission as social justice educators inside broader theoretical positions that lend some larger social relevance to their work as urban educators. However, Ms. Grant suggests the readings also provide stimulus for ongoing reflection on the ideas and dialogues raised by the texts:

> . . . the inquiry group is a time not only to reflect but also to share out with other members of the group. . . . When we were reading Freire, for example, or when we were reading MacLeod, there's certain issues that would come up that would cause me to reflect, because I would come to my students and throw ideas out to them and get questions from them about things that I have done. So after the sharing out there's more reflection on my practice, my practice of the week. So I'll go through each day sort of thinking about what did I do, how did I do it, why did I do it, how did it manifest, how did that affect the students? Am I actually promoting the ideas of "social justice and equity" in my classroom?

Ms. Grant is not alone in her reflections on the readings and their relevance to her practice. Each set of readings stirred important critical conversations about the oppressive culture of Power Elementary and the ways in which these teachers struggle to resist it in their own practice. In one such conversation, teachers saw the relevance of Finn's discussion of Bernstein's (1971) research on the impact of class-related habits of language usage on school success (Finn, 1999):

> Mr. Kinsman: I'm about half way through the Finn book and he talks a lot about explicit and implicit language . . . and how it relates to control and where you'll have, you know, like middle-class, upper-

middle-class kids that have a lot of explicit language that they're exposed to, where everything becomes explained in detail of why things are being done and that, I think, is one of the things that is truly remarkable to me, is I . . . I see the amount of things that are just implicit, whereas, you know, kids are just told to do something and if they think about not doing it they're given the evil eye. You know, there's a lot of nonverbal language that pushes them into conformity, but there's very little explanation, right. So, there's no . . .

Ms. O'Reilly: No "why?"

Mr. Kinsman: . . . there's no larger understanding of why they all need to be there waiting passively. It's just . . . it's the way it is.

Ms. Kim: So, have you tried doing anything with . . . with your student cause I had him on Friday, J (student at Power), and we tried doing the . . . with the discussions with him about being a rhino or . . .

Mr. Kinsman: Yeah. You know what I have explicit discussions with . . . with . . . but see, part of what was painful to me is I saw myself doing things that happened in some of these books that I . . . that I thought of as oppressive and I . . . there's times I still do and it's . . . one of your questions was about, you know, like are you a liberator, or are you an oppressor and you know, like can you possibly be both? And there's a part of me that goes, "Oh, my god. No, I'm just an oppressor." You know, I'm, you know [inaudible]. But I find myself on a regular basis, you know, I give explanations in detail to J and [inaudible] and you know, D [student at Power] about, you know, just why exactly it is that I need them to do something. And I . . . I think it's one of the things that really stood out to me is because you know, I try to be extremely explicit in my explanations of why I want students to do certain things, especially if they choose not to. You know, "Here's why I want you to do it. Is there any reason why you can't cause here's your chance to kind of tell me, you know, give me your understanding and your explanation of why it's not okay" and they'll, you know . . . usually I don't get anything.

The critical nature of the readings and the pursuant conversations, coupled with the intimacy of a small group meeting, provided these teachers the space to struggle openly with colleagues about their practice. Mr. Kinsman's reading of the word is used to engage in a highly personalized, critical, and self-reflective analysis of his practice—"Oh, my god. No, I'm just an oppressor." This type of honest dialogue amongst critical colleagues is essential for teachers to grow in their practice. Research bears out this conclusion, suggesting that a major challenge facing urban teacher development efforts is precisely the absence of these sorts of critical dialogues among urban teachers (Nieto, 2003; Oakes & Lipton, 2001).

The types of critical self-reflection we see from Kinsman can lead to very personal revelations about teachers' frustrations with their practice and the lack of support for improving. In one meeting where teachers were discussing the implications of Freire's (1970) *Pedagogy of the Oppressed* for their own pedagogy, the conversation shifted to conversations about the challenges of moving from theory to practice:

> Mr. Ballesteros: I hated myself for a while this year because I felt like I was being extremely oppressive. The more we read about a pedagogy for liberation, the more I realized mine was not. I'd love it if we could sit down and you could say that these are some things that you do well and these are some things that you really need to improve on, and then maybe I could learn from you too. There are a lot of things that I need to improve upon; anything that anyone can give me that I can improve upon from this meeting I would really value.

> O'Reilly: I really feel like I'm in the place where [Mr. Ballesteros] is. I know that when people make sweeping claims about classes out of control they are talking about me, and I expressed the desire to want help and no one offered me any. Why? Is it that they don't want to hurt my feelings or is it that they do what they do and they can't really articulate it? My feelings have been torn up a lot, I can handle that, but I want to be a better teacher.

This level of honesty about the very personal nature of teaching is essential for meaningful professional development. However, Mr. Ballesteros and Ms. O'Reilly alike point out that the desire to get better is not enough. Teachers need critical support and they need the type of safe and supportive professional spaces where they can be honest about these needs, or as Ms. Grant put it:

> . . . the group has the potential to offer a teacher a community. People to just sit with you in the darkness, listening to you, nodding their heads, letting you cry, scream, vent, and then STILL telling you that you gotta do it . . . that's damned powerful. A space where we can feel comfortable and safe to fall apart, (die), and be reborn, ready to keep moving. That's what it takes. No matter how many times it takes. Something like that doesn't come from staff developments, in-services about discipline and pedagogical practices, or even family and friends

who tell you to just get the [hell] out!! . . . Yeah, that's it . . . coming
back from the dead every day.

Without these types of spaces to "feel comfortable and safe to fall apart, (die),
and be reborn," it is unlikely that the performance of urban teachers will
improve. And while poor professional development should not excuse poor
pedagogy, Ingersoll (2003) would remind us that the dysfunctional nature of
the professional culture in urban schools can largely be attributed to the
absence of teacher support and control in the face of increasing expectations.

THEORY TO PRACTICE: DOES A TEACHER'S CRITICAL INQUIRY TRANSLATE INTO STUDENT LEARNING?

For urban teacher support to matter it has to impact what goes on in the classroom
and that impact has to be measured by student achievement. For the teachers in
the Power Elementary inquiry group, this analysis of their growth would come
from self-study of their practice. To engage in these studies, each of the teacher
pairs designed a curricular unit that addressed issues of social justice by drawing
from the principles being discussed in the group. To understand the impact of their
curricular interventions, the teachers also designed self-studies.

This section will focus on the collaborative research project of Kinsman
and O'Reilly and their part in the Power Elementary inquiry group presentation at the 2004 American Educational Research Association (AERA). O'Reilly
studied her second-grade class and Kinsman his first and second-grade split
class. Their study began with a statement of a problem they aimed to address
with their unit and a review of the literature that analyzes that problem. This
took place during the first two months of the school year.

STATEMENT OF THE PROBLEM AND LITERATURE REVIEW

O'Reilly and Kinsman chose to examine the education system as a mechanism
of social reproduction. They saw their school as part of a larger urban schooling
system that is not culturally responsive to the needs and learning capacities of
their students. They lamented Power Elementary's emphasis on physical control,
rote learning, and a set of cultural norms that fit the descriptions of urban
schools they found in much of the literature (Kozol, 1991; Rist, 1973; Valenzuela,
1999). They organized their literature review in four sections: processes of social
reproduction, effects of social reproduction, the role of the critical teacher, and
redefining student success.

In their examination of the processes of social reproduction in schools,
O'Reilly and Kinsman studied the impact of deculturalization in urban schools
(Ogbu, 1987; Spring, 1990). They used this work to pull from a second body
of literature (Anyon, 1981; Finn, 1999; Piaget & Inhelder, 1969) that argues

that an emphasis on physical and mental conformity is central to the process of deculturalization. They framed their understanding of this process in their AERA (2004) conference abstract:

> The banking model of education (Friere, 1970) creates a strongly disempowering experience for students, leaving the power of knowledge creation solely in the hands of authority figures. (Anyon, 1981, Finn, 1999)

To discuss the effects of these processes, they also drew on Freire (1970) and MacLeod (1995) to explain how these schooling conditions result in student feelings of disempowerment, resistance, and limited social mobility.

Having established the research perspective on the processes and effects of social reproduction, their literature review shifted to an examination of the role of critical teachers in alleviating these conditions in urban schools. Using Freire (1970) and Shor (1992), O'Reilly and Kinsman argued, "we find our position as 'domesticators' to be unacceptable. It is our responsibility to transform the system of urban schooling through critical pedagogy. *This* is our job." While they found the measure of their job to be student success, they felt it important to complicate popular notions of what that means. To establish their social justice perspective on redefining student success, they began with the No Child Left Behind Act definition of student achievement:

> Student progress and achievement will be measured according to tests . . . disaggregated according to race, gender, and other criteria to demonstrate not only how well students are achieving overall but also progress in closing the achievement gap. (U.S. Department of Education, 2003)

O'Reilly and Kinsman then used Piaget (Piaget & Inhelder, 1969) to critique the overemphasis on testing in this definition, and the growing support for educational reform efforts that lack more holistic assessments of student achievement: "If the aim of intellectual training is to form the intelligence, rather than to stock the memory, and to produce intellectual explorers rather than mere erudition, then traditional education is manifestly guilty of a grave deficiency" (AERA, 2004).

Expanding on Piaget's notion that traditional education has failed to produce intellectuals, they laid out a definition of student success that emphasized a "broader, lifelong definition of learning." Pulling from Piaget (Piaget & Inhelder, 1969) and Shor (1992), they outlined three learning goals attributable to intellectual growth: "self-motivation, active engagement, and involvement in cognitively demanding tasks for extended periods of time." Using this theoretically informed definition of student success, they designed, implemented, and studied their curriculum unit in which these goals were emphasized.

CURRICULAR INTERVENTION

O'Reilly and Kinsman focused on an educational history unit they designed to honor the fiftieth anniversary of the *Brown* v. *Board of Education* decision. Their unit expanded on a unit from the district-mandated scripted reading program, building in unit goals that were not measured as part of the reading program or state testing: gaining an understanding of the history of education in the United States and its relationship to urban students; gaining an understanding of the inequities and the process of deculturalization in education; and identifying and expressing acute areas of need in their educational experience.

They implemented theories of culturally relevant content and pedagogy, which they had been discussing in the inquiry group, in designing and teaching their unit, which covered: public education in the 1900s; the history of segregation in education; the struggle for integration in education; Bureau of Indian Affairs schooling, and contemporary immigrants and education. The unit culminated with standards-based assessment tests, as well as student-generated dramatizations and critiques of the history of schooling inequality for poor and non-white children in the United States.

UNIT ANALYSIS: DOES IT MAKE A DIFFERENCE?

In their analysis of this pedagogical approach, O'Reilly and Kinsman sought to understand the impact of teaching for social justice on their more holistic definition of student achievement. This definition of student achievement recognizes that social justice educators cannot ignore the existence of standardized tests as gatekeepers to social, political, and economic mobility. As they put it in their presentation, "preparing kids to achieve on these tests is part of transforming the system. But, it's *only* part of it." Another part of that transformation, they argue, is developing evidence-based practices that avoid the false dichotomy of teaching to the test or teaching for social empowerment. The pedagogy they propose prepares students with traditional academic and computational literacies, while also helping them to develop the critical intellectual capacities to be agents of social change.

To assess the impact of this approach, O'Reilly and Kinsman employed a mixed-methods research protocol. Their quantitative methodology used three traditional areas of standardized testing data on literacy and cognitive development to measure their students' academic growth. They also used qualitative analysis of student work, student interviews, and video of classroom interactions to understand the impact of their pedagogy on the two broader learning goals (self-motivation and active engagement) that are not easily measured by tests.

Their quantitative data reveals that, indeed, this pedagogical approach can produce testing gains that outpace traditional approaches. Having regular interactions with their grade-level colleagues, they knew that none of them were involved in critical inquiry or the use of social justice pedagogy. For this reason, they compared their classroom data to school-wide grade level testing data to build a case for the effectiveness of their approach to teaching. Across all three testing areas (fluency, comprehension, and cognitive demand) their classes outpaced the growth of their colleagues' classes during that period. Figures 11.2 and 11.3 reflect larger growth in the literacy gains of both

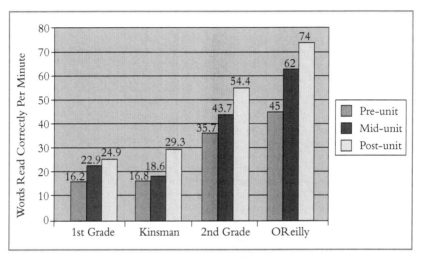

Figure 11.2. *Fluency Assessment Data.*

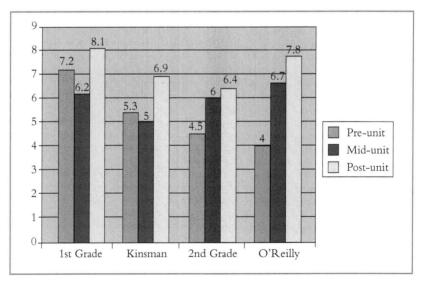

Figure 11.3. *Comprehension Assessment Data.*

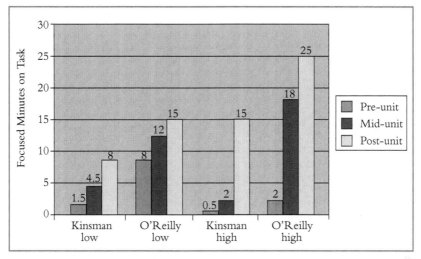

Figure 11.4. *Cognitive Demand and Time on Task.*

Kinsman's and O'Reilly's classes in comparison to their grade level colleagues: 8 percent and 5 percent higher in fluency and 19 percent and 26 percent higher in comprehension, respectively.[1]

However, the greatest leaps in student achievement are reflected in Figure 11.4; their students showed tremendous gains in the area of high cognitive development (97 percent and 92 percent, respectively). O'Reilly and Kinsman attributed this growth to their use, throughout the unit, of high cognitive demand learning activities—analysis, evaluation, and creation (Bloom, 1956) in order to teach for what Piaget (Piaget & Inhelder, 1969) defined as intellectual growth.

While this test score data provides traditional evidence of student growth, O'Reilly and Kinsman used their qualitative data to reveal student growth in the less quantifiable areas of self-motivation and active engagement, areas that the literature identifies as central to a broader definition of student success. These gains were most clearly reflected in their analysis of the unit's culminating task, which required students to dramatize the history they learned. It is the writing and performance of these dramatizations that they saw as central to the students' development of self-motivation and active engagement. As they describe it:

> During this unit, Gloria came in after recess and told me that her group spent their recess time re-writing and fine-tuning their script and then rehearsing it. The level of commitment and organization it takes for them to get a group of five or six kids together, each willing to give up their highly valued play time, to work on school work . . . well that's just about unheard of, but it is also evidence that they are both enjoying what they are learning and valuing what they

are learning as well. I can't think of better evidence for me as a teacher that my kids are getting it, than when it spills out of the classroom into the playground.

For Kinsman and O'Reilly, the opportunity to narrate the experiences of Gloria and her classmates is a valuable tool for understanding the type of learning that is going on in their classroom. The import of these kinds of qualitative inquiries into classroom practice and student learning is an implicit critique of the overemphasis on teacher development and assessment that focuses exclusively on raising test scores. However, their use of test score data reflects their understanding that this method of assessing learning also requires their attention. Ultimately, their analysis of the unit, using various methods of assessment, suggests that their critical pedagogical response to urban schools as mechanisms of social reproduction and control holds important implications for achievement and for educational social justice.

CONCLUSIONS

The participants in the Power Elementary inquiry group are like many teachers in urban schools. They vary in their life experiences, their experiences in the profession, and their success levels with their students. They continue to care deeply about their students and their jobs despite the virtual absence of institutional resources and support to address the enormous challenges of teaching in urban schools. To a person, they stay because they believe that urban teachers can right the ship. To a person, they believe that for the profession to be successful in that endeavor teachers must have increasing support in, access to, and control over critical dialogue about pedagogical practices in urban schools.

It is hard to know the precise relationship between professional development and teacher growth. There is little doubt that it matters, but teaching is not a simple matter of saying if you plug in 'A,' you get out 'B.' Teachers are also learners who develop their practice over time. Each set of teachers will have a different set of needs that emerge at different times in their careers. For this reason, a rigid scientific-methods research model likely will not produce conclusive evidence about the type of professional development that works best in urban schools. Instead, to meet the needs of teachers, researchers will have to better understand the critical, dynamic, teacher-centered systems of support that offer an alternative to the current over-investment in one-size fits all teacher training. Such alternative systems: (1) expose less effective teachers to successful teachers, their practice and their ideology, supported by ongoing critical dialogue and collegial accountability, and (2) place highly effective teachers in regular conversations where they critically evaluate, reflect, and share their practices.

The prospect of becoming an effective social justice educator is a daunting one for most urban educators. Critical inquiry groups can generate a professional climate that supports both teacher growth and development of social justice educators. Critical teacher inquiry can go a long way in addressing what Nieto characterizes as the staggering disconnect between the kinds of support urban teachers get and the kinds of critical dialogue and support they need to be successful (Nieto, 2003). The research on urban teacher development and urban student achievement tells us one thing very clearly—what we are doing right now is not working. The experiences of the teachers in the Power Elementary critical inquiry group suggest that we can do better for them and that this will result in them doing better for their students. At the end of the day, that seems to be the very least we should be doing for urban schools.

NOTE

1. On Graph 2, Kinsman's students started with an average score lower than the rest of the first grade, so while his students were still below the average score of the first grade on the final assessment, their gain was proportionately higher—1.3 points compared to the rest of the first grade which was .9 point.

REFERENCES

American Educational Research Association. (2004). "Holla back: Urban teachers examining critical social justice pedagogy in practice." Symposium, San Diego, CA: Author.

Anyon, J. (1981). Social class and school knowledge. *Curriculum Inquiry, 11*, 3–42.

Bernstein, B. (1971). *Theoretical studies toward a sociology of education.* London: Routledge and Kegan Paul.

Cochran-Smith, M., & Lytle, S. (1993). *Inside/outside: Teacher research and knowledge.* New York: Teachers College Press.

Cochran-Smith, M., & Lytle, S. (1999). The teacher research movement: A decade later. *Educational Researcher, 28*(7), 15–25.

Dana, N. F., & Yendol-Silva, D. (2003). *The reflective educator's guide to classroom research: Learning to teach and teaching to learn through practitioner inquiry.* Thousand Oaks, CA: Corwin Press.

Finn, P. (1999). *Literacy with an attitude: Educating working class children in their own self-interest.* Albany: State University of New York Press.

Fox, D. L., & Fleishcher, C. (2001). The power of teacher inquiry: Toward meaningful professional development and educational reform. *English Education, 33*(3), 187–189.

Freire, P. (1970). *Pedagogy of the oppressed.* New York: Continuum.

Goswami, D., & Stillman, P. (1987). *Reclaiming the classroom: Teacher research as an agency for change.* Upper Montclair, NJ: Boynton/Cook.

Hubbard, R. S., & Power, B. M. (2003). *The art of classroom inquiry: A handbook for teacher-researchers.* Portsmouth, NH: Heinemann.

Hunter-Quartz, K., Olsen, B., & Duncan-Andrade, J. (In press). The fragility of urban teaching: A longitudinal study of career development and activism. In F. Peterman (Ed.), *Resiliency, resistance, and persistence in transcending traditional boundaries: Communities partnering to prepare urban teachers.* Mahwah, NJ: Erlbaum.

Ingersoll, R. (2003). *Who controls teachers work?* Cambridge, MA: Harvard University Press.

Kozol, J. (1991). *Savage inequalities: Children in America's schools.* New York: Harper-Collins.

Lortie, D. C. (1975). *Schoolteacher.* Chicago: University of Chicago Press.

MacLeod, J. (1995). *Aint no makin' it.* Boulder, CO: Westview Press.

McFarland, K. P., & Stansell, J. C. (1993). Historical perspectives. In L. Patterson, C. M. Santa, K. G. Short, & K. Smith (Eds.), *Teachers are researchers: Reflection and action* (pp. 12–25). Newark, DE: International Reading Association.

Nieto, S. (2003). *What keeps teachers going?* New York: Teachers College Press.

Oakes, J., & Lipton, M. (2001). *Teaching to change the world.* Boston: McGraw-Hill.

Ogbu, J. (1987). Variability in minority responses to schooling: Non-immigrants vs. immigrants. In G. Spindler (Ed.). *The interpretive ethnography of education: At home and abroad* (pp. 255–280). Hillsdale, NJ: Lawrence Erlbaum.

Piaget, J., & Inhelder, B. (1969). *The psychology of the child.* New York: Basic Books.

Public Education Network. (2003). *The voice of the new teacher.* Washington, DC: Author.

Richardson, V. (1994). "Teacher Inquiry as Staff Development." In S. Hollingsworth & H. Sockett (Eds.), *Teacher Research and Educational Reform: 93rd NSSE Yearbook, Part I* (pp. 186–203). Chicago: University of Chicago Press.

Rist, R. (1973). *The urban school: Factory for failure.* Cambridge, MA: Massachusetts Institute of Technology Press.

Shor, I. (1992). *Empowering education: Critical teaching for social change.* Chicago: University of Chicago Press.

Spring, J. (1990). The purposes of public schooling. In *American education: An introduction to social and political aspects* (5th ed.) New York: Longman.

U.S. Department of Education. (2003). *No Child Left Behind Fact Sheet.* Retrieved January 15, 2005 from http://www.ed.gov/nclb/intro/factsheet.html.

Valenzuela, A. (1999). *Subtractive schooling: U.S.-Mexican youth and the politics of caring.* Albany, State University of New York Press.

12 *Literacy with an Attitude* and Understanding the Water We Swim In

John Otterness

JOHN OTTERNESS, FACULTY, UCLA School Management Program, observes that many teachers teach the way they were taught, and for teachers of poor and working-class students that almost always means domesticating education. He describes his experiences in helping administrators and teachers, in schools in the Los Angeles area, change their attitudes using a "walk-through" of three classes with a wide range of teaching practices. The teachers saw little to admire in the more student-centered classes but much to admire in the rigid teacher-centered class. In a second walk-through, after reading part of *Literacy with an Attitude* using the "insert method," teachers saw problems in the teacher-centered class and much to emulate in the other two classes.

When I mentioned Patrick Finn's book, Literacy with an Attitude: Educating Working-Class Children in Their Own Self-Interest *(1999), to a colleague, she said that she had given a copy to her Physical Trainer and he told her he was insisting that all his friends read it. I asked her why and she said her trainer's mother was from El Salvador, but he was born here in California and attended a local elementary school. His mother cleaned house for a person who was on the board of a prestigious private school. She took an interest in her cleaning lady's child and got a full scholarship for him at this school. From there he went on to a private college and is now working on his masters degree in physical therapy. His younger sister, however, is attending a large urban public school and having a very different type of education. When he read Finn's book, he found explanations for many of the situations in his life he had puzzled about, and he found areas of concern he didn't even know about. This is why he has been pushing all his friends to read it, including his 13 year old sister, who really struggled with it, but he was relentless and she learned from it! His conversation is now filled with the same passion, indignation, and desire to do something expressed in* Literacy with an Attitude. *This story indicates something of the book's power and appeal and why we use it in our work with schools.*

The "School Management Program" (SMP) is a joint initiative of the Anderson Graduate School of Business and the Graduate School of Education and Information Studies at UCLA. SMP was formed in 1992 as a university initiative to take a larger role in public education. The Los Angeles Unified School District (LAUSD) was our first client as we were selected to guide their LEARN school reform project. The role of SMP has changed over the years, from working exclusively with LAUSD schools, to working with schools throughout the state of California that want to provide a more successful education for their students, as well as schools that have been identified as underperforming by the state of California or the No Child Left Behind law. SMP faculty are the trainers and coaches who have assisted the leadership teams from approximately 700 schools with their local school reform efforts. SMP draws their faculty from the ranks of practitioners: administrators (principals, directors, superintendents); teachers, and practitioners from industry. We work with all levels of teachers: kindergarten through high school; administrators: from school site administrators and coordinators to district offices and school boards; and parents: as members of school leadership teams.

We use a wide variety of structures in our work with schools: Institutes around specific concepts such as the Data Institute; the Writing Institute; Classroom Walk-Throughs; Bridges to Understanding (English Language Learners); and Critical Friends Groups. These range from two to five days in length and are held away from the school site. We also provide services tailored to an individual school or district's need, including such items as coaching, workshops, observation and reports, or other structures that will be of assistance to the progress of the schools.

SMP has used *Literacy with an Attitude* both internally, to enhance our own understanding of the schools we work with, and externally to help schools begin to think beyond the tests and subject content as they work to improve their student's capabilities for school success. In the following pages I will refer to the work of Jean Anyon (1980), Basil Bernstein (1971), Paul Willis (1977), and Lois Weis (1990, but in every case I am referring to their work as reported and discussed in *Literacy with an Attitude*.

The schools we deal with are predominately working class and minority; understanding the influences and effects of factors other than subject area content is a necessary condition for improving their students' outcomes. Our purpose has been to help schools see themselves as part of a social class system, and to understand how that system, and the different cultures associated with it, governs schooling. We believe this knowledge can help them make good choices about schooling and improve their ability to educate their students "in their own self-interest" (Finn, 1999). There is an expression, "If you want to know about water, you don't ask a fish." We use *Literacy With an Attitude* in these contexts in order to "make the fish aware of the water"—to provide a different lens through which to observe schooling.

UNDERLYING CONCEPTS AND CHANGE

We grow up in an industrial society, although one that is changing. The stories that form the foundation of our country are stories of mass production: the interchangeability and uniformity of the pieces that make up a machine. The idea that you can design the pieces that make up a car, make each part according to specifications, assemble the pieces, and then drive away in your new Chevrolet, has a powerful hold on our psyche. This model has been touted as the *Great American Success Story,* and it carries over into other aspects of society. It is also the model of education, in the view of most people— parents, teachers, and the general public—which has the most generally accepted credence. If we design all the parts (teach the basics), and make sure the students meet the specifications (meet the standards), then they should be able to assemble the parts and drive away (read Shakespeare or science or history with understanding).

Reading *Literacy with an Attitude* helps our participants begin to develop a different view of how learning happens and what, besides content, needs to be considered to help their students achieve success in our society. Most of our schools are large urban/suburban schools with entrenched populations of interest groups, so the idea of a massive restructuring of public education remains in the future. But through the use of *Literacy with an Attitude,* we help them begin to envision a different and more successful system of teaching and learning for their classrooms and their local educational environment.

STRUCTURED INSTITUTES

SMP Institutes focus on processes that allow schools to better understand:

- Their students,

- Their educational community,

- Their teaching practices,

- The system they operate in,

- How these interrelate, and

- How these can lead to changes that get different results for their students.

Within these Institutes, our focus ranges from increasing practitioners' understanding of the issues that impact their subject area, to assisting school and district administrators to more effectively manage their leadership positions for better results.

My first introduction to *Literacy with an Attitude* came when I was given a copy by a former colleague in a high school where we both taught. I read it at one sitting, and in each section the phrase that rang through my mind was, "So that's why . . . happened!!" The insights Finn (1999) provided made it possible for me to make connections between research, classroom practice, and results. I brought the book to the attention of the SMP faculty and we were able to provide copies for all members of SMP. We had several discussions about the meaning of the various pieces of research and analysis and its relation to our work with schools. Additionally, we were fortunate to be able to spend a morning with Patrick and Mary Finn at UCLA where we were able to question them about their current work and what they saw as the effect of the book. This led to the incorporation of all or portions of the book in many of our Institutes.

FIRST USE IN AN INSTITUTE

The first use by SMP of *Literacy with an Attitude* was in a three-day institute for Elementary Teachers of Mathematics. The Institute was designed to provide a different view of mathematics in order to overcome the traditional drill and fear methods of understanding and teaching elementary math. We focused on developing insight into how children were understanding the mathematics they were being taught, and to provide a window through which to view their thinking. Another major focus was recognizing how much of mathematics is being able to recognize the same concepts or ideas when the notation is different. For example, in the following questions, the same concept is expressed in two different ways: (1) If five candy bars cost $3.95, how much would 7 candy bars cost? (2) If five percent is $3.95, how much would 7 percent be?

Teachers generally teach percentage as a separate skill. However, when teachers recognize and use their understanding and knowledge to help their students see this idea, their students deepen their understanding of mathematics from simply memorizing patterns of solutions to being able to manipulate the mathematics to succeed in new situations. But in order to help the teachers see math from a different viewpoint and have a different understanding of students' responses, we realize it is important for them to see the whole of education from a different perspective. We wanted them to realize that many times it was not just the content that was difficult for their students, but it was how the children approached the content and interpreted what the teacher and the school were requiring of them, that caused the difficulty.

READING THE BOOK

There are several sections of *Literacy with an Attitude* that provide a linkage for teachers, helping them form a different view of mathematics, and to develop a different perspective on the whole of education. Specifically, we asked Institute participants to focus on Finn's (1999) analysis of Anyon's (1980) work on students' social class and its impact on the style of instruction they received. One of the techniques we employ to help teachers go more deeply into a reading is what we call the Insert Method. As they read the chapter or section, they are asked to annotate the reading with symbols such as:

? — I have questions about this section
★ — this is an important idea
! — Wow, this is something new!!
X — I really disagree with what the author says

Depending on the group and the reading, we may add other indicators.

We group them when they are done reading, usually in triads, and ask them to do round-robin descriptions of their annotations, describing the section and why they marked reading as they did. We also ask them to complete this task before they have a discussion about their annotations. Our purpose in doing this is to assure that everyone's voice gets heard before the conversation starts. After the rounds are completed, the discussion is open. This is where the insights into their own practices and school culture begin to develop. These conversations are usually quite lively! Many times, the participants have to confront their own confirmation bias—the tendency to notice what fits our understanding and ignore what contradicts it. As they talk, other views come out and can be challenged or affirmed. We then ask the group to choose one or two points, and the insights they illustrate, and present them to the group. The theory behind this approach derives from a combination of the ideas of Piaget (1971, 1985), Vygotsky (1962), Bernstein (1971), and Freire (1970, 1973).

First, it is important that the participants freely express their own ideas, positions, and reasoning. To have a possibility of change, there must be an awareness of something to change from. Often the ideas that we operate under are implicit in our actions but not brought to the level of conscious awareness. Asking participants to express their own interpretations provides an opportunity to surface the implicit beliefs that underlie the ideas that drive their practice.

Second, after they express their ideas, the discussion that follows gives them the opportunity to hear and discuss different interpretations of the material with others who have also read the material. And because the teachers have this exchange of interpretations, there is now the possibility of change—moving from Piaget's (1985) "assimilation" (fitting new experiences and events into existing mental structures) to "accommodation" (adjusting the mental structures to accommodate new information).

When the triad finally chooses several ideas to present to the whole group, how they choose to present their ideas helps them understand the material on a deeper level. We then do a group debrief, asking them to look at both the process and the content and to imagine Jean Anyon visiting their school. They talk about where their school would have been placed on her continuum from "working class," to "middle class," to "affluent professional," to "executive elite" (Anyon, 1980). The questions we used for discussions were:

- What could you do differently to give your students a different kind of education?

- What would look different at your school if you tried to change it?
- How would a visitor know?

MATHEMATICS INSTITUTES

As we linked those ideas back to mathematics, the consensus among the participants was that there would have to be more discussion and interactive activities for their students and less of the fill-in-the-blank, drill and fear, and teacher-talk typical of a working-class school. They felt that if their students were to succeed, they would have to provide them the type of student-centered education Anyon (1980) classified as affluent professional, which is characterized by activities, student interactions, choices, and respect for the students, their families, and their communities. Their discussions revolved around finding ways to make what they saw as their school's culture more open to the affluent professional teaching style and to overcome the prevailing idea that their students couldn't be taught that way. One of the participants, a second grade teacher with many years experience, said to the group, "I've been doing it wrong all these years. I'm going back and figure out a different way to run my class."

BRINGING A DIFFERENT CULTURE TO THE CLASSROOM

We bring relevant outside information to the attention of school communities as an integral part of all our work. Schools have a tendency to rely on what we call the GAU—the Generally Accepted Understanding—that informs the way the school does its work. As various studies have shown—and our own experience verifies—for many educators their ideas about how to teach are driven primarily by how they were taught. Even as teachers are trained in new methods of teaching, when they return to the classroom they modify the new methods to conform to their earlier beliefs and their teaching doesn't change. It may look different, because it is possible to have a working-class school where the students are seated in groups, but the work can still be characterized as working class—teacher-dominated drill and fear (Finn, 1999).

Because teaching is, in fact, a cultural activity, how it is carried out depends on the culture in which it is embedded. Trying to change the how of teaching without changing the culture it is embedded in often leads to failure and rarely (if ever) changes the teaching. In addition, it often leads those charged with making the change to explain the failure by asserting, "Well, the teachers just want don't want to change!" or, "They're not smart enough to see what they need to do!" These are statements I have heard and they are similar to the reasons teachers give for students' disruptive behaviors, such as the students' resistance Finn (1999) described in his discussion of Willis' (1977) "lads," who openly mocked the teacher, refused to follow instructions, paid little attention to lessons, and generally disrupted the class whenever an occasion to do so arose. So a good portion of our work focuses on changing the culture, both the culture of teaching and the culture of expectations, aspects of school that are intrinsically linked.

There is a common saying in many cultures that, "*We see what is behind our eyes.*" We use the information and organization Finn (1999) has provided to help our participants see what is behind their eyes in order to change what they say and do in their profession. One of the most important points Finn makes is in describing a teacher conducting the reading period for a class of 1st graders: "She did what she thought any good teacher would do" (p. 93). When teachers respond without knowing what goes on "behind our eyes," they do it—as this teacher did—with the best of intentions. In my thirty-five year career of teaching, from kindergarten through college, I have never met a teacher who intentionally did not want the best for his or her students. But what teachers perceived as best was determined by the expectations they held of the skills and ability of their students, and by their perception of their job as teachers.

Even the teacher who was not only very authoritarian with her students, but also verbally abusive, explained, when asked why she treated the students that way, "It's a hard, mean world out there and these students are going to have to learn to cope with people who don't like them. So they need to start learning that now." Until teachers can see a better way to help their students become successful, the culture they bring with them into teaching will remain with them in the classroom. And this culture, formed by, "We see what is behind our eyes," is the major challenge to efforts to change teaching and schools so that all students have an education "in their own self-interest" (Finn, 1999).

The culture of expectations is also related to the specific subject matter and the perception of who can learn it and who can't. The math teacher who believes that ". . . some students can get it, some can't get it, and some could get it if they'd only do their homework," and who taught in a way Anyon (1980) characterized as working class, saw a daily reinforcement of those beliefs. Some got it (by his standards), most didn't, and those who did were the ones who turned in their homework. This teacher sees no reason to change since his understanding is continually reinforced as being correct. But, of course, the students in these classrooms resist as Willis' (1977) lads did, and as those in Anyon's (1980) working-class schools did: side talk, heads down on desk, doodling, turning around, et cetera.

Changing the culture means changing the expectations for and about the students; this requires understanding not only the content of the subject differently, but also the culture the student brings to the classroom, as well as its effect on the classroom. When teachers and administrators walk into a classroom, they too, see what is behind their eyes as they observe the physical and social environment of the classroom. They need to learn to see what they are looking at with different understanding; that is part of the change process we try to initiate.

USING THE CLASSROOM WALK-THROUGH
TO CHANGE WHAT IS SEEN

We use a process called Classroom Walk-Throughs to help schools see differently and change what goes on in the classroom. Our Classroom Walk-Through Institutes are designed to foster a nonjudgmental way for teachers to look at school through the workings of classrooms. The Institute involves interactive exercises, such as role-playing a virtual classroom visit using a video of an actual classroom in session, reading about the culture of schools in *Literacy with an Attitude* and other articles, and developing focus questions for the Walk-Throughs and for the conversation afterwards. All of these activities have seeing schools differently as their goal—changing the "What's behind their eyes."

As part of the training, we also do actual Walk-Throughs in classrooms in schools that have volunteered to let us use them for our practice. Sometimes these are schools whose teachers have been through our Institutes. We do two visits on consecutive days in the same classrooms at approximately the same times, followed by a group debrief in response to a focus question addressing both what we saw and how we saw. We try to find a question that will lead to deeper discussions about what has been seen. For example: "What evidence do you see that the students are engaged in their learning?" Even though we have an anticipatory discussion about what we will look for, and what we might see in response to the focus question, the initial visit is always an eye-opener. Such a question often leads to descriptions that look very similar to the lads of Willis' (1977) study and Weis' (1990) study of the Rust Belt schools.

During one Walk-Through Institute, I took a group from generally low performing, working-class, language minority schools to a high school that performed at a much higher level. The school we visited had, in addition to the regular, gifted, and Advanced Placement classes, an International Baccalaureate (IB) program. We visited an honors 10th grade Social Studies class, a regular Algebra I math class, and the World History IB class. The IB class was filled with discussion among the students about their presentation of ideas and included their questioning both the teacher and each other. The honors class was more structured with the students preparing a presentation according to a sheet of directions that included some choices. The Algebra I class was highly structured, what could be described as a traditional math class—explain, work samples, and practice.

Even though the participants' debrief focused on evidence they saw of students "engaged in developing their own understanding," the Walk-Through teachers expressed a high degree of satisfaction with what they saw in the Algebra I class, which they interpreted as students "engaged in developing their own understanding." They saw the same thing to a lesser degree in the 10th grade Social Studies class. They dismissed the IB class as not possible for their students. The different levels of structure and instruction in the classes they observed were invisible to them. They only saw that worksheets and classroom organization were absent in the IB class.

In the discussion that followed these Walk-Throughs, the participants' own belief systems were apparent in their descriptions of what they saw. They focused on behavior—"quiet" meant "learning," and "structure" meant "how the teacher controlled the class." In general, the evidence they reported as observations of students involved in developing their own understanding matched Anyon's (1980) description of a working-class school. Any evidence of learning that was more attuned to an affluent professional school was absent from their observations.

At another time, we took a group to visit a school with demographics similar to their own. Again, the classes they described in the debrief as having the most learning were the ones that matched the characteristics of teaching in a working-class school, characteristics that matched their own idea of how teaching and learning takes place. What was interesting in this situation was that the school we visited had been working to provide an education more toward Anyon's (1980) middle-class or even affluent professional type schooling. While we did observe some of the affluent professional type classrooms, the visiting teachers did not recognize those classrooms as engaging students in their own learning.

Following this school visit, we had the teachers read Finn's (1999) description of Anyon's (1980) research, again using the Insert Method. In the discussion that followed, teachers' comments indicated they had seen evidence that even within a school there were different educations for different students. But the discussion around how they interpreted what they were seeing was even more significant. They acknowledged that they had previously interpreted the structured, teacher-directed, quiet classes, where students were working individually, as places where learning was occurring, and that they had not seen activities involving interaction among students in other classes as evidence of learning. Following the discussion, they worked in groups to devise another focus question for a follow-up visit based on what they had seen and read. On the return visit they saw the classrooms differently—even though they were viewing the same students with the same teachers.

As teachers began to see schools and teaching through the lens of Finn's (1999) discussion of Anyon's (1980) work, they began to question their own practice. The discussions we had during visits to their schools were much richer now, with more questions than before. We also found less use of statements of opinion as fact: "These kids are just lazy. They don't want to learn." There was also more talk about ways to involve their own students more effectively in their learning.

The section of Finn's (1999) discussion of Anyon (1980) that seemed to resonate most clearly with teachers was the section where he reported the responses of two of his students whom he asked whether their own school experiences verified Anyon's findings (p. 24). As the teachers discussed Finn's students' responses, they remembered how rare were the occasions in their own education that they experienced activities like those described by Finn's student who taught in the affluent professional school. In schools they attended, only one teacher or one class had activities that promoted independence and creativity. They described their own teaching situations, which most often resembled the second student's experience in a working-class school. The examples of ways the Institute teachers' own classrooms were similar included: handing out Xeroxes of teacher's notes with words missing, giving students grid paper so they would keep their math problems lined up, and having their students copy the outline they had on the board or the overhead and answering low level questions.

One Institute participant, who teaches in the Special Education program at a large, predominately minority Hispanic urban middle school, gave the Finn (1999) chapter on Anyon to her students. She had them work in pairs to help each other with the reading. Then she asked them to write about where their school fit into continuum from working-class to executive elite schools. Over several days they continued the conversation and discussion. The students all agreed that their school was most similar to the working-class model. The teacher posed these questions for her students: "What kind of school would you like to attend?" and "How could you make that happen?" This discussion is ongoing.

STRUGGLING WITH EXPECTATIONS

The real underlying struggle teachers faced in our Institutes was their belief that what they were doing was all they—both teacher and student—could do; no more was possible. Even though each of their schools, as they described them, had a mission or vision statement that included a phrase similar to "All children can learn," the word that was never expressed in these statements was "except"—as in except those who won't do their homework, or except those who don't want to learn, or except those who's parents don't care, and many more excepts. They thought this not because they didn't want their students to be successful but because their experiences seemed to give them evidence to support their beliefs about why their students couldn't be successful. The challenge for us as a school change organization was to find ways to change this perception.

BRIDGES TO UNDERSTANDING: ENGLISH LANGUAGE LEARNERS AND *LITERACY WITH AN ATTITUDE*

California's Proposition 227 changed the landscape of education for students who come to school with no, or limited, command of the English language. The proposition mandated a maximum of one year of support for a student with limited English followed by placement in a classroom where all instruction is done in English. The English only proposition was driven by a belief about the best way to learn a language, and about what was needed to help language minority students succeed in school.

At SMP, we developed the *Bridges to Understanding Institute* to help teachers caught between the demands to teach in English and, at the same time, assure that students do not fall behind in the content area. The typical materials they were provided tended to be of the "teach them the skills of reading" educational philosophy. In our Institute, we provide ideas and techniques to expand the repertoire of the participants' ability to help their students. But more important, we help them understand the work that needs to be done beyond the skills of reading as a way to change their perceptions about their students.

In these Institutes we use Finn's (1999) chapter on Anyon (1980) as a beginning point for expanding the teachers' understanding of what is needed. We also bring in Finn's (1999) analysis of Bernstein's (1971) work on the impact of social class on language and discourse, important factors in students' school success. Bernstein's (1971) descriptors of the working-class language environment include an emphasis on solidarity, which translates into a tendency toward authoritarian discipline and conformity, as well as a way to address a sense of powerlessness. The result is a habit of language use among working-class families that depends on knowing what others think, and therefore makes implicit language most useful in this society of intimates. But the language of school is explicit, a mode of discourse that fits nicely with the middle-class families' habits of language use that are developed from a sense of powerfulness and from placing a high value on individuality. Economic and cultural capital in the middle and upper classes allows for travel and membership in organizations outside the family and local community and results in the need for explicit language in this society of strangers.

Using this analysis, we ask teachers to look at their community to see where there are similarities and where there are differences between working-class and middle-class language usage. Just as Bernstein's (1971) working-class communities are defined by implicit language usage, so are many of the schools' communities in which we work. In addition to being working-class communities, they are also language minority communities. This brings an added emphasis to the implicit language uses Bernstein (1971) describes.

Finn (1999) describes a second grade classroom that Mary Finn observed, where the teacher's language use varied according to the social class of the students who were grouped by reading ability. The teacher was very explicit with those in the highest reading group, who were also from higher SES families—sitting back in her chair and directing them verbally to the page and sentence she wanted them to read. With the lowest reading group (whose members were children from the lower SES families), the teacher moved into the center of the circle where she could reach each student's book and physically turn the pages and point to where she wanted them to read. This excellent, caring teacher was reproducing in her students their habits of language use instead of recognizing the need to teach the explicit school discourse to those whose families did not use it habitually.

In many schools you can observe a similar situation. In the high schools in which I have worked, there were often students who could wander the halls freely and if a teacher saw them, they would get a smile and a nod. Other students were always stopped and questioned. One of the reasons for this difference that *Literacy with an Attitude* helped me understand was the implicit-explicit language experiences of the students. Those who wandered at will were familiar with and generally used explicit language—the language of the staff. Those who were stopped were those whose language patterns were implicit.

As the teachers of English language learners began to understand the implications of Finn's (1999) analysis of Bernstein's work for their students, they began to look for ways to structure their classes so there were more activities that allowed the habitually implicit language use students to be successful, while turning the students' attention to their need to understand that school success is related to explicit language use. Since everyone can use language explicitly when they understand that the occasion calls for it, a focus on this understanding in classrooms with working-class students can lead to changes in their language habits and patterns of use.

In the same way, as we begin looking at the role of parents of English Language Learners, we are finding ways to help parents become more explicit in their native language in order to help their children develop habitual use of these characteristics. Instead of trying, as many schools do, to train parents to be teachers at home, we provide parents with questions they can ask that move their children to answer explicitly. For example, if a student who is learning to read in English has parents with limited fluency, we would have the student read the story to their parent in English and then retell the story in their native language. The parent then asks "why" questions about events in the story, moving beyond the who-what-when-where questions. In this way, we maintain the language of the parents in a positive manner while helping move the child and parent into a more school oriented language use.

LOOKING AT DATA THROUGH THE EYES OF *LITERACY WITH AN ATTITUDE*

Another way to begin changing teacher's perceptions of their students is to look at student work with different eyes and, additionally, to use different types of student work in order to see students differently. To this end, one of our Institutes involves learning various protocols for looking at student work and teacher assessment dilemmas. While the Institute itself does not use *Literacy with an Attitude* as a reference, when I have worked with schools using these protocols, the book becomes a reference point for me to develop questions to ask about student work. Initially, for teachers, looking at student work means finding what students did right and what they did wrong. The end result teachers set for themselves is to structure their lessons and present their material so that the students will not get it wrong.

Using references from *Literacy with an Attitude,* it is possible to help move teachers toward asking the questions another way. As teachers begin asking, "Why did they answer this question this way?" instead of "What did they get right or wrong?" they begin to change the way they perceive their students and deepen their understanding of why the students responded as they did. This can lead to perceiving students as people trying to make sense out of the school world in which they find themselves, rather than as individuals who need correcting. Similarly, in my work with several middle school math departments, as we looked at student work after reading portions of *Literacy with an Attitude,* the teachers began to wonder how and, more importantly, why students were interpreting their instruction as they did.

Data in schools usually serves two purposes: placement of students in their "appropriate groups," and identifying which teachers are doing the best as defined by test scores. In our Data Institute, we look at the variety of data schools collect, how data is presented and used currently, and how it could be presented and used to understand the results differently. Student work is just one aspect of the data schools generate with the intent of improving students' performance, whether on standardized tests—both norm referenced and criterion referenced—or in local assessments. We also look for data that isn't in the normal realm of school data. We ask the Institute participants to bring samples of the data they use at their schools—both school generated and teacher generated. As we work through the different types of data, the questions we keep in the forefront are, "What does this tell you about your student?" and, "What does your choice of assessments tell you about your understanding of how learning happens?"

As part of the homework on the second day of the Data Institute, we ask participants to read Finn's (1999) chapters on Anyon's (1980) and Bernstein's (1971) research using the Insert Method. The purpose of both these readings is to help them put a human face on the numbers and graphs they are interpreting. The purpose is also to help them see what other kinds of data they might need to look for in order to better understand their schools. Finn's (1999) chapter on Anyon gives us an entrée to looking at what the data tell them about the type of school they are working in. The Bernstein chapter provides us with the question of what other kind of data we need to look at in order to advance our students. The language usage of working-class students takes on a greater importance as we look at our school populations. Out of the readings done in the Data Institute comes the possibility of changing teachers' work with students.

LITERACY WITH AN ATTITUDE AND CHANGING THE CULTURE OF THE SCHOOL

Finn's work assembles and presents research on factors that determine success in school above and beyond the subject area content and provides us with a way to help schools see themselves differently. As teachers read the research Finn (1999) describes, whether it is from Anyon (1980) or Bernstein (1971) or Willis (1977), and reflect on what it means for their school, they can begin to change how they perceive their career as a teacher, their role as a member of a school community, and their responsibility to their students. Esther Dyson (1997) distinguishes between culture and community: "Culture is a set of rules, perceptions, language, history, and the like. . . . Culture can be learned. . . . By contrast, community is a set of relationships."

The strength of *Literacy with an Attitude* is that it allows a school to see its culture. And, as a community, they have the power to change that culture. But that change depends on how they understand, and even if they understand, their culture. Culture is the air we breathe or, to use the fish analogy, the water we all swim in. Until something is different, we don't notice our culture—it is our GAU, our Generally Accepted Understanding embedded in our day-to-day practice. Finn gives us the tools to open the community to their culture and as they change, he describes a path toward a different culture, one that can result in greater success for the entire school community.

REFERENCES

Anyon, J. (1980). Social class and the hidden curriculum of work. *Journal of Education, 162*, 2.

Bernstein, B. (1971). *Theoretical studies towards a sociology of education.* London: Routledge and Kegan Paul.

Dyson, E. (1997). *Release 2.0: A design for living in the digital age.* New York: Broadway Books.

Finn, P. (1999). *Literacy with an attitude: Educating working-class students in their own self-interest.* Albany: State University of New York Press.

Freire, P. (1970). *Pedagogy of the oppressed.* New York: Continuum Press.

Freire, P. (1973). *Education for critical consciousness.* New York: Continuum Press.

Piaget, J. (1985). *The equilibration of cognitive structures: The central problem of intellectual development.* Chicago: University of Chicago Press.

Piaget, J., & Inhelder, B. (1969). *The psychology of the child.* New York: Basic Books.

Vygotsky, L. S. (1962). *Thought and language.* Cambridge, MA: Massachusettes Institute of Technology Press.

Weis, L. (1990). *Working class without work: High school students in a de-industrializing economy.* New York: Routledge.

Willis, P. (1977). *Learning to labor: How working-class kids get working-class jobs.* Westmead, England: Saxon House.

13 Popular Education in Los Angeles High School Classrooms: The Collective Bargaining Education Project

Linda Tubach

LINDA TUBACH, TEACHER AND DIRECTOR, Collective Bargaining Education Project, Los Angeles Unified School District (LAUSD), explains how Freirean popular education is used to teach about social justice and the labor movement through a six-part curriculum that engages students, their teachers, and volunteer professionals from both labor and management in simulations of labor-management negotiations. Through group discussions and analytical writing assignments, students explore the issues of power, equity, and dignity in the workplace from multiple perspectives. Teachers are introduced to the benefits of popular education pedagogy and they are often moved by the leadership and critical thinking qualities their students exhibit. Students learn the value of negotiation from a position of strength and they see the importance of working together for a common goal.

The tension was building at the bargaining table. "I can't understand this," said Veronica. "The company's made you a very generous offer, and all you can say is . . ."

Chris, the union's spokesperson on wages, cut her off. "Understanding? You're not respecting us. We're the one's making this company rich. We do the work. Either you satisfy us now or we go on strike!"

Suddenly the entire union team stood up and stormed out of the high school lunchroom, stunning the management team.

"Now what should we do?" asked Shawn.

By the end of the collective bargaining simulation, 100 high school seniors in Mr. Bromley's Economics classes had answered this question in a variety of ways and they were eager to discuss what they had learned from the experience. Several common themes emerged as the students reflected on the weeklong role-play conducted through the Collective Bargaining Education Project in the Los Angeles Unified School District (LAUSD).

"Without a union," Mario said, "there is no bargaining in the workplace. You have to take what management gives you." "Every person has the power to make a difference, especially working together as a group," Sandra added.

Dozens of students agreed with Tony who said, "It was great! Every class should be taught this way. And every student should take this class so they can understand the need for unions and have better opportunities."

Using "popular education" techniques inspired by the teaching of Brazilian educator Paulo Freire in his most famous work, *Pedagogy of the Oppressed* (1970), the Collective Bargaining Education Project is bringing the labor movement to life in Los Angeles classrooms. Fellow social studies teacher Patty Litwin and I have compiled a six-part curriculum to engage students and their teachers in the past, present, and future of labor-management relations.[1] In addition to the collective bargaining simulation, the curriculum now includes role-plays of the Homestead Strike of 1892 and the 1934 West Coast Longshoremen's Strike from *The Power in Our Hands* (Bigelow & Diamond, 1988); a simulation of a contemporary union organizing campaign and union election; a workshop on labor law and workplace rights, and a case study on globalization and child labor in the garment industry from the Resource Center of the Americas.[2]

Every week Patty and I visit a different high school; we are invited by social studies teachers to work directly with students in their classrooms. Each lesson lasts a week or more and features background reading, preparation in small groups, and negotiations and/or "community meetings" to consider different points of view and make important decisions about labor relations. The collective bargaining simulation includes professionals from both the labor and management sides of the table, who volunteer to mentor the students on bargaining day. On the final day, students reflect on what they have learned through group discussions and analytical writing assignments. These reflections explore the issues of power, equity, and dignity in the workplace from multiple perspectives. The results are not predetermined; instead, students experience the world of work, labor-management conflict, and public policy as a range of possibilities. They create the outcomes themselves.

Our program is unique in two respects. It is the only full-time labor education program for high school students in the country, thanks to ongoing support from our local labor movement; and its success is based on the power of popular education techniques in the classroom. Kent Wong describes the rationale of educators who use these techniques:

> Popular educators embrace a vision of education that links theory and practice, a philosophy that supports social change and that challenges existing power relationships, and a methodology that is learner centered and values the knowledge and experiences of the . . . [learner]." (Wong, 2002)

USING POPULAR EDUCATION METHODS TO TEACH ABOUT SOCIAL JUSTICE AND THE LABOR MOVEMENT

After my first year of teaching high school economics and U.S. history, I knew I had to do something differently. More than half my students had failed my classes. My social justice themes seemed compelling to me, but my lectures clearly were boring to many students whose attention drifted elsewhere; more and more students became disruptive as the months of lectures, notes, chapter assignments, and tests wore on. My mentor teachers gave me some memory games, like "Jeopardy," to ignite greater student interest in my lessons. But the excitement of competition wore off quickly and the games seemed to deepen the inequities that had already emerged in my classroom—differences between the students who succeeded on my multiple choice tests and those who failed, between those who did their homework and those who didn't, between the cooperative and the disruptive students, and, even more disturbingly, differences along class, gender, and race lines. In fact, I was reproducing the very hierarchies I wanted my students to learn to challenge in their workplaces and communities.

For guidance I turned to some members of a collective I had joined in college called "Praxis," which attempted to implement Freire's (1970) ideas in our teacher preparation program. Bill Bigelow, social studies teacher in Portland, Oregon and editor of *Rethinking Schools*,[3] sent me a lesson plan for a role-play of the 1934 West Coast longshoremen's strike that he had created with Norm Diamond, our former professor. As the lesson unfolded in my classroom, students who had been unresponsive to lectures, memorizing facts for tests, and textbook assignments suddenly came to life.

In this simulation, students directly experience the choices the actual strike participants faced. As they interact in five different social groups, students develop their points of view, negotiate with each other, and propose solutions to the strike. They decide whether the governor should call in the National Guard to reopen the port and protect strikebreakers, and what action they will take if he does. I was astounded by my students' mastery of the information and their ability to create and evaluate possible resolutions to the labor conflict. In an article for *Rethinking Schools*, Bigelow (1993) explains:

> As Paulo Freire says, "Conflict is the midwife of consciousness," and the simulated conflict in role-plays like this allows students to reflect on much larger issues: When are alliances between different social groups possible? What role should the government play in labor disputes? Can people unite for worthy goals? [These are] big and tough questions, but because they draw on an experience every student helped create, they are concrete rather than abstract. Regardless of past academic achievement, the activities and discussion challenge every student. (Bigelow, 1993)

RESULTS FOR HIGH SCHOOL STUDENTS

Students often tell us that both the process and content of the lessons in our labor education curriculum have had a deep impact on them. Why? As Bigelow puts it, "Role-plays: Show, don't tell" (Bigelow, 1994). The students learn by doing, by using ideas and information to make important decisions and solve meaningful problems. Both educational research and our own practical experience in the classroom have demonstrated that the role-play is a very powerful learning strategy. "Not only is it fun," one student told us, "but I really learned something and I feel that I had a part in learning, instead of someone just telling me." Many students report that these lessons are the best learning experience they have had in high school.

The content of the curriculum is highly relevant to the students' experience and to their futures, another vital element in effective learning. Research on the learning process shows that people retain ideas and information best that they perceive to be useful for survival (Jensen, 1996). Most of the students we work with are from working-class communities. They are often familiar with aspects of their parents' work. Many work part time themselves in low wage jobs.

By engaging in role-plays, students are able to consider multiple points of view on how to achieve a better workplace, and they learn firsthand about the benefits of unionizing and collective action in our workplaces and communities. They learn that the choices they each make as individuals and in groups make a difference. At the end of each class, dozens of students sign up for more information about careers in the labor movement, labor studies programs, and internship opportunities. Some of our students have gone on to become labor organizers (and social studies teachers!) themselves.

We also have found that whether we're working with students identified as highly gifted, or with students at an underperforming inner city school, their responses to the curriculum are qualitatively the same. Well-constructed role-plays on substantive issues serve to level the playing field in the classroom, enabling all students to access the content and demonstrate their abilities.

RESULTS FOR TEACHERS AND UNION COACHES

After several years of working in classrooms all over the LAUSD, we have improved both the content and the structure of the curriculum. With constant practice and feedback from students and teachers, we have devised ways to ensure greater participation and to enlarge the scope of the ideas for debate and discussion in each lesson. For example, we defined new tasks, such as the "discussion coordinator" in small groups to facilitate greater student participation, added or deleted steps to more effectively build the momentum of each role-play, and included new issues or new roles to deepen the curriculum.

The lessons also have a considerable impact on the teachers who invite us into their classrooms to demonstrate them. They are often moved by the leadership and critical thinking qualities their students exhibit and are introduced to the benefits of popular education pedagogy. "I've never seen my students focus so intently on any previous project," one teacher told us. "Students learned the value of negotiation from a position of strength. They saw the importance of working together for a common goal, compromising when necessary, and unionizing to gain power." Teachers tell us that students are participating who rarely have ever spoken in their classes before.

The success of our demonstration lessons raises teachers' expectations and respect for their students, and gives teachers an incentive to revise their teaching practice. We get a lot of requests for additional role-play and simulation curricula to address other social studies subjects. Teachers have also been motivated to become more involved as rank-and-file members of the teachers' union.

The labor union staff and leaders, who serve as coaches for the students' collective bargaining teams, have also expressed enthusiasm for the program. They frequently volunteer over and over again, and our volunteer pool grows every year as coaches invite their peers to join them in educating and organizing our youth. For many coaches, this is a rare opportunity to interact with young people, learn about their hopes and aspirations, and model the value of unionization to "the next generation." These union leaders recognize the importance of predisposing teenagers favorably toward unions, and they are spreading the word in the labor movement.

HOW WE BECAME A FULL-TIME LABOR EDUCATION PROGRAM

Over ten years ago, the California Federation of Teachers' (CFT) "Labor in the Schools Committee" launched a "Collective Bargaining Institute" field trip for Los Angeles high school students, modeled after a program created by Professor Irving Brotslaw at the University of Wisconsin's School for Workers. The Collective Bargaining Institute field trip event has been coordinated ever since by the UCLA Center for Labor Research and Education and the United Teachers of Los Angeles, with support from the L.A. County Federation of Labor, the L.A. Trade Tech College Labor Center, and the Federal Mediation and Conciliation Service.

Each December, 100 high school students are recruited from schools throughout the LAUSD to participate in a simulation of collective bargaining held at the teachers' union building. Students are divided into small labor and management teams and are coached by staff and leaders from dozens of local labor unions. Their teachers have the opportunity to observe the students in action and are introduced to additional curriculum resources on labor issues.

The annual Collective Bargaining Institute field trip, and other exciting lessons compiled by the CFT "Labor in the Schools Committee," laid the basis for our full-time Collective Bargaining Education Project in the Los Angeles schools today. The success of the Collective Bargaining Institute, combined with other CFT "Labor in the Schools Committee" curriculum resources, prompted the Southern California chapter of the Industrial Relations Research Association to apply for a Federal Mediation and Conciliation Service grant to implement an expanded labor education program in Los Angeles high school classrooms.

The grant was awarded and Patty and I were released from our own classrooms to develop the *Workplace Issues and Collective Bargaining in the Classroom* curriculum, and to train teachers throughout the school district by modeling the lessons in their classrooms. Over 150 high school teachers have participated in the program, more than 300 local union and business leaders are actively involved, and thousands of high school students have learned about the importance of unions in the history and future of working people.

Our Collective Bargaining Education Project has received widespread support from students, teachers, unions, labor attorneys, mediators, and management representatives from the business community in Los Angeles. Recognizing that the decline in popular knowledge about unions is a major obstacle to union organizing, our Central Labor Council and local unions have been especially effective lobbyists for our program. As a result, the LAUSD has included the Collective Bargaining Education Project in the superintendent's discretionary budget each year since 1999. We continue to receive invitations from Central Labor Councils and teacher unions around the country to help launch similar programs. And, thanks to publicity in the magazines of the American Federation of Teachers and the National Education Association, we also receive a steady stream of requests for our curriculum from individual teachers across the nation.

CONCLUSION

Through a learning process that involves direct experience around relevant issues, young people can begin to understand the sources of conflict and injustice in our society and explore possible resolutions. Our program exposes students to labor history and to contemporary bargaining and organizing practices, which prepares them to participate in unions and in organizing at their workplaces. The role-play and simulation tools we use, based on popular education techniques, also create more equitable student participation and achievement in our classrooms.

Teachers who observe and participate in our labor lessons are inspired to change their teaching practices and become more involved in their own unions. Activists in our local labor movement have the opportunity to coach students through mock collective bargaining, and in so doing, organize our emerging labor force. In short, using popular education methods in high school classes on labor issues can revitalize not only the labor movement but education itself![4]

NOTES

1. The six-part curriculum, *Workplace Issues and Collective Bargaining in the Classroom*, is available at the Collective Bargaining Education Project, (213) 386-3144, or send e-mail to cbep@lausd.k12.ca.us. See attached samples of collective bargaining fact sheets, planning form, and negotiations chart.

2. The Minnesota-based Resource Center of the Americas develops education programs, organizes anti-sweatshop campaigns, and provides educational resources. See www.AMERICAS.org.

3. Founded in 1986 by activist teachers, *Rethinking Schools* is a nonprofit, independent publisher of educational materials, including a quarterly journal as well as other books and booklets. *Rethinking Schools* materials advocate the reform of elementary and secondary education, with a strong emphasis on equity and social justice. See www.rethinkingschools.org.

4. This chapter is adapted from an article in L. Delp, M. Outman-Kramer, S. J. Schurman, & K. Wong (Eds.), *Teaching for change: Popular education and the labor movement*. Los Angeles: UCLA Center for Labor Research and Education, 2002.

REFERENCES

Bigelow, B. (1993). Getting off the track. *Rethinking Schools, 7*(4), 1.

Bigelow, B. (1994). Role-plays: Show, don't tell. In B. Bigelow, L. Christensen, S. Karp, B. Miner, and B. Peterson, *Rethinking our classrooms: Teaching for equity and justice* (pp. 114–115). Milwaukee, WI: Rethinking Schools.

Bigelow, W., & Diamond, N. (1988). *The power in our hands: A curriculum on the history of work and workers in the United States*. New York: Monthly Review Press.

Freire, P. (1970). *Pedagogy of the oppressed*. New York: Seabury.

Jensen, E. (1996). Completing the puzzle: The brain-compatible approach to learning. Del Mar, CA: Brain Store.

Wong, K. (2002). Introduction. In L. Delp, M. Outman-Kramer, S. J. Schurman, & K. Wong (Eds.), *Teaching for change: Popular education and the labor movement* (pp. 1–3). Los Angeles: UCLA Center for Labor Research and Education.

APPENDIX 13.1 UNION COLLECTIVE BARGAINING FACT SHEET

A collective bargaining session is about to begin. You will represent the Solidarity Workers Union, which includes 750 workers at Giant Grocery, a profitable grocery store that is part of the Mega Grocery Corporation, a very successful chain of 350 grocery stores nationwide. The bargaining unit includes food and general merchandise clerks, meat cutters, and clerk's helpers on all three shifts at five locations in the area. A different union that has supported the grocery workers in the past represents the delivery and the warehouse workers. The issues in your negotiations are:

1. Wages

2. Medical Benefits

3. Health and Safety

4. Seniority

Your goal is to negotiate the best wage and benefit package you can for a one year contract for your workers. The union has taken a strike vote and is prepared to walk out if its demands are not met. Any contract you negotiate is a tentative agreement, and must be voted upon by the union membership.

HERE'S SOME BACKGROUND:

1. Wages: This is one of the most important bargaining issues. The average wage of a bargaining unit member is $12.00/hr. You feel that past contracts have not kept up with inflation and that the company has not been sharing its profits with the workers whose labor creates the profits. You want this contract to make up for this. Your goal is at least a 5.5% increase in wages. Your initial demand is 8% or approximately $1.00/hour (Each wage increase of 1% = $180,000 cost to the company.)

2. Medical Benefits: Over the years, the union members have won an excellent medical insurance plan at the local HMO (Health Maintenance Organization) that is fully paid for by Giant Grocery. (Giant Grocery pays the HMO an average of $400/month for each employee's medical insurance, single and family rates combined, totaling $3.6 million/year for 750 workers.) You know the HMO is raising its rates for medical insurance and Giant Grocery wants relief for the increasing cost of medical benefits. The union members want to maintain their current benefits and this is a strike issue for them. Your initial demand is to maintain 100% company-paid medical insurance since you believe that management could pay for any cost increases with a small portion of Giant Grocery's growing profits.

3. Health and Safety: The union wants Giant Grocery to provide health and safety training to all employees every year. In addition, the union wants the company to establish a health and safety steering committee that reviews recommendations from union health and safety committees at each store. All committees would meet on company time, get updated training, conduct safety assessments at each worksite, analyze workers compensation costs, and make recommendations for reducing repetitive motion injuries and other hazards. The union believes that Giant Grocery's current pay incentive plan for supervisors who reduce injury rates in their departments is not improving workers' health and safety. Your cost estimate for this health and safety program is $50,000 for time and materials.

4. Seniority: The union wants seniority (length of service with the employer) to govern worker's selection of shifts (day, evening, and night shifts). The workers feel that currently the supervisor's favorites always get assigned to the day shift. (You could point to a pattern of race and/or gender discrimination here.)

APPENDIX 13.2. MANAGEMENT COLLECTIVE BARGAINING
FACT SHEET

A collective bargaining session is about to begin. You will represent the Giant Grocery, part of the Mega Grocery Corporation, a very successful chain of 350 grocery stores nationwide. The Solidarity Workers Union represents 750 grocery store employees on all three shifts at five locations in the area, including food and general merchandise clerks, meat cutters, and clerk's helpers. The delivery and warehouse workers are represented by a different union and have traditionally supported the grocery workers in bargaining. The issues in your negotiations are:

1. Wages

2. Medical Benefits

3. Health and Safety

4. Seniority

Your goal is to negotiate the least costly wage and benefit package you can, for a one year contract. You want to attract the best employees, yet stay within Giant Grocery's budget. The Chief Budget Officer (CBO) has instructed you to avoid spending over $1.5 million of new money on increasing wages and benefits. The CBO also wants to avoid a strike.

HERE'S SOME BACKGROUND:

1. Wages: Wages will be the most important and expensive issue you negotiate. The average wage for an employee in the bargaining unit is $12.00/hour. You want to hold wage increases to 3% to keep pace with the "cost of living" as measured by the federal government's Consumer Price Index (CPI). Each wage increase of 1% = $180,000 cost to the company. You want to keep wage costs down in order to increase the annual dividends that the company pays to stockholders. Since profits have increased a lot over the last few years, you believe that increasing dividends will encourage investors to buy more stock in the company. You could inform the union negotiators that higher wages might mean cuts in medical benefits or possibly downsizing and layoffs.

2. Medical Benefits: Giant Grocery has provided fully paid medical insurance for its employees at the local Health Maintenance Organization (HMO) that has cost $3.6 million each year (or $400/month for all employees, averaging single and family rates together). However, you have just been informed that the HMO is raising its rates 15% for the

medical benefits package you purchase. Faced with this 15% increase in the cost of fully covering your employees' health care insurance, you believe the employees should share some of the burden. So Giant Grocery can reduce labor costs, you want the employees to start contributing $60.00/month as a copayment to the HMO in order to maintain their medical insurance.

3. Health and Safety: The union is requesting a health and safety committee system that management feels is an unnecessary burden. Management believes that Giant Grocery has an above-average health and safety record and is in compliance with all relevant Occupational Safety and Health Administration (OSHA) standards. All employees already receive a health and safety handbook when hired. The Human Resources office documents all workplace injuries and encourages employees to report injuries promptly to their immediate supervisors. Giant Grocery also has an incentive pay plan for supervisors who reduce injury rates in their stores. Management believes that no additional resources are needed to address health and safety at Giant Grocery stores.

4. Seniority: You feel your supervisors should have the right to schedule the workers' shifts on "as needed" basis. The union feels scheduling should be based on seniority (length of service with the employer). You might be open to the union demand, if the union could sell cost sharing of medical costs to their members.

Issues	Union 1	Mgmt. 1	Union 2	Mgmt. 2	Union 3	Mgmt. 3	Tentative Agreement
1. Wages	8% Cost: 1% = $180,000						
2. Medical Benefits	Maintain full coverage						
3. Health and Safety	Committees and training Cost: $50,000						
4. Security	Shift Assignments By Seniority						

Figure 13.1. *Negotiations Chart*

Wages: Initial proposal and supporting reasons	Medical Benefits: Initial proposal and supporting reasons
Health and Safety: Initial proposal and supporting reasons	Seniority: Initial proposal and supporting reasons
Power: Consider the source of your power to achieve your goals. Where does it come from? What statements can you make or actions can you take to demonstrate your power to the other side? Be sure to integrate these ideas into your supports for the issues above.	

Figure 13.2. *Planning Form*

14 "We Cannot Avoid Taking Sides": Teacher Unions, Urban Communities, and Social Justice in Historical Perspective

Lauri Johnson

LAURI JOHNSON, ASSOCIATE PROFESSOR in Educational Leadership and Policy, University at Buffalo, State University of New York, tells the story of the Teachers Union of New York City whose members worked from the 1930s through the 1950s to make the communities where they taught a better place for their students and their families to live. This historical case provides a vivid example of how unions might educate teachers for social justice and how teachers, teacher educators, parents, and community members can work together to address equity issues in the larger society. She suggests that as progressive teacher educators we must reclaim these submerged historical narratives in order to provide today's teacher education students, a majority of whom will become members of teachers unions, with a vision of social justice unionism. She urges teacher educators to collaborate with teachers unions that forefront teachers as public intellectuals and view urban schools as sites of educational and social reform.

Today's teacher unions and teacher education programs inhabit an uneasy, and often conflictual, relationship with urban communities. First, urban teachers are overwhelmingly white and middle class, while urban students are predominately students of color and often poor. In Buffalo, New York, for example, students of color constitute 74 percent of the student population and over 77 percent of the students qualify for free and reduced lunches (New York State District Report Card, 2004). The predominately white teaching force, on the other hand, lives in middle-class enclaves within the city limits or nearby suburbs and represents some of the highest paid city employees. Most teacher education students in local universities and colleges grew up and attended school in these same white, middle-class suburbs and have had little exposure to the realities of urban neighborhoods.

In our financially strapped community, teacher union leaders gain the public spotlight chiefly when they press for higher salaries for teachers, defend contractual demands, and block school reform efforts, such as charter schools. As in many urban communities that experience chronic unemployment, deteriorating city services, and budget crises, teacher unions are often viewed by local parents and community activists as self-serving, out of touch with community concerns, and obstructionist in the face of school reforms that give more power to urban parents.[1] As Karp (1994) notes, today's teacher unions are seen as "defenders of privilege and bureaucracy rather than as agents of change or allies of the communities that public schools serve."

Teacher union reformers and community activists alike agree that a new vision of teacher unionism must be built in city schools that moves beyond a traditional industrial approach and recognizes that teacher unions can help teachers create better schools and work with parents and community activists as part of a broader movement for social progress. Peterson (1999) terms this "social justice unionism," a position that defends the rights of teachers as workers but goes beyond teacher professionalism and bread-and-butter issues and grounds itself in a commitment to social justice (p. 16).

The key components of social justice unionism are articulated in the document *Social Justice Unionism: A Working Draft* that was developed by 29 teacher union activists at a three-day institute sponsored by the National Coalition of Education Activists in 1994 (NCEA, 1999). In their view, social justice unionism should:

1. Defend the rights of its members while fighting for the rights and needs of the broader community and students;

2. Recognize that parents and community members are key allies and build strategic alliances with parents, other labor unions, and community groups;

3. Involve rank-and-file members in running the union and initiate widespread discussion on how education unions should respond to crises in education and society;

4. Put teachers at the center of school reform agendas, ensuring that they take ownership of reform initiatives;

5. Encourage those who work with children to use curriculum and pedagogy that promote racial and gender equity, combat racism and prejudice, encourage critical thinking about society's problems, and nurture an active, reflective citizenry that is committed to real democracy and social and economic justice;

6. Forcefully advocate for a radical restructuring of American education;

7. Aggressively educate and mobilize its membership to fight for social justice in all areas of society (pp. 129–130).

These activists conclude: "Without a new model of unionism that revives debate and democracy internally and projects an inspiring social vision and agenda externally, we will fall short of the challenges before us" (p. 130).

In fact, this is not the first time in the history of teacher unions that reformers have advocated a larger vision of unionism that views the school as a primary site for social change and embraces the notion of teachers working with urban parents and community activists for school reform. The militant Teachers Union of New York City (TU), which reached the height of its influence in the 1930s and early 1940s, proved unique in the history of American teacher organizations for its radical agenda of economic and social reform. I believe it provides a potent example of how unions might educate for social justice and nurture a community of teachers and teacher educators who are a force for change in urban schools and neighborhoods.

This chapter provides a historical narrative of the TU's community organizing efforts and professional development activities with a particular focus on the leadership of union activist Lucile Spence and the Harlem Committee. And I ask how we, as progressive teacher educators, might reclaim this radical vision of teacher unionism in order to provide alternative models for our students that foster collaborative work in urban communities.

SOCIAL JUSTICE UNIONISM IN THE PAST:
THE TEACHERS UNION OF NEW YORK CITY

The Teachers Union of New York City (TU) began in 1916 with 600 teachers but by the late 1930s reached a top membership of 6,500. With union members who represented a spectrum of ideological views on the Left, including liberals with prolabor sentiments, pacifists, suffragists, Socialists, and avowed Communists, the TU supported issues such as academic freedom and civil liberties, equal educational opportunities, progressive education, and the truthful presentation of African American life and history (Zitron, 1969). Yet their legacy as a teacher organization that both defended the rights of teachers and fought for social justice in the larger community has been largely forgotten.[2]

The TU affiliated as Local 5 of the American Federation of Teachers (AFT) and took the position from its inception that teachers were workers, "skilled workers to be sure, but workers nevertheless" (Zitron, 1969, p. 17). As Dr. Henry R. Linville, the first president of the union put it, "Teachers are just as surely employees of the interests in power as are the men who slave in factories" (p. 17). However, the TU opposed simple bread-and-butter unionism and instead advocated a platform of radical social and economic reform. Advised by school officials shortly after organizing to avoid controversial political and trade union issues, the TU paper responded: "We cannot avoid the taking of sides. Who is it that wants us to remain passive? A searching of the genesis of ideas will lead us straight to the lair of those who want the economic relations existing in American life to remain as they are" (Zitron, 1969, p. 20). The TU would remain a thorn in the side of the school bureaucracy and other teacher organizations throughout its fifty-year history.

In 1935, charging political infighting and "communist domination," President Henry Linville, several of the TU officers, and about a third of the membership split to form a rival New York City union known as the Teachers Guild. Eager to obtain the charter as New York City's chapter of the American Federation of Teachers, the Teachers Guild repeatedly lobbied the national AFT membership throughout the late 1930s to expel the TU from the national organization on charges of "communist domination." At the 1941 AFT Convention in Detroit, the Teachers Guild garnered enough support to expel the TU from the AFT, and the TU then affiliated as Local 555 of the United Public Workers of the Congress of Industrial Organizations (CIO).

The few historical studies of the TU and the Teachers Guild often focus on this political split between the two groups and the charges of "communist domination" leveled against the TU, particularly during the Cold War era. In this chapter I examine what the TU actually did in terms of community organizing and the professional development of teachers. Meanwhile, the Teachers Guild grew in membership throughout the 1950s and won a citywide vote to represent New York City teachers as the United Federation of Teachers (UFT) in 1960.

After the split, the remaining TU members (about 1,600), including Lucile Spence and a handful of African American teachers from Harlem, regrouped and escalated their radical agenda. A graduate of Hunter College with a Master's degree from Columbia University, Spence began her career teaching biology at Harlem's Wadleigh High School in 1926, becoming one of the first African American teachers employed at the school. She would later serve as Secretary of the TU and a leader in school reform efforts in Harlem. Although the TU participated in a number of battles with New York City school officials around teacher's working conditions, it was their work in promoting intercultural curriculum, advocating the professional development of teachers around issues of race, and community organizing for school reform that set them apart from other teacher unions. Lucile Spence would prove a key leader in these efforts and a bridge between Harlem's African American community organizations and the predominately white TU.

UNION LEADERS AS COMMUNITY ACTIVISTS:
THE ORIGINS OF THE HARLEM COMMITTEE

In 1935, Lucile Spence helped found the Harlem Committee of the TU to focus public attention and garner resources for the Harlem schools. Alice Citron, a Jewish teacher who had taught in the Harlem schools for 20 years (and was an active member of the Harlem chapter of the Communist Party), was also a key member of the Committee. Adopting a broad view of school reform, the Harlem Committee aimed to increase student achievement, agitate for building repairs and new building construction, incorporate black history in the classroom, combat discriminatory attitudes and actions by school employees, and hire more African American teachers and administrators. The goals and focus of the Committee were a direct outgrowth of the material conditions present in Harlem during the 1930s.

The depression years had proved difficult for all New Yorkers, but particularly the residents of Harlem. At 60 percent (a conservative estimate), the unemployment rate in Harlem was double that of whites, and almost half of the families in the neighborhood were on relief. It was the Harlem Riot on March 19, 1935, however, that brought local and national attention to Harlem's economic and social problems. Lino Rivera, a black Puerto Rican teenager, was arrested for shoplifting a pen knife from E. H. Kress, a white-owned store on 125th Street that had historically refused to hire African American employees.

As the police hustled Rivera out the back entrance of the store, a rumor spread through the assembled crowd of shoppers that the young man had been beaten and was near death. Efforts by shoppers to inquire about his condition were rebuffed by the police. In a spontaneous outpouring of anger and frustration at police brutality, worsening economic conditions, and ongoing racial discrimination in Harlem, the majority of stores along 125th Street (Harlem's main thoroughfare) were looted that night, resulting in $2 million of property damage and three deaths, including an African American teenager who was shot by the police as he ran from a looted store.

In response, Mayor Fiorello La Guardia created an interracial commission to study the conditions in Harlem that led to the riot. Dr. E. Franklin Frazier, professor of sociology at Howard University, was hired by the mayor to head up the study. With a staff of 30 assistants he conducted an eight-month-long investigation that included 25 community forums in which a cross section of Harlem residents aired their grievances about the lack of social services, employment discrimination, police brutality, and overcrowded, substandard schools ("Riot Report Bared," 1936).

Several TU members testified at the Harlem Commission's hearings, many anonymously, for fear of losing their jobs. They vividly described unsanitary and dilapidated school buildings, overcrowded classrooms on double shifts, outdated curriculum materials, the lack of psychological and social work services, and the prejudiced attitudes of many white teachers who often regarded assignment to a Harlem school as "punishment." The resulting commission report was a detailed sociological study that convincingly demonstrated the need for comprehensive social reform in Harlem (*The Complete Report*, 1969). These recommendations became fuel for the organizing efforts of teacher union activists in the Harlem Committee.

The group proved particularly adept at creating broad-based community coalitions and gaining media coverage. On March 19, 1936, the first anniversary of the Harlem Riot, the Harlem Committee sponsored a meeting of 450 delegates representing over 70 organizations at St. Martin's Chapel in Harlem. At this meeting, a coalition of church groups, labor and community organizations, and political activists announced the formation of an umbrella organization known as the Permanent Committee for Better Schools in Harlem, electing Rev. John W. Robinson, a Harlem religious leader, as chairman and Lucile Spence of the TU as secretary of the organization.

From 1936 to 1939, Lucile Spence worked tirelessly to promote the group's school reform agenda, contacting Harlem churches, civic organizations, and labor leaders to gain support. She accompanied Rev. Robinson and scores of parents and community leaders to lobby the mayor and the Board of Education for new school buildings and African American representation on the school board ("Mayor Fails to See Group," 1936). Their organizing efforts also included frequent mass meetings to publicize the deficiencies of the Harlem schools.

On January 27, 1937, the Permanent Committee for Better Schools in Harlem held a mock hearing at the Abyssinian Baptist Church, in which they conducted a "People's Trial" of the New York City Board of Education members, charging them with discrimination and neglect of the school children of Harlem. The charges included overcrowded and dilapidated school buildings, the lack of recreational facilities, and the intentional (and illegal) racial segregation of high schools in Harlem through attendance zoning practices that ensured that African American students were tracked into underresourced (and all black) training programs in dressmaking and shut out of the more technically skilled (and predominately white) vocational curriculum. A panel of jurors made up of prominent Harlemites found the Board of Education guilty on all counts and urged the Mayor to reconvene his Commission on the Harlem Riot to investigate school conditions in Harlem (Johnson, 2002).

PROFESSIONAL DEVELOPMENT FOR TEACHERS AS PUBLIC INTELLECTUALS

In addition to community organizing, the TU also carried out professional development activities to help teachers and community members examine issues of race, inequality, and democratic schooling. In 1937, under the banner of "Education for Democracy: Democracy in Education," the TU began sponsoring yearly conferences. Often attended by over 2,000 teachers, the TU conferences typically included workshop sessions on progressive education, equal educational opportunities, black history, academic freedom, civil liberties, and teaching for world democracy. Leading scholars on race relations from Columbia University and City College, and progressive New York City politicians frequently participated side-by-side on panels with union members.

Lucile Spence was a featured speaker at many of the TU annual conferences. In 1940, for instance, she chaired a panel on equal educational opportunities with civil rights activist Thurgood Marshall of the National

Association for the Advancement of Colored People (Teachers Union of New York City, 1940). The published proceedings of these conferences included photographs of the sessions, transcripts of major speeches, and summaries of issues raised by attending teachers during small group discussions. Booklets of these conference proceedings were produced yearly and distributed throughout the New York City schools (see, e.g., Teachers Union of New York City, 1938, 1941).

Every year the union also presented an award for outstanding service in the cause of education for democracy during the previous year. The recipient of the award would give a featured talk at the annual conference when accepting the award. During the 1940s, winners of the democracy award included Eleanor Roosevelt, Franz Boas, and W. E. B. DuBois. An analysis of the scope and depth of topics discussed at the TU annual conferences provides a remarkable record of the union's attempt to move radical school reform from theory to practice by providing forums where university professors, progressive politicians, teachers, and administrators could address topical issues on an equal playing field. In short, TU activists approached teacher in-service education as if New York City teachers were public intellectuals who were interested in discussing political issues, creating democratic classrooms, and promoting social change.[3]

TEACHER UNIONS AND CULTURALLY RESPONSIVE CURRICULUM

In the late 1940s the Harlem Committee was renamed the Anti-Discrimination Committee and sponsored regular in-service courses on black history and race relations, and a yearly human relations film series (Teachers Union of New York City, n. d.-b), and developed a collection of multicultural children's books that were available on loan to teachers for classroom use at the union's teacher center (Teacher Union of New York City, n.d.-a). They began the production of a yearly Negro History Week supplement, in which Lucile Spence wrote a series of articles supporting racial integration of the schools.

Other regular features of the supplement included poetry by Langston Hughes, bibliographies of recommended books on black life, revisionist articles on reconstruction and the history of slave revolts, and a yearly quiz entitled "What's Your Negro History Quotient?" The Negro History Week Supplement was distributed to teachers in school districts across the country and continued production for several years. In the early 1950s, the union also produced curriculum supplements on Puerto Rican history ("Puerto Rico Day," 1954), Jewish history ("Jewish Centenary," 1954), and Italian American history ("400 Years of Italian-American History," 1955).

Lucile Spence (1954) summed up the Harlem Committee's far-ranging efforts to infuse African American history in the New York City school curriculum in her lead article in the Negro History Week supplement:

> Our struggle has been not to get separate courses or to have one
> Negro History Week, but to get the placing of the history and con-
> tributions of the Negro in every level of social studies, literature, and
> science wherever it naturally comes. We want this written into our
> courses of study for all the children of our city—to engender pride
> for the Negro child and appreciation for the white child. (p. 1)

TEACHER UNION ACTIVISTS UNDER SIEGE

In 1949, in the wake of the red-baiting of radical groups during the Cold War
era, the TU came under fire from conservative forces on the New York City
Board of Education and in the New York state legislature, which passed the
Feinberg Law, making membership in "subversive" organizations grounds for
disqualifying teachers for employment in the public schools. In the fall of 1949,
Lucile Spence, along with four other New York City teachers, filed suit against
the New York State Feinberg Law in the New York Supreme Court. In the
record of the court proceedings, one of the teachers anonymously noted their
motivation for the suit: "I couldn't face my pupils if, after teaching democracy
all my life, I remained silent while the constitution was being destroyed"
(Opinion of Mr. Justice Harry E. Schirick, 1949). They won their case before
the State Supreme Court, but the New York State Board of Regents appealed
the decision and the U.S. Supreme Court eventually ruled that the Feinberg
Law was constitutional.

In 1950, eight leaders of the TU (including Alice Citron of the Harlem
Committee) were called out of their classrooms, interrogated by Board of
Education officials, and immediately dismissed when they refused to answer
questions about their political affiliations. Lucile Spence protested the dismissals
along with other TU members, Harlem parents, and students who demonstrated
and signed petitions to reinstate the teachers. On June 1, 1950, the TU was
officially banned from representing New York City teachers by a school board
resolution (Teachers Union of New York City, 1950). In 1952, as the witch hunts
escalated, the Senate Internal Security Subcommittee held public hearings into
the political affiliations of New York City teachers and college professors.

Spence was subpoenaed to testify, along with several other TU leaders.
Most of the teachers took the Fifth Amendment and were subjected to disciplinary proceedings by the New York City Board of Education. Over 300
New York City teachers were fired or resigned under the pressure of these
McCarthy-type hearings. Spence was one of only a handful of teachers who
swore under oath that she "was not and had never been a member of the
Communist Party" ("Senate's Communist Inquiry Reaches into Local Colleges," 1952). In fact, during the Popular Front era of the 1930s and early
1940s, many progressive African Americans in Harlem, who were unaffiliated
worked with Socialist and Communist party members on specific reform
efforts (see, e.g., Caute 1978; Naison, 1983; Biondi, 2003).

Throughout the trials and tribulations of the Teacher's Union in the 1950s, however, Lucile Spence remained loyal to the organization. She continued to serve as secretary of the union, worked with other union members to produce a study of bias and prejudice in New York City textbooks (Teachers Union of New York City, 1948), and assisted with a series of surveys to document the lack of African American teachers in the New York City schools (see, e.g., Teachers Union of New York City, 1951, 1955). The union continued to work with parent and community groups around school integration issues after the Brown v. Board of Education of Topeka case, but the Cold War investigations marked the beginning of a protracted and costly legal battle by union activists to defend their jobs as teachers and the direction of their union. The union officially disbanded in the early 1960s, and many teachers who were fired were not reinstated until 1972 (Buder, 1972).

Although Spence retired from teaching in 1961, she remained active as an educator and activist on the international scene. She taught with Operation Crossroads in Liberia and Ghana, a volunteer organization often cited as the forerunner and inspiration for the Peace Corps, that was started by Rev. James Robinson in 1960 to enlist American college students in providing educational and technical services to African countries ("200 U.S. Students to Work Five Weeks in African Villages," 1960). She also served as chairwoman of the Women's Africa Committee of the African-American Institute, founded in New York City in the late 1950s to assist in African development and strengthen African American links to Africa. In a final tribute, Lucile Spence was inducted into the Hunter Alumni Hall of Fame in 1973 in recognition for her long career as a Harlem teacher and labor activist (Hunter Hall of Fame, 1973). She died in Harlem on August 14, 1975 (Lucille Spence, 1975).

SOCIAL JUSTICE UNIONISM IN THE FUTURE: THE LEGACY OF THE TEACHERS UNION

On the one hand, the fate of the TU represents a sad chapter in the history of teacher organizing and community activism. Their experiences underscore the chilling effect of government censorship in education and the importance of protecting academic freedom and safeguarding the rights of teachers and other workers to organize for social reform without government interference. One might also argue that this legacy of radical teachers and teacher unions has been suppressed in the historical record as well. In standard accounts, the activities of the TU are often discounted as "Communist dominated" and partisan, with little attention paid to their role in promoting antiracist and antifascist curriculum and their community engagement with African American parents in New York City neighborhoods like Harlem, Bedford-Stuyvesant, and the South Bronx. These lessons, of the power of government surveillance and selective memory of the past, should not go unnoticed in our post-9/11 America that privileges "national security issues" over political protest, and where efforts to educate students for democratic citizenship can be reduced to "patriotism based on fear."

On the other hand, the process of excavating the history of Lucile Spence and other activists in the Harlem Committee of the TU proved personally inspirational to me, and can inspire today's progressive teacher educators as well. As an urban teacher educator who spent much of her career working in the New York City schools, I was unaware of the heroic struggles of teachers and parents to promote diversity and structural reform in the New York City schools in the 1930s and 1940s. I have taken heart from the courage and resolve of teacher union activists who risked their jobs to promote progressive causes and the determination and political savvy of parents and community members who advocated for better schools and culturally responsive curriculum and pedagogy for communities of color long before it became popular in educational literature. As a multiculturalist, discovering this legacy has given real meaning to the notion of "standing on the shoulders" of a long line of diversity advocates who have come before.

In addition, as a teacher educator I have gained new insights into how university faculty might work with teacher union activists to develop powerful professional and community development activities that promote social justice in urban communities. I was particularly impressed with the TU's ability to engage progressive academics, politicians, and urban teachers in ongoing discussions and inquiry into specific school reform issues. In the 1930s and 1940s the TU conducted a number of action research projects with the assistance of university faculty, which documented the lack of teachers of color in urban neighborhoods, the lack of diversity in textbooks and curriculum materials, and surveyed teachers' views on progressive curriculum projects. These investigative reports, widely publicized in the New York City media, became organizing tools to rally parents and community members at mass meetings to press for policy changes in urban schools. Today, this would be called "constituency building" in school reform work, and the TU played a key role in bringing diverse stakeholders together around the need for change in urban schools. Their work provides an example of how today's teacher educators might work with unions to marshal the evidence and build pressure for educational policy changes that result in more equitable funding, assessment practices, and culturally responsive curriculum for urban schools, as well as socially just economic policies (Anyon, 2005).

The TU also enlisted well-known anthropologists, sociologists, historians, writers, and teacher educators from Columbia University and New York University to present ongoing in-service courses, institutes, and workshops throughout the 1940s, free to New York City teachers, which explored new scholarship on race relations and African American history and literature, and gave urban teachers a platform to present their own intercultural curriculum projects to other teachers. This ongoing staff development, where scholars presented side-by-side with classroom teachers, proved a more sophisticated version of what we now term "teacher resource centers," where local teacher unions provide in-service workshops for teachers. It points the way to how interdisciplinary teams of educators from local universities might work with teacher unions to establish on-site staff development in urban school districts that seriously addresses the real work of improving urban teaching.

The activities of the TU in the 1930s and 1940s also provide us with a valuable glimpse of what social justice unionism might look like. This model links unions and teacher educators in an effort to improve the living conditions in urban neighborhoods; recognizes that any movement for school reform must involve urban parents and community members as equal players; develops and promotes curriculum and instruction to combat racism and ethnic prejudice; and nurtures an active and reflective teaching force and citizenry to create democracy and social justice in schools and society. Peterson (1999) notes that today's teacher unions, which are increasingly under attack, will not survive unless they are seen as advocates of social justice school reform. In short, it is only by building alliances (as the TU did) with the community, urban parents, and progressive teacher educators that teacher unions will be able to withstand the current conservative onslaught. It is in the interest of progressive teacher educators to foster these alliances and make sure that progressive teacher unions survive.

Today's teacher educators and future urban teachers in our university classrooms have no collective memory of how teacher unions might be different, or how urban teachers might act as public intellectuals rather than bureaucrats and technicians. As progressive urban teacher educators, we must reclaim and revoice the historical narratives of urban education's radical past in order to create new spaces and opportunities where our work might connect (and reestablish) a more progressive heritage of teacher unionism and teacher education activism. We must present powerful counternarratives about union activists like Lucile Spence of the Harlem Committee, Layle Lane of the American Federation of Teachers (Johnson, 2004), and Margaret Haley of the Chicago Teachers Federation (Rousmaniere, 2005), in order to name different realities and keep the memory of radical teacher unionism alive. We must use these narratives to fashion a new vision of how teacher educators can support social justice unionism. As Fielding (2005) puts it, we must "put our hands around the flames of our own stories to protect them and help us see the presence of possibility in the gloom of troubled times" (p. 63).

In these troubled times, when teachers and teacher unions are encouraged to support the status quo of uninspired prepackaged curriculum, relentless high-stakes testing, and undemocratic practices in urban schools, we cannot avoid taking sides. As progressive teacher educators, we either stand with our students, their parents, and union activists as agents of change in urban schools and neighborhoods, or we end up propping up a bankrupt educational system that is not serving the needs and best interests of poor and working-class students in urban schools. Which side are you on? I'm taking my cue from

Lucile Spence and the other committed teacher union activists of the Teachers Union of New York City.

NOTES

1. In a series of interviews I conducted with local parent activists in Buffalo the educational unions were frequently mentioned as major stumbling blocks for school reform efforts.

2. Portions of this account of Lucile Spence and the Harlem Committee of the Teachers Union of New York City appeared in Johnson (2002) and Johnson (2004).

3. My use of the term public intellectual is similar to Giroux's (1985, 1990) notion that teachers should be transformative intellectuals who combine scholarly reflection and practice to work for social change and to educate students for democratic citizenship.

REFERENCES

Anyon, J. (2005). *Radical possibilities: Public policy, urban education, and a new social movement.* New York: Routledge.

Biondi, M. (2003). *To stand and fight: The struggle for civil rights in postwar New York City.* Cambridge, MA: Harvard University Press.

Buder, L. (1972, September 21). City acts to rehire 31 teachers ousted in McCarthy era. *The New York Times,* 1, 26.

Caute, D. (1978). *The great fear: Anti-communist purge under Truman and Eisenhower.* New York: Simon & Schuster.

The complete report of Mayor LaGuardia's commission on the Harlem Riot of March 19, 1935. (1969). New York: Arno Press & *The New York Times.*

Fielding, M. (2005). Putting hands around the flame: Reclaiming the radical tradition in state education. *Forum,* 47(2 & 3), 61–70.

400 years of Italian-American history. (1955, September 30). *The New York Teacher News,* 1–4.

Giroux, H. A. (1985). Teachers as transformative intellectuals. *Social Education,* 49(5), 76–79.

Giroux, H. A. (1990). Curriculum theory, textual authority, and the role of teachers as public intellectuals. *Journal of Curriculum and Supervision,* 5(4), 361–383.

Hunter Hall of Fame, Alumni Association of Hunter College (1973). New York: Hunter College Archives.

Jewish centenary. (1954, November 27). *The New York Teacher News,* 1–4.

Johnson, L. (2002). "Making democracy real": Teacher union and community activism to promote diversity in the New York City public schools, 1935–1950. *Urban Education* 37(5), 566–587.

Johnson, L. (2004). "A generation of women activists: African American female educators in Harlem, 1930–1950. *Journal of African American History, 89,* 223–240.

Karp, S. (1994). Rethinking teacher unionism. *Z Magazine*. Accessed on January 10, 2006 at http://zena.secureforum.com/Znet/zmag/articles/karp1.htm.

Mayor fails to see group. (1936, April 18). *The New York Amsterdam News*, 2.

Naison, M. (1983). *Communists in Harlem during the depression*. Urbana: University of Illinois Press.

National Coalition of Education Activists. (1999). Social justice unionism: A working draft. In B. Peterson and M. Charney (Eds.), *Transforming teacher unions: Fighting for better schools and social justice* (pp. 128–132). Milwaukee, WI: Rethinking Schools.

New York State District Report Card. (2004). District comprehensive information report: Buffalo City School District, 2003–2004. Retrieved on January 10, 2006. http://emsc33.nysed.gov/repcrd2004/links/d_140600.html.

Opinion of Mr. Justice Harry E. Schirick of the Supreme Court of the State of New York Declaring the Feinberg "Subversive Activities" Law Unconstitutional, Nov. 28, 1949, Schomburg Center Clipping File, 1925–1974, Teachers NYC, Sc004, 843.

Peterson, B. (1999). Survival and justice: Rethinking teacher union strategy. In B. Peterson and M. Charney (Eds.), *Transforming teacher unions: Fighting for better schools and social justice* (pp. 11–19). Milwaukee, WI: Rethinking Schools.

Puerto Rico Day. (1954, November 13). *The New York Teacher News*, 1–4.

Riot report bared. (1936, July 18). *The New York Amsterdam News*, 1–4.

Rousmaniere, K. (2005). *Citizen teacher: The life and leadership of Margaret Haley*. Albany: State University of New York Press.

Senate's communist inquiry reaches into local colleges. (1952, September 25). *The New York Times*, 1.

Spence, Lucile. (1975, August 18), *The New York Times*, 28.

Spence, L. (1954, January 16). The struggle for integration. *The New York Teacher News*, 1.

Teachers Union of New York City. (n.d.-a). *Recommended list of books for better human relations*. New York: Author.

Teachers Union of New York City. (n.d.-b). *Reference list of human relations films*. New York: Author.

Teachers Union of New York City. (1938). *Education for democracy: An abstract of speeches and discussion*. New York: Author.

Teachers Union of New York City. (1940). *Education for democracy: 1940 annual educational conference program*. New York: Author.

Teachers Union of New York City. (1941). *"Education—Democracy's first line of defense": Proceedings of the fifth annual educational conference*. New York: Author.

Teachers Union of New York City. (1948). *Bias and prejudice in textbooks in use in New York City schools: A Teachers Union report*. New York: Author.

Teachers Union of the City of New York. (1950). *The Timone Resolution, July 6, 1950*. New York: Author.

Teachers Union of the City of New York. (1951). *A survey on the employment of Negro teachers in New York City public schools.* New York: Author.

Teachers Union of the City of New York. (1955). *A survey on the employment of Negro teachers in New York City.* New York: Author.

200 U.S. students to work five weeks in African villages. (1960, May 30). *The New York Times,* 1.

Zitron, C. (1969). *The New York City Teachers Union, 1916–1964: A story of educational and social commitment.* New York: Humanities Press.

15 For Further Thought

Mary E. Finn

MARY E. FINN, RETIRED DIRECTOR OF THE Urban Education Institute, Graduate School of Education, University at Buffalo, examines some of the assumptions that underlie teacher education with an attitude, assumptions about democracy, equality, individual opportunity, collectivity, and solidarity. It extends the argument for social justice teacher educators to collaborate with progressive worker educators by looking at both historical and contemporary works that shed light on the topic of preparing teachers to strengthen democracy through education.

MERITOCRACY OR DEMOCRACY?

Educators, like most other members of the human race, live comfortably with contradictions and unresolved conflicts in the assumptions that underlie their beliefs and practices. One such example is the conflict between meritocracy and democracy, where meritocracy suggests that the hierarchical ranking of individuals reflects the fact that those at the top have more merit than those below them and thus deserve more of society's benefits, and where democracy implies that all citizens are fully and equally entitled to share in certain social (citizenship) rights and benefits regardless of their social rank (Finn, chapter 1). These opposing assumptions are important in considering academic testing, which too often is used to maintain the hierarchical status quo, with its large economic and education gaps between the top and the bottom social classes.

Aptitude tests are designed to measure one's ability to acquire what can be called cultural capital—society's accumulated knowledge and skills that have been deemed worthy of being transmitted to future generations and that provide a foundation for creating new knowledge and skills. Although the American dream advertises that access to cultural capital is available to all comers, cultural capital, like economic capital, is largely controlled by the dominant social classes. Those whose access is denied are rightly angered. Among them are the parents of children in schools with low test scores who realize the impact these scores have on their children's future opportunities for educational and personal success. Parents know that eliminating testing is not the answer and demand instead the resources necessary to attain more equitable educational outcomes.[1]

Withholding the resources necessary to develop each child's potential to achieve is a form of violence, a social hurt that carries grave consequences for children and for society (Galtung, 2001). Both educational and economic resources are needed to develop potential. Elite families go to great lengths to insure their children's education provides powerful learning experiences that develop critical analytic, inquiry, and communication skills. Children of working families need educational experiences that develop the same skills, experiences that also acknowledge the disparities built into the social and economic hierarchy and that motivate the children to learn in order to reduce or eliminate the disparities. As Finn (chapter 1) proposed, oppositional identity and resistance to acquiring cultural capital because it is seen as belonging to "those other folks" can be overcome with such "Freirean motivation."

There is also the need to address what research has established are the educational consequences of both inadequate economic resources and the culture of racism (Rothstein, 2004). The emotional and physical consequences of uncertain income and the inability to secure adequate shelter, food, clothing, and medical care for one's family are the most obvious. These insecurities, however, also affect one's view of the future, and whether there is any point in making plans for it, and they contribute to the culture of underachievement, a lack of faith, based on historical and personal experiences, that hard work and educational success necessarily result in good jobs and secure income.

Rothstein (2004) cites research that confirms the educational consequences of social class differences in economic resources and child rearing that Finn (1999) describes. He adds important data about the size of vocabulary to which young children are exposed in their homes, and the way they spend time after school and in summers, as factors that also affect preparation for school success. All these factors make it more difficult for working-class families to give their children a good preparation for learning than for upper class families. So while all children do learn in school, "those from lower classes, on average, do not learn so much faster that they can close the achievement gap" that results (Rothstein, 2004, p. 15).

Academic testing, which is extremely "family-background sensitive" (Lehmann, 1999, p. 156), compounds the problem. That is, tests tend to reflect the social class differences in family economic and educational background that contribute significantly to a child's preparation for school success. Tests can only discover talent or aptitude that has had a chance to develop through adequate preparation. Government policy, however, has not acknowledged the need to assure that families have the economic and educational assets to reduce the preparedness gap.

Instead of assuring there is no preparedness gap, government policy views testing as a fair way to determine who gets what sort of education by assigning students to their place in the meritocractic hierarchy, the vertical ranking of individuals from most deserving of high quality education, to those least able to benefit from it. The objectivity of this process masks its unfairness and reinforces the deeply embedded resistance to economic reforms that could equalize the family background characteristics that contribute to differences in school preparedness. Critics prefer to blame and punish schools, teachers, and students for low test scores, even though the Civil Rights-era Coleman Report showed that differences in the achievement gap were largely explained by educational and economic differences in students' families.

The Coleman Report was supposed to supply the evidence necessary to move Congress to provide massive amounts of aid to schools attended by large numbers of African American students. Coleman discovered instead, to his own dismay, that differences in educational and economic assets of black and white students' families were more important than their schools' resources (Lehmann, 1999, p. 160; Rothstein, 2004, pp. 14-15). Because black students who attended integrated schools fared better than those who didn't, many civil and educational rights reformers relied on greater school integration through busing to close the achievement gap, rather than infusing black schools with adequate resources (Lehmann, 1999, p. 160). This solution has been largely abandoned today because it resulted in white flight from cities and nearly complete resegregation of schools in many urban districts.

The most serious consequence of the Coleman Report today is that educational critics and policy-makers concluded they could largely ignore differences in school resources, and they assumed they had no responsibility for the social class differences in students' families. Both conclusions were wrong. Forty years of research confirms Coleman's core findings (i.e., "no analyst has been able to attribute less than two-thirds of the variation in achievement among schools to the family characteristics of their students") (Rothstein, 2004, p. 14). But this does not mean that schools have no impact. Research also indicates the achievement gap does not grow during the regular school year, so although schools are "probably doing a great deal to narrow [the gap] during the regular school day, these efforts are offset by gap-widening experiences in the after-school hours" and by the way children spend time during the summer break (p. 58).

Lareau (2003) attributes these different out of school experiences to social class differences in child-rearing. Middle- and upper-middle-class families practice what she calls "concerted cultivation," which involves, among other things, organizing family time around children's extensive schedule of team sports, lessons, and performances. Working-class children are more likely to be raised in a spirit of "natural growth"; they spend more time with other children in self-directed or open-ended play. These differences are a matter of both economic resources and habits and beliefs (Talbot, 2003).

Rothstein (2004) concludes that it is not possible to equalize achievement between children of different social classes without reforming "the economic and social institutions that ensure unequal achievement, on average, for children of different social classes" (Rothstein, 2004, 94). He offers a more radical and probably more accurate reading of Coleman's findings by arguing for massive spending, not on schools per se, but on working families and their young children so that when their children reach school they are on a more nearly level playing field with children from elite families. While it could cost as much as $156 billion annually to close the school preparedness gap by providing working-class children with the necessary early childhood experiences, this figure "is only about two-thirds of the average annual cost of federal tax cuts enacted since 2001" (Rothstein, 2004, p. 145).

So, schools matter, and could matter more if all children were raised in families with the resources necessary to prepare them for success in school. But we'll never get resources equitably distributed so that aptitude tests no longer correlate highly with social class unless we acknowledge the conflict between the concepts of democracy and meritocracy, and the way both are related to our ideas of opportunity. Lehmann (1999) tells how an IQ-like academic aptitude test, the Scholastic Aptitude Test (SAT), came to have such influence on our educational system and society as a whole. His story reflects our faith in both of these contradictory concepts and goes a long way toward explaining why there has been no groundswell of enthusiasm or demand for the economic remedies Rothstein (2004) suggests would lift entire classes of people.

The SAT is one of the main determinants of academic merit today; that is, decisions about who has the aptitude for and thus deserves to have a powerful higher education are strongly influenced by SAT scores. This test filled the need of higher education reformers after WWII to recruit and educate an elite based on aptitude for scholarly endeavor. This new merit-based elite was to replace the older hereditary elite (based on families' accumulation of economic and cultural assets) that had long used such venerable institutions as Harvard and Yale to pass on their social status to their children. The new elite, with higher academic aptitude than the hereditary one, would provide the research and scholarship to meet the new world leadership needs of the United States in the post–World War II period.

The SAT's role was to discover potential border-crossers, individuals from nonelite families whose higher levels of aptitude for scholarly work might have been overlooked in the ordinary scheme of things; scholarships then provided them entrance to elite colleges and universities. Today, however, the new meritocratic elite is much like the older hereditary one; its beneficiaries busily work to solidify their status and pass it on to their children, whom they groom for elite status beginning with highly selective preschools, and whom, if they do not exhibit sufficient natural academic aptitude, they bolster with an army of specialists and expensive SAT test prep tutoring (Lehmann, 1999, p. 345).

Although the meritocratic system claims to be "a way of determining fairly who gets America's material rewards," one would design the system we have today only if one believed that high SAT scores and academic performance "are the same thing as merit" (Lehmann, 1999, p. 344), which is exactly what the founders of the SAT-based American meritocracy (Harvard's Conant, Berkeley's Kerr, and Educational Testing Service's [ETS] Chauncey) presumed: "to reward educational performance was to reward merit itself" (Lehmann, 1999, p. 120).

Denying opportunity has long been morally unacceptable in America. But equally unacceptable in a democracy is a system where competition for the opportunity to acquire a high status education takes place as early in life as possible, and in the school arena, where the "influences of parentage, of background culture and class are at their highest and most explicit," and which results in schools reproducing the social structure, not altering it (Lehmann, 1999, p. 345). Any hierarchy or meritocracy that is based on aptitude or achievement tests that are clearly family-asset sensitive denies the very equality of opportunity it pretends to offer. And any form of hierarchy based on a concept of opportunity that compares individuals through testing, ranks them vertically, and strictly parcels out rewards accordingly, is a challenge to democracy.

Michael Young (1958), the British sociologist who invented the term "meritocracy" to describe a social order that he viewed as an "object of horror," had serious doubts about individual opportunity (Lehmann, 1999, p. 343). For Young, even if tests provided equality of opportunity through a nonhereditary form of selection for places on the social pyramid, an increase in social justice and democracy could not be guaranteed as long as the hierarchical structure was in place. The people at the top might now have more academic ability than those from older hereditary elites, and they may have worked harder to earn advancement and thus be seen as more deserving of their high places, but the inequality between the top and the bottom would not necessarily change.

As long as people buy into the idea that equal opportunity means anyone can climb to the top of the social and economic pyramid, no matter how unrealistic that is, and that everyone should have that as a goal, those at the top will feel justified in trying to keep their place and to pass it on to their children. They will, therefore, stand in the way of efforts to make the system more equitable and democratic, to flatten the hierarchy, and they will have the social, economic, and political power to guarantee success in keeping the structure intact. So the way schools (and society) use tests keeps the hierarchy safe. A few border-crossers benefit, but political will to give the working classes collectively the benefits of a powerful education will still be lacking.

New thinking is needed about alternative ways to structure society and to distribute rewards, one where the reward for talent is access to the resources needed to develop it, for instance, and where there is greater equity of educational outcomes. It is hard to hold onto such alternative views, however, when society focuses so completely on individuals as the primary unit of worth, and when we each feel so individually autonomous. How have the working classes themselves thought about the problem and what solutions have they proposed? What can progressive, social justice teacher educators learn from them?

WORKER EDUCATION MODELS
FOR DEMOCRATIC TEACHER EDUCATION

Organized labor's clear-headed view of the class structure of American society, and their experience educating and organizing working-class adults, offer valuable suggestions for preparing teachers to educate for understanding the social and economic power structure, and to actively engage in making educational and economic policy decisions more just and equitable.

Worker educators in the early part of the last century, in both Britain and the United States, understood that schools for the working classes were organized around the interests of the dominant classes, and that those interests clashed with the interests of the working classes. They knew the working class would never acquire the type of analytic skills necessary to understand how the structure of society continued to cause their distress if they only received an education that the dominant class determined to be suitable for them, the type of working-class education Anyon (1981) described. A healthy union movement, they concluded, required an independent education for workers.

In their history of British working-class education, Horrabin and Horrabin (1924) distinguished between the Extensionists, who wanted to extend the benefits of culture to adults members of the British working class, and the Independents, who wanted "a particular kind of education, aiming primarily at meeting the specific needs of the workers themselves independently of, and even in opposition to, the ordinary existing educational channels" (Horrabin & Horrabin, 1924, pp. 9–10).[2]

The Independent's goal for working-class education was to "bring men [sic] out of ignorance of the principles on which societies are formed and governed." Workers who are provided their own education, inquire and investigate until they understand why "they only, of all classes of society, have always been involved in poverty and distress" (Horrabin & Horrabin, 1924, pp. 17–19). The first step in understanding why an "independent" education is needed for the working class is to realize that no education is neutral or nonpartisan. Independents agreed that education was the means to working-class emancipation, but the traditional education system was suspect because it sought "to train up youths . . . to be submissive admirers of 'things as they are' " (Horrabin & Horrabin, 1924, p. 27), clearly a partisan position.

The status quo is not maintained by engaging in overt indoctrination, but rather by denying that social class or group conflict exists (Altenbaugh, 1990, p. 5). Independent worker educators in Britain understood that:

ordinary education . . . elementary or "higher," is definitely propaganda for the existing order. Propaganda does not consist simply of the dogmatic assertion of certain conclusions. It is much more effective when it relies on the quiet taking for granted of certain assumptions. And the fundamental assumption of all education which does not consciously challenge the existing order of society is that the existing order is, on the whole, desirable and likely to be permanent. (Horrabin & Horrabin, 1924, p. 73)

So Independent worker education curricula focused on sociology, history, and economics, the subjects that "naturally lent themselves to keen debating on all those problems which lay closest to the everyday life of the workers" (p. 58), and which provided skills for asserting their collective self-interest and for "building of a new social order" (p. 72).

The U.S. worker education movement, similar in time and goals to the British movement, produced several resident labor colleges, of which the best known was Brookwood, established in upstate New York in 1921. The curriculum at Brookwood continued the British Independents' focus on analysis and inquiry into the history and structure of society and the worker's place in it, as well as the need for powerful literacy in order for workers to articulate their positions and negotiate just solutions to the inequities they encountered. One instructor noted that the students came for knowledge but then they needed "to learn how to use facts after they have them—how to express their ideals so the crowd will get them and be moved to *action* by them; how to put ideas into print so people will read and understand them." These were the tool (or powerful literacy) courses (Altenbaugh, 1990, p. 93).

In addition to Brookwood's progressive curriculum, there was a clear articulation of the pedagogy that was most effective with workers—reflective, participatory, active, and experience-based pedagogy. Traditional pedagogy was seen as a form of oppression because "the more completely students accepted the passive and subservient role imposed upon them by the traditional class-room, the more they would adapt to . . . society instead of functioning as active agents for social change" (Altenbaugh, 1990, p. 130). When Brookwood came under attack by the American Federation of Labor (AFL) for the radical views of some of the faculty, John Dewey defended the school. Brookwood, he said, "more than most educational institutions of whatever sort, has been truly educational in living up to its effort to lead students to think—which means, of course, to think for themselves" (Dewey, 1929, p. 214).

With the demise of the independent labor colleges in Britain and the United States during the economic crisis of the Great Depression, worker education continued to develop in universities and in classes offered in local union halls. The larger goal of a new social order, however, received less attention in these less independent educational environments. For example, as one historian noted, the consequence of closing the London Central Labour College was that the "sociological subjects which enable the adult worker to understand society in its concrete interrelated totality" received less emphasis (Craik, 1964, p. 158). And more practical classes, useful "for the everyday domestic work of a trade union," (e.g., running meetings, organizing, and managing an office, bookkeeping, record keeping, etc.) received greater emphasis

(Altenbaugh, 1990, p. 96). Without the residential labor colleges, with their focus on social, political, and economic theory and visions of a new social order, fewer new labor leaders and educators were being prepared with the knowledge and analytical ability "indispensable to the intellectual equipment of the workers for the conquest of political power" (Craik, 1964, p. 156).

This eventually took a toll on the labor movement in both the United States and Britain. The AFL underwent tremendous growth and then steep decline and significant change after Brookwood closed its doors in 1937. Beginning with the merger with the Congress of Industrial Organizations (CIO) the percentage of U.S. workers who belonged to unions climbed to nearly a third of the workforce in the 1950s; today, "it's barely one in ten" (Bai, 2005, p. 40). Americans' overall approval of labor unions increased from 55 percent in 1981 to 60 percent in 2001 (Cole, 2004) and *Business Week* reported that the number of nonunion workers who say they would vote for a union at their company increased from 30 percent in 1984 to 47 percent in 2003, yet potential union members "are often intimidated by illegal firings of union supporters." Such firings increased in frequency from 8 percent in 1964–1965 to 25 percent in 1998–1999 (Business Week, 2004, p. 84).

This important topic, however, finds little or no space in the educational curriculum. A recent poll indicates that Americans' chief source of knowledge about labor unions comes from personal experience, people they know in unions, and the media, (which frequently focuses on the hardship consumers suffer when unions strike rather than the hardships of the workers (Martin, 2004). "Learning about unions in school was not even mentioned" (Cole, 2004, p. 1). As Schurman (chapter 2) explains, popular educators have had some success using Freirean pedagogy to educate and organize workers, and Tubac (chapter 13) describes ongoing efforts to introduce the topic of trade unionism into classrooms. Much more of this sort of work is needed, however, to stop the decline in industrial trade union membership and power.[3]

Service industry and teachers unions have become the largest unions in the country. The 2.7 million-member National Educational Association (NEA) has members in every congressional district; the smaller American Federation of Teachers (AFT) has 1 million members. Many supporters of public education fear the voucher and charter school movements are attempts to further the conservatives' goal of breaking the union movement by reducing the membership of the teachers unions and thus eliminating a source of powerful support for such issues as equity in educational funding, increase in the minimum wage, and other economic policies that would benefit the education of the children of working families (Rethinking Schools, 2004, p. 4).

The future of both public schools and teachers unions today may depend, as Counts and Brameld (1941) noted decades ago, on rallying public support not only for the schools, but for "the fundamental place of trade unionism in a democracy. . . . Issues of crucial importance to an intelligent understanding of labor in our society are warped or completely avoided in thousands of educational institutions in the U.S." (Counts and Brameld, 1941, pp. 256–257). In addition, "The training of teachers thus far has not led to the correction of this situation in the schools." Teachers have forgotten to ask, "What kind of society should we strive to build?" In addition, "The training of teachers has not only largely neglected such questions, but university faculties . . . abet such neglect by preserving 'above-the-battle' disdain for the world of economic and social realities which awaits outside" (Counts and Brameld, 1941, pp. 250–251).

Collaboration between teacher education and organized labor could help teachers realize "first, that democracy is itself successful only in the degree that the great majority of people share in the control and use of the resources which make for security, growth, happy living; and, second, [echoing John Dewey] that the teachers are themselves in status, interests and ideals, affiliated with this majority" (Counts and Brameld, 1941, p. 259). In urging teachers to join the American Federation of Teachers, Counts and Brameld argue:

> Affiliation with organized labor brings about more understanding by the teacher of the lives of working people, of the weaknesses and strengths of trade unions; and other matters about which teachers are traditionally ignorant. . . . Such understanding in turn leads to greater probability that the study of American history, economics, and politics will receive honest treatment in the classroom. (Counts and Brameld, 1941, pp. 260–61)

Realizing this result requires a "vastly greater emphasis . . . on the social and philosophical foundations of education than is now commonly the case" (Counts and Brameld, 1941, p. 262). Just the opposite, unfortunately, has happened in many teacher education programs in the ensuing 65 years.

To put collaboration between progressive teacher educators and progressive labor into practice, Counts and Brameld (1941) suggested teacher education students get hands-on experiences in labor organizations through internships [or field experiences] in unions' research and education departments, and that joint committees of teacher educators, their students, and members of local unions be established to plan specific campaigns around economic policies [such as minimum wage], that impact all parties. For their part, unions could hold open houses and invite teachers to social events to open lines of communication that might lead to establishing parent-teacher groups within union locals and teachers participating in central labor bodies through membership on their various committees (Counts & Brameld, 1941, pp. 266–267).

Teacher education with an attitude can prepare teachers who work within the public school system to provide this sort of independent working-class education, if, as Noguera (2005) says, we have the will. But this requires more openness to a collective view of education and a society that focuses on the common good (Tomasky, 2006), based in what Williams (1958) called a "common culture."

HOW CAN A COMMON CULTURE CONTRIBUTE TO DEMOCRACY?

One of the most difficult aspects of preparing teachers for success with urban students from working families is overcoming the culture gap. Today's teacher education students are predominately white, suburban, middle class, and female (Lauricella, 2005, p. 123). Teaching in urban neighborhoods is not the first choice of these future teachers. In fact, the Research About Teacher Education study found that over 85 percent of prospective teachers "preferred to teach in contexts other than urban neighborhood schools where there are often differences between them and their students in terms of culture, language, race, and class" (Howey & Post, 2002, p. 267).

Those individuals who do end up teaching in urban schools need help in bridging the cultural divide that separates them from their students. Critical multicultural, antiracist, and sociocultural education reforms have aimed to do just that by creating greater understanding and appreciation for cultural differences (Banks, 1998; Sleeter, 1996; Oakes & Lipton, 2002). Following the argument of Raymond Williams (1958), however, it also may be helpful for educators to consider ways to further a common, democratic culture to which all social classes, races, and ethnic groups contribute.

Williams (1958) wrote about culture in Britain from 1780 to1950, but he also had many challenging and provocative things to say about democracy, equality, social class, education, art and communication that have relevance for twenty-first-century American society. Especially interesting for those who prepare teachers of working-class children is his discussion of popular or working-class culture versus real or middle-class culture. "If the major part of our culture, in the sense of intellectual and imaginative work, is to be called, as the Marxists call it, *bourgeois,* it is natural to look for an alternative culture, and to call it *proletarian*" (p. 320). Williams does not find this a very useful distinction, however. "The body of intellectual and imaginative work which each generation receives as its traditional culture is always, and necessarily, something more than the product of a single class." While there will always be dissident elements in a culture, he believes "the area of culture . . . is usually proportionate to the area of a language rather than to the area of a [social] class" (p. 320).

Williams (1958) does believe, however, that not all social classes have equal access to the common cultural tradition, nor do they have equal power to determine the standards by which to judge what is culture and what is not. The process of selecting what is valued in a culture will always tend "to be related to and even governed by the interests of the class that is dominant" (p. 320). But that is not the same as saying the existing culture is the product and legacy of the dominant class only. The dominant class may, in fact, believe that they alone produce culture and thus they might argue, "if their class position goes, the culture goes too" (p. 321). And the "new rising [working] class" may still see culture as something belonging only to the upper class and thus "either be tempted to neglect a common human inheritance or, more intelligently, be perplexed as to how, and how much of, this bourgeois culture is to be taken over" (p. 321). So Williams broadens the definition of culture to include not just intellectual and imaginative work but, essentially, "a whole way of life" to which all members and social classes of society contribute. He argues, therefore, against the assumption many make that culture and the dominant class are necessarily one and the same.

Williams (1958) makes an important observation, however, about the different ways the dominant class and the working class view the nature of relationships within society. The dominant or middle-class idea of social relationships, what is usually called individualism, is "an idea of society as a neutral area within which each individual is free to pursue his [sic] own development and his [sic] own advantage as a natural right" (p. 325). This idea, he says,

> can be sharply contrasted with the [collectivist] idea that we properly associate with the working class: an idea which . . . regards society neither as neutral nor as protective, but as the positive means for all kinds of development, including individual development. . . . The human fund is regarded as in all respects common, and freedom of access to it as a right constituted by one's humanity. . . . Not the individual, but the whole society will move. (p. 326)

Because of its sense of the interdependence of modern life, the culture the working class has produced

> is the collective democratic institution, whether in the trade unions, the cooperative movement or a political party. Working-class culture . . . is primarily social (in that it has created institutions) rather than individual (in particular intellectual or imaginative work). When it is considered in context, it can be seen as a very remarkable creative achievement . . . [though] to those whose meaning of culture is intellectual or imaginative work, such an achievement may be meaningless. (Williams, 1958, p. 327)

But Williams (1958) cautions those "liberals" who support the positive use of government to promote the social mobility ladder, and the view that it is a benefit to the working class. To Williams, the ladder is,

> the perfect symbol of the bourgeois idea of society, because, while undoubtedly it offers opportunity to climb, it is a device which can only be used individually: you go up the ladder alone. This kind of individual climbing is of course the bourgeois model: a man [sic] should be allowed to better himself. . . . Many indeed have scrambled up, and gone off to play on the other side; many have tried to climb

and failed. Judged in each particular case, it seems obviously right that a working man [sic], or the child of a working-class family, should be enabled to fit himself [sic] for a different kind of work, corresponding to his ability. Because of this, the ladder idea has produced a real conflict of values within the working class itself. (1958, p. 331)

Williams concludes that the ladder is dangerous because "it weakens the principle of common betterment . . . and it sweetens the poison of hierarchy, in particular by offering the hierarchy of merit as a thing different in kind from the hierarchy of money or of birth" (1958, p. 331).

The working-class idea of solidarity is a truer basis of community and of a common culture because it views "the common interest as true self-interest," and finds "individual verification primarily in the community" (Williams, 1958, p. 333). Working-class solidarity, however, is not without problems; it can increase intolerance and resistance to diversity. Williams believed these tendencies must be countered if working-class access to and participation in culture is to be achieved on an equal basis with the dominant class:

Solidarity, as a feeling, is obviously subject to rigidities . . . [therefore] it is necessary to make room for, not only variation, but even dissidence, within the common loyalty. . . . Thus, in the working-class movement, while the clenched fist is a necessary symbol, the clenching ought never to be such that the hand cannot open, and the fingers extend, to discover and give a shape to the newly forming reality. (1958, p. 335)

One result of the differences between individualist and collectivist views of social relationships is conflict over the proper role of government in a democracy. Should it be a force that regulates the market so everyone benefits (a working-class collectivist view); or a force that restrains the power of government so everyone has freedom to acquire material rewards based on their individual abilities (a middle-class individualistic view)? Much of the political contention in the United States today is a reflection of this divide, with conservatives and liberals fighting over the "rights to government help" (such as Social Security) that FDR solidified in the New Deal (Sunstein, 2004, A26). As Kennedy (2004) notes, since the 1980s "a confused and pernicious form of individualism" has displaced the progressive social ethos that guarantees the education, employment, housing, food, and medical care necessary to ensure individual freedom means something. Otherwise, as he quotes Isaiah Berlin, "To offer political rights, or safeguards against intervention by the state to men [sic] who are half-naked, illiterate, underfed, and diseased is to mock their condition" (Kennedy, 2004 p. 23).

Individualism is well entrenched in the American psyche and will be difficult to dislodge, partly because of the "persistence of largely delusional

expectations of social mobility, and tensions along the racial and ethnic fron-
tiers," and also because of the political weakness of organized labor, the voice
of collectivism (Kennedy, 2004 p. 23). The negative view of the role of government, as well as the way schools and classrooms are organized in the United
States, are reflections of the individualist thinking that prevails in the dominant
social class. A great deal of the opposition and resistance on the part of
working-class students to accepting the education offered them may be reluctance to buy into the competitive, meritocratic thinking that individualism
represents, and with good reason. Meritocracy has not and cannot work for the
vast majority of working families; only a few border-crossers benefit.

Overcoming students' oppositional identity and resistance requires social
justice teachers who see the negative implications of schools' reliance on
competition over collaboration. Many teachers who typically pursue an individualistic pedagogy in their classrooms avidly pursue their collective self-
interest through membership in teachers unions. Yet organized labor goes
unrecognized in their pedagogy. They ignore, in fact avoid, any discussion or
teaching about the benefits of collective action and its role in our history and
our current democracy. This paradox, the result of the false promise of professionalism, reinforces domesticating education. Social justice teacher educators
have a responsibility to help teachers examine their underlying assumptions
regarding individualistic pedagogy, as well as design ways in which their classroom activities can connect what they view as necessary in their own lives—
collective action through union membership to guarantee their rights—to
their students' needs and rights. Education with an attitude is about helping
teachers understand how an entire class of people can get the powerful education they need to further their collective self-interest.

CONCLUSIONS

Taken together, we hope the chapters in this volume contribute to new visions
of teacher preparation, ones that foster a social justice-Freirean pedagogy where
progressive teacher educators and popular labor educators collaborate to instill
in their students an understanding of how knowledge (and society and reality
and culture) is socially constructed, and a sense of social responsibility for
demanding economic and education policies that support their efforts to do
their job well. Such critical teachers of urban working-class students and adults
will "play a central role in the fight for democracy" (Fraser, 1997, p. 185).

One might reasonably ask, however, what steps can be taken to create
such a teacher education program. And the answer must be, by the same
process that social justice teachers are prepared: through inquiry groups that
investigate how teacher education contributes to reproducing the social and
economic status quo, followed by reflection and dialogue on the findings, and
powerful, critical campaigns in collaboration with local community organizations and labor unions. In this way teacher educators can connect social justice

theory to practice through actions that build social change movements to demand more equitable economic policies from the government, the sort of new civil rights movement for which Anyon (2005) has called.

This is admittedly a tall order, but the process could begin by holding dialogues with faculty, students, and staff (including secretaries and janitors) about the current state of our democracy and teacher education's role in perpetuating it. What do we know about the power structure? Who in our dialogue-inquiry group benefits, and who doesn't? What is our relationship to unions and do we ever consider the topic of unions and social class in our instruction? Are we walking the talk about democracy that we are so free with in criticizing others, and for which so many of the products of our educational systems are called upon to make the ultimate sacrifice in war? Are we preparing them well to make choices in their—and our—collective self-interest? Do we see our teacher preparation programs as sites for the struggle for equity and democracy?

The ideas, experiences, and proposals contained in this volume call on us to broaden our definition of the role of teacher education in a democracy to include the critical approach and to consider the opportunities these authors offer to match our democratic rhetoric to our teacher preparation reality.

NOTES

1. The Coalition for Economic Justice (chapter 3) has organized to halt the exit exam in California until the schools are provided the resources to educate students to the level needed to pass the exams.

2. In Britain, these two categories of worker education became the Workers Education Association (WEA), which originated out of philanthropic impulses and wanted to create the worker-gentleman Alfred Marshall envisioned (Finn, chapter 1), and the National Council of Labour Colleges (NCLC), which sought to empower poor and working classes through "education of the workers in the interests of the workers as a class" (Horrabin & Horrabin, 1924, p. 51), much as Freire (1970) envisioned half a century later.

3. See Delp, Outman-Kramer, Shurman & Wong (2002) for other examples of union organizing using popular education.

REFERENCES

Altenbaugh, R. J. (1990). *Education for Struggle: The American labor college of the 1920s and 1930s.* Philadelphia: Temple University Press.

Anyon, J. (1981). Social class and school knowledge. *Curriculum Inquiry*, 11.1.

Anyon, J. (2005). *Radical possibilities: Public policy, urban education, and a new social movement.* New York: Routledge.

Bai, M. (2005, January 30). The new boss. *New York Times Magazine*, 40.

Banks, J. (1998). *An introduction to multicultural education.* Upper Saddle River, NJ: Prentice Hall.

Business Week. (2004, September, 13) 84.

Cole, P. (2004). *Labor's untold story.* Albany: American Labor Studies Center.

Counts, G., & Brameld, T. (1941). Relations with public education: Some specific issues and proposals. In T. Brameld (Ed.), *Workers' education in the United States.* New York: John Dewey Society.

Craik, W. W. (1964). *The Central Labour College, 1909–1929: A chapter in the history of adult working-class education.* London, UK: Lawrence & Wishart.

Delp, L., Outman-Kramer, M., Schurman, S., & Wong, K. (Eds.). (2002). *Teaching for change: Popular education and the labor movement.* Los Angeles: UCLA Center for Labor Research and Education.

Dewey, J. (1929, January 9). Labor politics and labor education. *The New Republic,* 212–215.

Fraser, J. (1997). *Reading, writing, and justice: School reform as if democracy matters.* Albany: State University of New York Press.

Galtung, J. (2001). *Peace by peaceful means.* Thousand Oaks, CA: Sage.

Horrabin, J. F., & Horrabin, W. (1924). *Working class education.* London: Labour Publishing Co.

Howey, K., & Post, L. (2002). A strategy for the reform of teacher preparation in urban centers in the United States. *Asia Pacific Journal of Teacher Education, 5*(2), 256–272.

Kennedy, D. (2004, September 19). The second Bill of Rights: A new New Deal. *New York Times Review of Books,* 23.

Lareau, A. (2003). *Unequal childhoods: Class, race, and family life.* Berkeley: University of California Press.

Lauricella, A. M. (2005). Community Walk-About: Finding the Hope in Hopelessness. In L. Johnson, M. Finn, & R. Lewis (Eds.), *Urban education with an attitude* (pp. 121–124). Albany: State University of New York Press.

Lehmann, N. (1999). *The big test: The secret history of the American meritocracy.* New York: Farrar, Straus and Giroux.

Martin, C. (2004). *Framed! Labor and the corporate media.* Ithaca, NY: Cornell University Press.

Noguera, P. (2005). The racial achievement gap: How can we assure an equity of outcomes? In L. Johnson, M. Finn, & R. Lewis, (Eds.), *Urban education with an attitude* (pp. 11–20). Albany: State University of New York Press.

Oakes, J., & Lipton, M. (2002). *Teaching to change the world* (2nd ed.). New York: McGraw-Hill.

Rethinking Schools. (2004, Fall). Editorial: A nation at risk, 4.

Rothstein, R. (2004). *Class and schools: Using social, economic and education reform to close the black-white achievement gap.* New York: Teachers College, Columbia.

Sleeter, C. (1996). *Multicultural education as social activism.* Albany: State University of New York Press.

Sunstein, C. (2004, October). Economic security: A human right. *The American Prospect*, A24–26.

Talbot, M. (2003, November 2). Too much. *New York Times Magazine*, 11–12.

Tomasky, M. (2006). Party in search of a notion. *The American Prospect, 17*(5), 20–28.

Williams, R. (1958). *Culture and society 1780 to 1950*. New York: Harper & Row.

Young, M. (1958). *The rise of the meritocracy*. Bristol, England: Thames and Hudson.

Contributors

VLADIMIR AGEYEV is Clinical Professor of Educational Studies at the University of Buffalo, State University of New York. He is co-editor (with A. Kozulin, B. Gindis, & S. Miller) of *Vygotsky's Educational Theory in Cultural Context*. Cambridge: Cambridge University Press (2003).

KAHLLID A. AL-ALIM is a parent in the Los Angeles Unified School District. He has been involved in the Coalition for Educational Justice (CEJ) for 5 years, is on its steering committee, and also serves on a South LA neighborhood council.

SUZANNE BOROWICZ is Director of the Western New York Writing Project at Canisius College, Buffalo, New York. Together with Suzanne M. Miller, she has published *Why Multimodal Literacies? Designing Digital Bridges to 21st Century Teaching and Learning* (2006).

ALEX CAPUTO-PEARL is a teacher in the Los Angeles Unified School District, a founding member of the Coalition for Educational Justice (CEJ), and a member of its Steering Committee.

JEFFREY M. R. DUNCAN-ANDRADE is Assistant Professor of Raza Studies and Education and Co-Director of the Cesar Chavez Institute's Educational Equity Initiative at San Francisco State University.

MARY E. FINN is the former director of the Urban Education Institute in the Graduate School of Education at the University of Buffalo, State University of New York and co-editor (with L. Johnson and R. Lewis) of *Urban Education with an Attitude* (SUNY Press, 2005).

PATRICK J. FINN is Associate Professor Emeritus of Learning and Instruction at the University at Buffalo, State University of New York, and author of *Literacy with an Attitude: Educating Working-Class Children in their Own Self-Interest* (SUNY Press, 1999).

PETER HOFFMAN-KIPP is Assistant Professor of Education at Sonoma State University. His teaching and research interests center on the development

247

of teachers' pedagogical and political identities, and the influence of multicultural teacher education on teacher identity.

LAURI JOHNSON is Associate Professor of Urban Education in the Department of Educational Leadership and Policy at the University of Buffalo, State University of New York. Her research focuses on educators' conceptualizations of race, historical and contemporary studies of parent and community educational activism, and successful urban school leadership. She is the co-editor (with M. E. Finn & R. Lewis) of *Urban Education with an Attitude* (SUNY Press, 2005).

FRANCES A. MARTIN is a recent graduate of the Los Angeles Unified School District. She has been involved in the Coalition for Educational Justice (CEJ) for 4 years, is on its steering committee, and is now an undergraduate at California State University-Northridge, majoring in political science.

SUZANNE M. MILLER is Associate Professor of Learning and Instruction at the University at Buffalo, State University of New York and Director of the City Voices, City Visions Digital Video Project. Her monograph *Why Multimodal Literacies? Designing Digital Bridges to 21st Century Teaching and Learning* (with S. Borowicz) was published in 2006.

ROSEMARY K. MURRAY is Associate Professor of Graduate Education and Leadership at Canisius College, Buffalo, New York. Her research and teaching focus is adolescent literacy in urban settings.

BRAD OLSEN is Assistant Professor of Education, University of California, Santa Cruz. His research and teaching focus on teacher knowledge and identity development, critical pedagogy, and sociolinguistics.

JOHN OTTERNESS is a retired K–12 teacher and a faculty member of the University of California, Los Angeles (UCLA) School Management Program. His interest is in how students interpret the activities we require them to do in school settings and how that can inform our practice.

GILLIAN S. RICHARDSON is Assistant Professor of Graduate Education and Leadership and Director of the Literacy Center at Canisius College, Buffalo, New York.

ROSALIE M. ROMANO is Associate Professor of Educational Studies, Ohio University. Her research is centered in critical theory/pedagogy in teaching and learning and she directs the CARE program—Creative Active Reflective Educators for democratic education—as well as COST, an overseas student teaching consortium of fifteen U.S. universities.

SUSAN J. SCHURMAN is President of the National Labor College in Silver Spring, Maryland, the only accredited college in the nation dedicated exclusively to the education needs of union members and their families.

DENNIS SHIRLEY is Professor of Teacher Education, Special Education, and Curriculum and Instruction at the Lynch School of Education at Boston College. He would like to thank the Rockefeller Study and Conference Center at Bellagio, Italy, for providing him with a one-month residency that enabled him to write his chapter in this volume.

LINDA TUBACH is a teacher and the Director of the Collective Bargaining Education Project, Los Angeles Unified School District (LAUSD), the nation's only full-time labor education program for high school students.

DIANE ZIGO is Assistant Professor of Literacy Education at LeMoyne College, Syracuse, NY. Her research and teaching focus is on community literacy.

Index

action research, 66, 77, 226
activists
  parent, 49, 90, 219, 228
  social justice, 96, 100, 102, 142
  student, 56
  teacher, 211
  teacher education, 89, 91, 96, 227
  teacher union, 218–219, 221, 223–228
Alinsky, Saul, 4, 24, 80, 83–84
Alschuler, Alfred, 69, 72
American Federation of Teachers (AFT), 219–220, 238
analytic skills
  critical, 4, 33–34, 57, 66, 69, 72, 74–75, 85, 112, 118, 135, 168, 205–206, 232, 236, 238
  structural, 9, 51–53, 55, 69, 237
anti-racism, 1, 225, 240
  organizing, 47, 49–51
Anyon, Jean, 6, 17–19, 22–27, 31, 79, 82–83, 128, 183–184, 192, 194–197, 199–201, 203–204, 226, 236, 244
Aronwitz, Stanley, 51, 64

banking model, 10, 183
Bernstein, Basil, 19, 20–22, 26, 180, 192, 195, 201–204
Boas, Franz, 223
Bowles, Samuel, 6, 18, 34
Brookwood Labor College, 43, 237
Buffalo, New York
  high schools, 25
  neighborhoods, 122
  parents, 228
  Public School District, 112

Center for Labor Research and Education, UCLA, 209

Center X, UCLA, 141–142, 154
charter schools, 1, 81, 218, 238
Cochran-Smith, Marilyn, 88, 129–130, 174–175
community
  activists, 218–210, 225
  based curriculum, 53
  and civic engagement, 79, 81–82, 91, 225
  in educational settings, 29, 42, 106, 119–120, 122, 133, 144–145, 151, 193, 204
  of interest, 2, 99, 242
  organizations, 29, 80–83, 86, 88, 90, 220, 222, 243
  in professional development, 173, 182, 219
  service, 41
  teacher, 79
  in teacher education, 4, 10
Community Project, UCLA, 153
conscientization, 23, 27, 29, 68
consciousness-raising, 53–54, 96, 98
critical action, 95–96, 102–103
critical classroom, 37
critical consciousness, 3, 8, 33, 36–37, 43, 52, 64, 72, 76, 95, 124
Critical Friends Group, 192
critical pedagogy, 37, 47, 90, 128, 135, 178, 184, 188
  theory, 63, 65, 67–69, 76
critical readings, 40–41, 181
critical study of race, 142
critical teacher inquiry groups, 173, 176–178, 185, 188–189
critical teacher education, 244
critical teachers, 4, 9, 183–184, 243
critical thinking, 4, 9, 38, 40, 42, 64, 84, 114, 118, 127, 145, 185, 205, 208, 218

Made in the USA
Lexington, KY
17 October 2012